AIRLINERS

AIRLINERS

ROBERT WALL

Prentice-Hall Inc,
Englewood Cliffs, NJ

A QUARTO BOOK

ISBN 0 13 021105 2
First American edition published by
Prentice-Hall Inc, 1980

This book was designed and produced by
Quarto Publishing Limited
32 Kingly Court, London W1
Design and picture research: Roger Daniels
Editor: Jane Struthers

Phototypeset in England by
Brown, Knight and Truscott Ltd, Tonbridge
Colour originated in Hong Kong by
Sakai Lithocolour Co Ltd
Printed in Hong Kong by
Leefung-Asco Printers Ltd

To my colleagues of the Bristol
Aeroplane Company - *Ave Atque Vale*

By the same author: OCEAN LINERS
Endpapers: Big crowds and dancing girls
celebrate the dedication of the new Western
Air Express Airport in Alhambra; California in
April 1930, with an American-built Fokker F32
as the centrepiece.
Title page: This cut-away of an Armstrong
Whitworth Ensign formed part of an Imperial
Airways poster printed in German.
This page: The graceful shape of the Lockheed
Constellation.

CONTENTS

AF 086 / 4.ª e DOM

S. PAULO (CONGONHAS)*	RIO (GALEÃO)	DACAR (YOFF)	5.ª e 2.ª PARIS (CHARLES DE GAULLE)
P 18:30 ▶	P 20:00 ▶	C 02:10 ▶	C 07:00

AF 085 / 4.ª e DOM

PARIS (CHARLES DE GAULLE)	DACAR (YOFF)	RIO (GALEÃO)*	4.ª e DOM S. PAULO (CONGONHAS)
P 13:00 ▶	C 15:00 ▶	C 16:00 ▶	C 17:15

Concorde
AIR FRANCE

TWICE
THE SPEED OF
SOUND

'BRITISH AIRWAYS ANNOUNCE the departure of their Concorde Flight No BA 173 for New York. Will all passengers please extinguish cigarettes or other smoking materials and proceed to the aircraft. Please have your boarding passes ready.' These unexciting and rather mundane words initiate another routine journey on the most sophisticated transport system that man has yet been able to devise. The time is 0840 hours, and passengers have been checking in for the Concorde 'breakfast special' to New York. At the check-in desk, each passenger has been handed a boarding pass and presented with a complimentary flight bag. It is London, Heathrow, Terminal 3.

The Concorde lounge soon fills up. The place has an air of careful elegance and there is a mood of expectancy, especially for those passengers who are about to make their first supersonic flight. Few pause to reflect that the first powered flight by an aeroplane took place less than eighty years before. It lasted for 12 seconds and covered 120 ft (37 m) at a speed of about 30 mph (48 km/h). This morning, the passengers on Concorde will be in the air for three hours forty-two minutes, and will travel at 1340 mph (2156 km/h), or twice the speed of sound. But for the moment they are content to read a newspaper or accept an early morning cup of coffee. As a reminder that an extraordinary event is about to occur, a steward circulates with glasses of champagne, and even at this early hour most travellers accept the proffered drink.

By now it is 0850 hours, and a chart on the lounge wall reminds passengers that it is still only 0350 hours, local time, at their destination of New York's Kennedy Airport.

Outside on the tarmac, ground crews are preparing the sleek aircraft for the trip. The flight crew are already on board. There are only three of them – Captain, First Officer and Flight Engineer – and they are engrossed in the complicated series of pre-flight checks that test the satisfactory functioning of the aircraft systems. The machine itself is indeed remarkable.

The BAC/Aérospatiale Concorde SuperSonic Transport (SST) was built as a two-nation venture by the aerospace industries of Britain and France. Assembly lines were set up at Filton, near Bristol in England, and at St Martin, near Toulouse in France, following an agreement signed between the two nations in November 1962. Despite some initial difficulties, which are inevitable in international projects, a joint basic design was soon established and work went ahead. The first prototype, a French-built airframe, made its maiden flight on 2 March 1969 and the British version followed on 9 April of the same year. The power plants chosen for Concorde were four Rolls-Royce/SNECMA Olympus 593 medium-pressure turbojets. The original design of the Olympus dated back to the 1950s and it was one of the best tested and most powerful engines in existence. These monsters provided 38,050 lbs (17,259 kg) of thrust each and they were mounted in an airframe of simple and expressive elegance. The needle-like fuselage stretched to 203 ft 3 in (62 m) in the production version while the delta wing measured 83 ft 10 in (25 m) from tip to tip. Accommodation was provided for 128 passengers in twin seats 4 abreast, and a pay-load of 25,000 lb (11,340 kg) was produced from a loaded weight of 400,000 lb (181,436 kg). The aircraft cruised at Mach 2.05 for a maximum range of 3970 miles (6389 km).

This is impressive enough, but it becomes staggering beyond belief when compared to the first powered airplane of 66 years before. When Orville Wright took to the air on 17 December 1903 at 1035 hours in the Kill Devil Hills, Kitty Hawk, North Carolina, the machine that he and his brother Wilbur produced had a total weight of 750 lbs (340 kg), measured 40 × 21 ft (12 × 6 m) and was driven by a 12 hp engine! The fuel carried by the Wright biplane could not drive Concorde for more than one hundredth of a second.

However, the outstanding technical achievement that made Concorde the first supersonic airliner to be used in passenger service had to be bought at a price. Supersonic flight demands high-stress components and above-normal operating temperatures. To create such an aircraft, many thousands of hours of development work had to be absorbed into operating economics. Therefore, the SST was an unattractive proposition to international airlines already committed to the more profitable wide-bodied, mass-carrier jetliner which was epitomized in the Boeing 747. So, Concorde was only ordered for the national airlines of the producer countries and the production run amounted to a mere 16 aircraft – a derisory figure by world standards in the 1970s.

None of this troubles the minds of the Concorde passengers, however, as an attractive British Airways stewardess announces that the flight is ready to board. Inside the stylish cabin the windows are small, but because the aircraft cruises at around 55,000 ft (16,764 m), there is little to see beyond the dark blue of the sky. The five members of the cabin crew show passengers to their seats and check up on their pre-supplied information. How many passengers are on a diet? Who are the invalids, if any? Does anyone eat kosher food?

At precisely 0930 hours, the aircraft

'Time is money' – the theme of this Air France poster sums up the whole purpose of air passenger transport. Shorter journey times mean more time available for business activity, and it is on this simple adage that the whole of modern civil aviation has been founded.

moves out of its loading bay and rolls across the tarmac to the taxiways. As Concorde moves, the cabin crew go through the standard drill that takes place on all passenger-carrying aircraft world-wide. The passenger's attention is drawn to the location of emergency exits, where to find life-jackets and how to use the oxygen supply if necessary. The formality is soon over, but for most passengers it is a timely reminder of the ever-present requirements of air safety.

As Concorde eases forward to seek a place in the line-up for take-off, the breakfast menu is issued. Today it starts with chilled melon, mango and kiwi fruit. To follow, there is a choice of gammon steak and sausages, sauté of kidney turbigo or poached fillet of Dover sole with eggs in a cream sauce. A veteran traveller reflects that it is all a world away from his first airborne meal – tea and thin biscuits on one of

the Imperial Airways Paris-London flights of the 1930s.

The Captain's voice comes over the cabin address system, saying that Concorde will take-off at full power with the four Olympus engines on re-heat (the burn-up of additional fuel in the exhaust pipes to get about twenty per-cent additional thrust) and that it will be going supersonic in about twenty minutes. Passengers settle back in their seats for take-off, and some take a final glance at the airport scene around them.

The big airports of the world are cities in themselves, catering not only for passengers, but for all the varied staff and visitors who come in their thousands either on business or plea-sure. Despite the impression of confu-sion that the average airline passenger often receives, the modern airport is a masterpiece of organization, processing passengers in an orderly progression

Below: The impressive outlines of a BAC/Aérospatiale Concorde of British Airways dominates the runway scene as it taxies out prior to take-off. Right: The cabin interior of a Concorde of Air France. The windows are small due to the need to retain the integrity of the structure. The stewardess is standing near the machmeter, which records the aircraft speed for passengers. Although Concorde has not been a commercial success in terms of sales, it has pointed the way to collaboration between European manufacturers which has led to the Airbus project.

from check-in to take-off. The terminal must be large enough to deal with the peak crowds which occur at certain times of day and year, and public areas also have to take the host of visitors which accompany the passenger, who usually checks in early to take advantage of the shops and restaurants. This is important, as these facilities provide a large part of the airport's income. The traveller's baggage has to be processed, weighed and sent to the correct flight, and the passenger himself checked through passport control, immigration and customs before he arrives in the departure lounge. These days, security checks to guard against hijackers are all-important, and the passenger may also be faced with another ticket check before he takes advantage of the duty-free shops – another large source of income to the terminal.

Eventually, the flight will be called,

and escalators and high-speed moving walkways will lead the traveller to the correct gate either by jetty, mobile lounge or using his own feet up stairs.

The departure of just ten large aircraft can mean that 4000 people have to be processed in about one hour, and this number repeats itself a hundred or so times a day in a large airport.

The world's busiest airport is Chicago O'Hare, handling 44½ million passengers in 1977, and it is still growing. It has an aircraft movement every 45 seconds. At the time of writing, the second largest is Atlanta International, with 29 million passengers, and then Los Angeles, London Heathrow and Tokyo International airports.

London's Heathrow Airport is the busiest air terminal in Europe and rivals New York's Kennedy, Chicago's O'Hare, and the San Francisco International for the title of the world's busiest airport. Nearly 1000 aircraft arrive and depart daily at the peak summer season.

Owned and operated by the British Airports Authority, Heathrow employs 52,000 people and services 76 airlines. It possesses three major passenger terminals and these are all located on a central island, to which access is gained by a road tunnel and underground railway from central London. The main runways are arranged in a diamond pattern around the central island and the two main ones, Nos 1 and 5, handle the main bulk of traffic, while a cross-diagonal runway is always on standby.

Twenty-four million passengers a year pass through Heathrow – a figure approaching half the total population of the United Kingdom. Ten million alone use Terminal 1, the facilities there being used exclusively for British Airways, Britain's flag carrier. Terminal 2 is Heathrow's oldest terminal and has

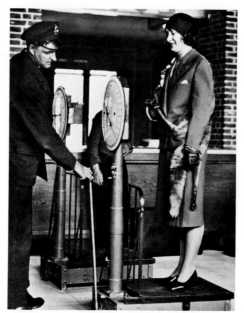

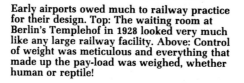

Early airports owed much to railway practice for their design. Top: The waiting room at Berlin's Templehof in 1928 looked very much like any large railway facility. Above: Control of weight was meticulous and everything that made up the pay-load was weighed, whether human or reptile!

The decision to transfer London's main air terminal from Croydon to Heathrow was taken at the end of the Second World War. The facilities were primitive until the central terminal was built. Here, passenger reception is seen carried out in tents.

Guide to the Airport of London (Croydon).

IMPERIAL AIRWAYS.

W.H.SCUDDER.

AIR MINISTRY.   PRICE 2d.

now been rebuilt to deal with the European traffic of 17 non-British flag carriers, including some prestigious names like Deutsche Lufthansa and Air France. Its annual throughput amounts to eight million persons. A further six million go through Terminal 3, which is the intercontinental building, housing the big names like Pan American World Airways (Pan Am) and includes the British Airways Concorde terminal.

Heathrow replaced the old and much-loved London Aerodrome at Croydon, which had been the British capital city's main airport from 1920 until the outbreak of the Second World War. However, when the development of aircraft raced ahead, the grass fields and short runways of Croydon could no longer safely handle the new generation of airliners that went into service during the war.

In the 1920s and 1930s, the name of Croydon was synonymous with Imperial Airways, whose headquarters were based there. It is said that Croydon was chosen as the London Airport because, as it was on the south side of the city, pilots approaching from the European capitals did not have to fly over the city and disturb residential areas below.

Even as long ago as 1920, local people had mixed ideas about the proposal to locate a busy air terminal on their doorstep. While the plans did not arouse the passionate opposition that is incurred by similar proposals today, there were still those who viewed the idea with distaste. Beddington and Wallington Urban District Council strongly objected to the proposal and *Flight* magazine reported in March 1920 that 'It would appear that exclusive Wallington is anything but pleased with its new neighbour'.

It was the start of a battle that has gone on between airport developers

Between the world wars, the London aerodrome at Croydon was a popular excursion for Londoners on weekends. The airfield was controlled and operated by the Air Ministry, which published this popular guide in the late 1920s. The airliners are Armstrong Whitworth Argosies.

The complex pattern of a modern airport is well illustrated in this plan of London Heathrow. The decision to locate terminals on the central island, taken in 1948, has led to development difficulties as the traffic has grown.

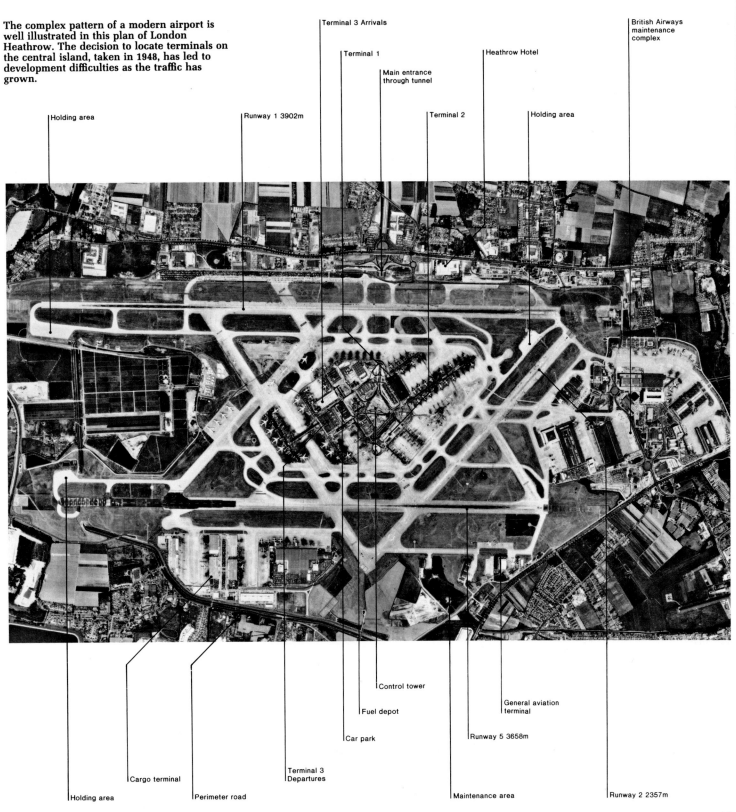

Terminal 3 Arrivals

Terminal 1

Main entrance through tunnel

British Airways maintenance complex

Heathrow Hotel

Terminal 2

Holding area

Holding area

Runway 1 3902m

Control tower

Fuel depot

General aviation terminal

Car park

Runway 5 3658m

Cargo terminal

Terminal 3 Departures

Holding area

Perimeter road

Maintenance area

Runway 2 2357m

and local residents ever since, and one that has been joined with increasing ferocity since the advent of the large gas turbine pure jet. The old piston-driven aeroengine has for some listeners an almost reassuring note, and the turbo-prop ran so smoothly that the large propellor-driven Bristol Britannia was to be called *The Whispering Giant* by the press.

The big pure jet has none of these virtues. In its crudest form it can be very inefficient, and trails brown plumes of soot and unburnt fuel which pollute the lower atmosphere. But its greatest drawback springs from the fact that it is man's noisiest creation – an inevitable and irrevocable result of the conversion of vast quantities of fuel into controlled and usable energy in the space of a few seconds. Therefore, the designers of Concorde knew from the beginning that their choice of the giant Olympus engine would lead to conflict with conservationists.

The struggle developed on both sides of the Atlantic. In the United Kingdom, there was an Anti-Concorde Campaign movement which sought to have the aircraft banned from the airways on two counts. The campaigners cited engine noise on take-off and also the effects on the environment of the shock wave and so-called supersonic boom as the machine passed through the sound barrier into the supersonic condition.

On the first count, Concorde is in fact no louder than many of its subsonic competitors, particularly the Boeing 707. Nevertheless, groups of protesters carried out demonstrations at both New York and Washington airports – the proposed terminals for the transatlantic services of both Air France and British Airways.

However, there are a number of practical measures that can be taken to cut

As modern airports have grown, so has public concern over their disadvantages, particularly noise pollution. A campaign of violence was led by students and farmers to prevent the opening of Tokyo's new airport at Narita. The opening was delayed for four years as a result of the action. Above: A Boeing 747 takes-off over a cloud of smoke from fires lit by demonstrators while airport buildings are assaulted and equipment destroyed (left). However, today Narita is one of the busiest airports in the East.

down noise on take-off. Engines can be fitted with hush kits – an intriguing series of baffles which damp out at least part of the full-throttle din. More importantly, some airports are restricted in the number of night flights allowed, to reduce the noise, and take-off patterns are arranged to achieve the greatest altitude in the shortest possible time.

This is not always as easy a procedure as it appears at first sight. The noise disturbance to nearby communities is least when an aircraft climbs steeply, but fuel consumption is much greater and pay-load penalties may have to be accepted. Noise monitors are located at the down-wind end of major runways, and pilots who break the local noise regulations can be the subjects of follow-up action by the authorities.

Precautions such as those outlined above have done little to satisfy protestors, although the value of aviation generally to mankind has long been recognized by thinking people. In some instances, protest has been taken to physical and political extremes.

The most famous instance is the prolonged campaign by Japanese farmers, students, conservationists and political activists, to prevent the opening of the new Tokyo International Airport at Narita, 40 miles (64 km) outside the capital. Regular airline operations were held up for four years while the police struggled to keep demonstrators away from the airfield perimeter and to clear away several large towers built to interfere with the approach path to the main runways. There were several casualties and many arrests before the airport finally opened to traffic on 21 May 1978. Up to the opening day, the pitched battles between police and protesters continued, and on the eve of the ceremony, all commercial flights in Japan were disrupted after saboteurs cut a power cable serving the main Tokyo Air Traffic Control Centre. Nevertheless, the official view eventually prevailed, and today Narita functions without incident and is one of the busiest airports in the East.

Concorde, therefore, will lift away from Heathrow at the steepest angle of climb consistent with safety. There is a muted roar and the aircraft is away, scything along the runway, while ground crews half a mile (0.8 km) away protect their ear-drums from the loudest noise on earth. Power is soon reduced, and the re-heat cut back to its minimum noise, as the aircraft makes a steady climb at 250 knots that will take it due west over its birthplace, the city of Bristol, and then over the Bristol Channel until the Atlantic is reached, south of the Irish coast. Only then does the Captain ease the throttles forward and the machmeter on the cabin bulkhead ease gently to the magic figures Mach 1. There is a barely perceptible nudge and it is supersonic. The Captain's voice comes on the tannoy to announce that Concorde will be accelerating to Mach 2 – twice the speed of sound – and flying at 57,000 feet (17,374 m). For those who know, or care to consult the records, these figures represented the world airspeed and height records for the years 1957 and 1947 respectively, such has been the pace of aeronautical advance in only three decades.

On the second count, the routing patterns of supersonic aircraft are controlled as much by environmental considerations as they are by the desire for economical operation. Evidence abounds that physical damage to buildings, and particularly to glass windows, occurs during close passage of supersonic aircraft, although much of this is challenged by aerodynamicists. This evidence, together with the so-called sonic boom, has led many governments to refuse permission for Concorde supersonic transit over populated areas and this in effect means over land at all times.

Routes have to take account of these restrictions, although on the transatlantic schedules ninety percent of all flying hours are in any event carried out over the ocean. Concorde is brought back to subsonic cruising well out from New York, Washington and Rio de Janeiro. On the eastern routes to Bahrain and Singapore, which are operated by British Airways and Singapore Airlines, routing is far more difficult, and tracks lead down the centre of the Adriatic to mid-Mediterranean, and then by desert areas to the Arabian Gulf. From there, the route leads completely around the Indian sub-continent, then north to avoid Sumatra and down the Malaccan Straits to Singapore.

The time is 1030 hours, and passengers are enjoying breakfast at Mach 2, while drinking another glass of champagne. The main noise now comes from the aircraft's air-conditioning system, which is a complicated transfusion of tapped engine intake air cooled in the aircraft heat exchanger system to do double duty in use for fuselage cooling and passenger comfort. The incredible speed at which Concorde is flying is unnoticeable, even though it now touches 1340 mph (2156 km/h). Through the cabin windows, the sky above takes on a deep, dark blue as the stratosphere thins away to the boundaries of space, and far away on the horizon, the curve of the earth can be seen clearly.

After breakfast the passengers relax, and some catch up on sleep. Others work on business papers, preparing for the working day that lies ahead in New York. Concorde will touch down at Kennedy Airport at 0815 hours local

Modern airport buildings have contained some of the best architecture of the late twentieth century. Below and right: The new Charles de Gaulle Airport of Paris at Roissy-en-France leads the way in Europe with futuristic passenger-moving walkways and well lit lounges.

The TWA terminal at Kennedy Airport, New York, was designed in 1956 by Eero Saarinen, and is a soaring allegory of flight in curves and pillars (above and left).

time, one hour fifteen minutes earlier than departure local time at London Heathrow.

In this simple statistic lies all the purpose of supersonic travel. With the advent of the jet airliner and the speed-up of air-routes world-wide, there came the unpleasant phenomenon which quickly became known as jet-lag. In the space of 10 to 12 hours, a traveller could be whisked halfway round the world and across half-a-dozen time zones. Human physiology refuses to grant instant adjustment to such cavalier treatment, and so may take two or three days to align the bodily functions of sleeping and eating to the new local time. Businessmen are among the worst sufferers, for if one's company spends a large sum of money to place one at a meeting in, say, St Louis, Missouri, it does not expect two days to be taken to recover from the ride across. By halving the time to cross the Atlantic, Concorde eliminates many of the worst effects of jet-lag and the business efficiency retained thereby goes far to compensate for the expensive supersonic flight.

Ahead now lies New York and the United States of America – a nation that dominates the skies and controls over eighty percent of the world's aviation industry, both in the construction and operation of airliners. Although the giant Russian state-owned Aeroflot holds the title of the world's largest airline in terms of fleet numbers and route mileage, the all-powerful 'top twelve' group of American airline companies (Allegheny, American, Braniff, Continental, Delta, Eastern, National, Northwest Orient, Pan Am, TWA, United and Western) operate the world's densest traffic patterns. Between them, they lift annually over 150 million passengers into the air, equivalent to roughly three-quarters of

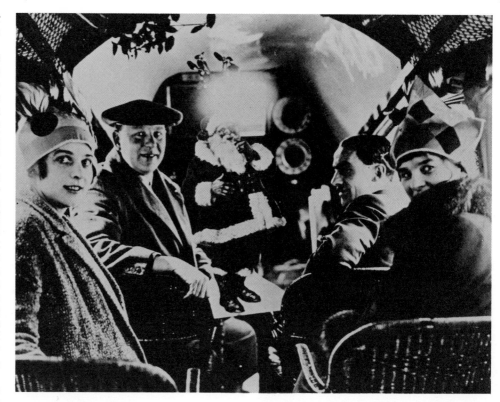

The changing world of air travel. Christmas in the air in the 1920s (above) in a cramped cabin with wicker chairs contrasts starkly with the space available in a modern Boeing airliner as seats are fitted. The pitch of seats is closely controlled by IATA, the international airline authority, which sets standards for passenger comfort and fares.

the entire population of the United States.

Supporting the major companies, there are scores of smaller airlines, many of which are, in terms of business achieved, larger than the national airlines of several European countries. On the 1979 register of airlines operating in the United States, there appeared the names of 308 companies that run fleets of three or more aircraft. These companies fly a vast network of services and there is no town of any size that does not possess its own airfield. Some of them are vast. O'Hare Airport at Chicago is the busiest in the world, and annually handles 750,000 aircraft movements (one every 45 seconds) and 43 million passengers. The country's other big international terminals are John F Kennedy at New York, Logan International at Boston, Dulles at Washington, Metropolitan at Detroit and Los Angeles, San Francisco and Seattle airports.

Airports are expensive to build and operate, and unless there is a throughput of not less than three million passengers annually, the venture is not likely to be profitable. In the United States, most airports are owned or run by city authorities, and function efficiently and economically. Income is raised not only from aircraft landing and parking fees, but from a host of other concessions, ranging from duty-free shops, hire cars, bars and restaurants to car parking lots. O'Hare has space for 14,000 cars alone.

To show how air travel is now integrated into the social and economic life of the American people, it is only necessary to take a close look at the architecture of some of the country's larger and newest airports. A nation tends to use its best designers on the buildings that it deems important. There is no better example of this latter truth than at the airport Concorde is approaching – Kennedy at New York.

Here, individual airlines and groups of airlines build and operate their own terminal, and so there is a pleasing variety of style. Two stand out from the others. I M Pei's design for National Airlines combined a giant support structure over a light spacious interior, but the real show-piece at Kennedy is the TWA building, designed in 1956 by the Finnish-American Eero Saarinen. In this building, Saarinen dismissed the angular box structure that still typifies world architecture and produced a curvilinear allegory of flight in soaring roofs and pillars. Saarinen went on to produce the plans for the terminal at Dulles International at Washington, DC, Concorde's other American destination.

Yet only a short half century separates the time of the modern giant airport from the grass fields that saw the pioneer flights of Alcock and Brown, Lindbergh and Amelia Earhart. In these later years of the twentieth century, when mass air travel is accepted as routine, it is difficult to imagine the sense of daring and adventure that even a short pleasure flight evoked only a generation ago. The early aviators were courageous innovators but it is unlikely that even a very few of them ever foresaw with accuracy the astonishing growth that would occur in the industry that they pioneered. It was a great step forward from the gossamer-like creations of the Wrights and Blériot to the lumbering 100 mph (160 km/h) machines of the 1920s, carrying perhaps 15 passengers in wicker armchairs for a few score miles. But who in 1927 could see the forerunner of the wide-bodied jets of today in Lindbergh's tiny *Spirit of St Louis*. In some of its high-density versions, the Boeing 747 is capable of carrying 500 passengers at nearly 600 mph (966 km/h) through distances ranging to 5000 miles (8047 km).

Aeronautical science continually progresses and development is never at an end. Who can doubt that this lovely Concorde, for all the economic and operational difficulties that have faced it, is really only the first in a long line of developing supersonic transports that will in some century or another weave a triumphant web of ultra-fast transport routes around the world.

Aviation is among man's newest skills, yet no other has so dramatically imposed itself on civilization in so short a time. Much of the progress has been achieved under the demands of military requirements, and stricken cities from London and Rotterdam through Cologne, Berlin, Dresden and Warsaw, to Hiroshima and Hanoi, have no great cause to praise aviation. Nor have those whose homes adjoin the runways of busy airports. But the history of civil flying since the end of the Second World War has seen the advent of mass air travel, and even the quieter engines of the new wide-bodied jetliners. The triumph of the airliner is that it has brought world travel within everyone's reach, and in the process has made the world a safer place.

The story of the airliners will be found in the pages that follow. In the meantime, the signs reading *No smoking – fasten seat belts* are illuminated above the seats and it is time to prepare for landing in New York. Suddenly, the green-blue water of Long Island Sound is flashing past below and rising rapidly to meet the airplane. There is a gentle bump beneath the seats, and the Concorde 'breakfast special' has landed. London is 3000 miles (4828 km) and three hours fifteen minutes away. In America, a new day is beginning. It is 0815 hours Eastern Standard Time.

FLYING GOGGLES AND BRANDY

THROUGHOUT THE MILLENIA that preceded man, the great flying lizards of the dinosaur age and then the birds travelled the air on their daily search for the food that ensured their continued survival. As soon as he was capable of conscious and controlled thought, man observed the birds and knew that flight was possible. Several hundreds of thousands of years were to pass before that possibility at last became the reality of modern mass travel by air.

The science of aeronautics can trace its beginnings in the writings of the ancient Chinese and their man-lifting kites. Evidence found in the tombs of the Nile Valley showed the interest of the Egyptians in the theory of flight, and later, in Italy, Leonardo da Vinci turned his attention to devising schemes for the construction of ornithopters, helicopters, parachutes and gliders.

Throughout recorded history, there are the stories of those who felt that man could fly, using artificial wings strapped to his arms and legs to agitate himself into the air. It is one of the supreme ironies of civilization that the problem of man-powered flight was not solved until nearly a decade after the first manned journey to the moon, with the Gossamer Condor. In fact, practical aeronautics are just two centuries old, if man's first excursion into the air is taken to be the first manned flight of a hot air balloon. François Pilâtre de Rozier and the Marquis d'Arlandes ascended from the Bois de Boulogne near Paris on 21 November 1783 in a Montgolfier balloon, 49 ft (15 m) in diameter. They came down 5½ miles (9 km) away after a journey lasting 25 minutes.

The development of the balloon and its eventual growth into the airship is described in Chapter Four. Sixty years passed before the first significant event in the history of heavier-than-air machines occurred. Sir George Cayley, baronet and English landed gentleman, was at first sight an unlikely candidate for the role of aeronautical researcher, yet he possessed possibly the best aviation brain of his time. Cayley started experimenting with model gliders in 1796 at the age of 23, and in 1804 he devized the first model aircraft with a mainplane. Sir George continued to experiment throughout his life, and it is now generally acknowledged that only the lack of suitable power plants prevented him from attaining sustained flight with both aeroplanes and helicopters at least fifty years before the Wright brothers.

In 1852, a 10-year-old boy, son of one of Sir George's servants, was carried into the air by a glider that the baronet had designed and built at his home at Brompton Hall, in Yorkshire, England. He was the first human being to travel in sustained flight in a heavier-than-air flying machine, but no record of this small hero's name has ever been discovered! The glider had been towed downhill in a breeze by Sir George's coach, and it is alleged that in the following year the coachman was used as the next cargo for his master's flight trials, but he resigned in protest.

Towards the end of his life, Sir George Cayley said 'The air is an uninterrupted, navigable ocean which comes to the threshold of every man's door'. His vision of manned flight was taken up throughout the remaining half of the nineteenth century by a number of pioneers, prominent amongst whom were the German Otto Lilienthal, the Frenchman Clement Ader and the Americans Samuel Langley and the Wright brothers.

Like most great human success stories, the Wright brothers' ultimate

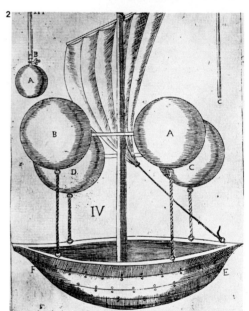

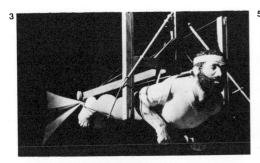

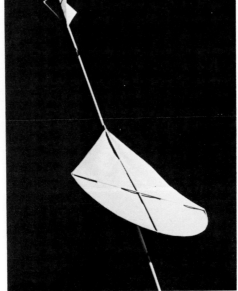

From man's earliest days, the dream of flying persisted. 1: Baldud, a legendary English king, is supposed to have fixed wings to his arms and jumped! 2: A Jesuit priest proposed this airship in 1670. 3: A scheme for a man-powered ornithopter, by Leonardo da Vinci (1452–1519). 4: An engraving which records Rozier's fatal attempt to cross the English Channel. 5 and 6: The English baronet Sir George Cayley built a series of model gliders which led to the 'boy lifter' of 1849. 7: Flying has always been portrayed as one of the most glamorous forms of travel.

triumph at Kitty Hawk on 17 December 1903 was not achieved without a great deal of patient trial and research. Before the first powered flight, the brothers had made over 1000 flights in their *No 3* glider, during which time they became the first aviators to use lateral (rudder) control and turn an aircraft by banking (tilting). They carried out the latter manoeuvre by wing-warping – a step which led to the later perfection of horizontal control surfaces and ailerons. From this continual and dogged improvement, it was but a short step to mount a petrol engine into the airframe and so produce the famous *Wright Flyer* of 1903. It is perhaps significant that no other pioneer aviator attempted to match the Wright brothers for nearly three years, so great was the advance that they had made.

Then, Alberto Santos-Dumont and Louis Blériot began their work in France which was to culminate in Blériot's channel crossing from England to France on 25 July 1909. In many ways, the implications for the future were the more astonishing results of Blériot's feat, rather than the flight itself. Practical flight had been demonstrated by travel from one country across the sea to another. The lessons were duly noted by at least some of the more forward-looking military staffs of the time, and the British army began to take an interest in flying machines. The Germans were already involved in the business of operating military airships (albeit not too successfully), and the American and French armies would soon follow suit.

However, before Blériot made his 22-mile (35-km) dash into the history books, the first passenger to travel in an aeroplane had made his odyssey. He was the forerunner of the millions that were to follow. No doubt well wrapped up

Above: Sir Hiram Maxim's large steam-powered aircraft broke away from its safety rails when under full power. Right: The German pioneer Otto Lilienthal made many flights in his lightweight hang-gliders before his death in an accident in 1896.

against the cold air of the slipstream, and without any of the creature comforts that sustain today's airline passenger, Charles W Furnas strapped himself alongside Wilbur Wright on the lower mainplane of *Flyer No 3* for a flight that was made from the Wright base in the Kill Devil Hills at Kitty Hawk. He was not a moment too soon. Fifteen days later Henri Farman flew with Ernest Archdeacon on board, who became the first European to fly as a passenger.

This same year of 1908 not only saw the shape of future events in the short passenger flights that took place. It was also forced to take notice of the sombre side of aviation and to accept the realization that there is no more demanding a science in terms of engineering accuracy and preplanned safety, and that errors can never be forgiven, and often not retrieved.

On 3 September 1908, Orville Wright began a series of demonstration flights for the United States Army at Fort Meyer, Virginia. All went well until 17 September, when a blade failed in one of the twin propellers of the Wright biplane. This placed too much stress on the one remaining airscrew, making it tear loose and foul the rudder controls, and causing the aircraft to nose-dive to the ground from 75 ft (23 m). Orville Wright was seriously injured and his passenger, Lieutenant Thomas Selfridge USA, was killed instantly, thus becoming the first person to be fatally injured in a powered airplane.

In the same year, just two months before Selfridge's death, the world's first woman passenger in an airplane (as opposed to a lighter-than-air craft) – Madame Thérèse Peltier – took-off with a French pilot from an Italian airfield in a Voisin biplane. In the United Kingdom, Mrs Samuel Cody became a

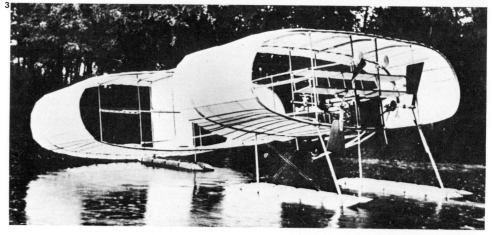

The Wright brothers continued to develop their aircraft after their initial triumph at Kitty Hawk in December 1903. Wilbur Wright demonstrated the Flyer A in France in 1908 (1) a year before Blériot's arrival in Dover on 25 July 1909 (2). A variety of designs proliferated in these years. The Blériot/Voisin with cellular wings (3) and the Koechlin Boxkite (6) owed much to the work of the Australian Lawrence Hargrave. Karl Jatho's aircraft (4) was an early German attempt, and Henri Fabre made the first flight from water (5). The Ecquervilly multiplane (7) and the machine of Trafan Vuia (8) could hardly leave the ground.

regular passenger in her husband's airplanes, from July 1909 onwards.

Aviation was progressing at an astonishing rate as the second decade of the century approached, and during these 10 years it would get added pace from the greatest accelerator of all human endeavour – the practice of war. In 1910, the industrial nations of Europe were clearly headed for military conflict, and the infant airframe business was to expand into a sizable industry by 1918. From this would come the first airliners and the foundations of the industrial giants that make up the aerospace industry of today.

By the end of 1909, world opinion had ceased to scoff at the airplane and recognized it to be a practical vehicle. America's lead had, to some extent, been overtaken by the European aviators, although the Wright biplane was probably still the most advanced aircraft of the time. It is often forgotten that the Wrights were not only the first men to build and fly a practical air-

plane, but that one or other of the brothers made the first flights of half a mile (0.8 km) and then 1 mile (1.6 km), the first flight of over one hour's duration, produced the first practical two-seat aeroplane, and made the world's first flight at over 1000 ft (305 m) altitude. All these were important milestones on the road to a workable passenger-carrying airliner, yet by the end of 1909, the main aviation records were all held by Frenchmen in wholly French-designed aircraft: speed by Louis Blériot at 47.85 mph (77 km/h) in his *Blériot XII*; distance by Henri Farman at 145 miles (233 km); height by Hubert Latham at 1486 ft (453 m) in an Antoinette.

The story of aeronautics in the next four years is of one liberally sprinkled with 'firsts' of all kinds, and also littered with broken records as faster, larger, safer and more powerful aircraft were produced. While most emphasis was placed on military development, the role of the airplane as a transport to

rival the ship and the railway was not altogether overlooked.

The next important developments took place in 1911. This was the year of the first tentative airmail flights. A French pilot, Henri Pequet, is credited with making the first official airmail flight, in February, from, of all places, Allahabad in India across the Jumna River to Naini in Uttar Pradesh. In September, a service using a Blériot monoplane opened between Hendon and Windsor in England. It was carried on for 15 days as a celebration of the Coronation of George V and the franked envelopes which commemorated it are now collectors' items of great value. On 23 September, the first official mail flights were made for the United States Post Office authorities by Earl Ovington, flying a Blériot over 6 miles (10 km) from Nassau Boulevard in New York City to Mineola Air Station on Long Island.

These flights were a small beginning but they represented another step

The boxkite evolved design was popular and successful in the first decade of the century. The Voisin (top) was typical of several designs. Paul Cornu's twin-roter helicopter (bottom) made the first flight by a rotary-wing aircraft on 13 November 1907. Aviation rallies (opposite) were popular events and a good way of showing aircraft to the public.

Above: Roger Sommer about to take off with 12
passengers aboard an aircraft of his own design
on 24 March 1911. The passenger aft appears to
be acting as carefully placed ballast! Sommer's
flight was aimed at surpassing the efforts of
Louis Breguet who had flown the previous day
with 11 passengers. Opposite page: In February
of the same year, Henri Pequet flew the first
official airmail from Allahabad in India.

ahead. Flights were becoming longer, as Pierre Prier showed when he made the first non-stop Paris-London hop, also in 1911. But the most important event of that year took place under the guidance of a member of a family whose name was to become one of the greatest in aeronautics – Breguet. Louis Breguet and his brother had already achieved the most astonishing success in aviation techniques to date, by getting daylight seen between the ground and the wheels of a primitive helicopter that they pioneered in 1908. Unfortunately, control of the craft eluded the brothers once it had left the ground, although Louis Breguet never lost his faith in helicopters – a belief which was justified forty years later. Louis therefore turned to fixed wing aircraft and his company, the Société des Avions Louis Breguet, is still in active and successful business today.

Work on the *Breguet I* was complete by June 1909, and it was demonstrated at the world's first aviation show at Reims in August. It was a biplane, with warping wings as ailerons and elevators for pitch control, and twin rudders mounted aft. The power plant was a 60 hp Renault, and was an immediate success. The following year Breguet rebuilt it, and in August 1910, he set a record by taking six people aloft, including himself. But Breguet felt that his machine was capable of even better performance, which he proved on 23 March 1911 at his field in Douai, when he took-off with 11 passengers on board. The distance travelled was a mere 3 miles (5 km), but it was with the largest number of passengers yet to be carried. As if this was not enough, and to emphasize that such loads would soon be commonplace, 12 passengers were taken up the very next day by Roger Sommer in a Sommer biplane, although

only 2625 ft (800 m) were covered, and it appears that Sommer was simply engaged in one-upmanship over Breguet.

The world now required an aircraft of greatly increased carrying capacity if a practical airliner was to be developed. Not only did it have to seat at least 10 passengers, but it needed cargo space for mail and freight as well, and this pay-load had to be transported safely through a range that made international flights a possibility. Such a machine was available by 1913 and it came from an unlikely source – the aircraft factories of Tzarist Russia.

Igor Sikorsky was born in Kiev on 25

May 1889, and educated at Kiev University, and then in St Petersburg and Paris. He showed an early interest in aeronautical engineering and, like Louis Breguet, turned his attention to helicopters. It was to remain a lifelong interest and eventually Sikorsky would perfect the type.

However, the technology available in 1912 could not cope with the complex requirement of helical control and Sikorsky, like Breguet, turned to the study of airplanes. He impressed the Imperial General Staff with his proposals and was soon appointed Director of the Aeronautical Department of the Russian Baltic Railway Car Factory at

St Petersburg. In 1913, he produced the *Baltiski Bolshoi (Baltic Great)* biplane and originally provided it with two 100 hp Argus engines. These did not provide sufficient power and were supplemented by another pair, the new engines being fitted in tandem behind the original ones. The *Bolshoi* had a wing span of 92 ft (28 m) and was the first to have an enclosed cabin for all on board, including crew and passengers. It was the first four-engined aircraft to fly and was by far the largest in the world at the time. Behind the cabin was the first open promenade deck ever fitted to an airplane, where it was intended that the passengers could get a breath of fresh air in flight!

The *Bolshoi* never went into service, but Sikorsky had demonstrated that large aircraft were a practical possibility and he started work immediately on an enlarged version. This emerged as the giant *Ilya Mourometz*, which flew in January 1914. Although designed as a bomber, it was the only machine to be produced before the First World War that had anything like the performance and size of the modern airliner. It had a wingspan of 101 ft (31 m), an enclosed and heated cabin, and a rear fuselage promenade deck (the second and last example ever fitted to an airplane). Named after a tenth-century Russian hero, the big machine was also the first of its size to be produced in quantity, and 75 were in the service of the Imperial Navy during the First World War. Sikorsky developed the *Ilya* rapidly and flew with 16 passengers on 11 February 1914. In June he flew from St Petersburg to Kiev non-stop – a distance of 1590 miles (2559 km). The day of the long-range airplane had dawned. Two months later, Russia and the rest of Europe was at war.

So preoccupied were the Europeans with great affairs of international concern, that few people noticed the start of the first scheduled air service in the world. Using a tiny Benoist two-seat flying boat, pioneer Anthony Jannus linked the Florida towns of St Petersburg and Tampa. (This is discussed in more detail in Chapter Six.) Jannus had been the pilot for Captain Albert Berry when the latter made the world's first parachute descent over St Louis, Missouri, in March 1912. Unfortunately, the infant airline proved unprofitable and was soon abandoned.

The struggle between the world powers was to last four years, and civil aviation was almost forgotten during the conflict. Although the war was predominantly fought on land, and therefore the air weapon was seen largely in tactical rather than strategic terms, there was pressure for improved performance. Hence the war years saw much technical progress and, in particular, powerful and reliable aeroengines were developed.

By 1918, Rolls-Royce of England had produced the eighth version of their Eagle – a 12-cylinder, liquid-cooled, in-line V engine which had powered the big Handley Page bombers and was fitted to the new Vickers Vimy. Designers had realized the limitations of the rotary engine used to power many Allied fighter aircraft and the static air-cooled radial was now being developed. In 1919, the Cosmos Engineering Company worked on their nine-cylinder Jupiter, but the development costs proved too difficult for Cosmos to finance, and the Bristol Aeroplane Company took over. It went on to make the Bristol Jupiter – one of the best aeroengines of the 1920s. Equally important engine work was done in the United States by Liberty and the Wright Company, and in Europe by Renault,

Tsar Nicholas II uses a ladder to inspect Igor Sikorksy's four-engine *Russki Vityuz* in 1914. The machine was the first to have four engines mounted for tractor propellors (Sikorsky's first aircraft *Baltiski Bolshoi* had four in tandem pairs) and was the forerunner of the giant *Ilyu Mourometz*, the world's first practical load carrier, of which (inset) 75 were built for the Imperial Russian Navy between 1914 and 1917.

£1 2s. 6d. *Including Government Landing Fee.* No. **2174**

AVRO JOYRIDES.

HOUNSLOW AERODROME.

Mr., Mrs., or Miss *Bean*

Date *7-6-19*

Avro No. *K.105.*

Pilot's Name *Dobyk*

G. L. P. HENDERSON,
Lieut-Col., late R.A.F.

After the Second World War, aviation came to the masses mainly through travelling air circuses and joy-riding. A popular machine of the day, in which thousands had their first experience of flight, was the Avro 504K, seen (above) during a joy-riding tour to publicize the newly-formed Qantas in 1921. Opposite page: A DH16 of Air Transport and Travel Ltd, the pioneer British airline which opened the world's first international daily scheduled service on 15 July 1919 between London (Hounslow) and Paris (Le Bourget). The DH16 was developed from the DH4s and DH9s which formed the early fleet of the airline.

Benz, BMW, Mercedes and Maybach.

Even while the war raged, and Allied commanders willingly accepted 30,000 casualties a day on the Western Front, there were some visionary souls who thought in positive terms about the return of peace and the possibilities of air travel. So it was that on 12 October 1916, in London, Britain's first civil airline company was registered as the Aircraft Transport and Travel Ltd – the brain-child of George Holt Thomas. However, the wartime emergency regulations specifically forbade civil flying throughout the United Kingdom, and he could only await the end of the war.

In America there was no such ban and, even before the war ended, the first serious attempt to set up a regular airmail service was being made. The first flights were between New York and Washington in May 1918, using the popular Curtiss JN-4 Jenny – a biplane

that had been retired from the Air Corps as no longer suitable for military training. The Jenny covered the 200 miles (322 km) between the cities at a speed of 60 mph (96 km/h), which was no faster than the mail trains. Even when the United States Post Office put faster machines on the run, there was not any significant advantage over surface travel, and the New York–Washington service eventually ceased in May 1921.

It is one of history's curiosities that for the better part of a decade after the end of the war, the United States airline companies concentrated on carrying mail, rather than passengers, by air. This had much to do with the lucrative mail contracts available from the United States Post Office which gave a new airline the necessary financial backing, whereas investment in passenger lines had to be attracted on the

open market. Nonetheless, the nation that would eventually dominate the airline industry in all its varied facets was among the late starters when the war finally ended.

Incredibly, civil aviation was not permitted in Britain until 1 May 1919. This was to allow officialdom sufficient time to set up a Civil Aviation Department of the Air Ministry, and for Parliament to pass an Air Navigation Act, which gave the Secretary of Air powers to set up air traffic regulations. No doubt this administrative arrangement was vitally important for safety in the skies over the United Kingdom, but the delay led to another ironic situation in the early history of the airliner. It was in defeated Germany, in that first desperate winter of the peace while thousands starved, that Deutsche Luft Reederei opened the first regular daily passenger service by air on 5 February 1919. The service ran between Berlin and Weimar and was operated with ex-military AEG and DFW biplanes. There was a surplus of old air force machines at the end of the war and hundreds of skilled pilots were only too ready to return to the skies. In Germany, France and the United Kingdom, converted bombers were to bear the brunt of providing the first airline services.

Many of these ex-service airplanes were totally unsuited for passenger operations. For example, the AEG JII, that flew between Berlin and Weimar, was a twin-seat, ground-attack aircraft that had flown first in 1916. The passenger was carried in the rear cockpit which had been used in wartime by the gunner. As the gunner had always stood, there was no seat provided. This inconvenience was surmounted by wiring a suitable piece of wood across the fuselage spars, on which the unfortunate commuter perched for the two

Deutsche Luft Reederei were the first airline in Europe to open inter-city scheduled services. They started in February 1919 with airmail services between Berlin and Weimar (main picture) using a LVG C VI biplane. These aircraft were all of the open cockpit type and passengers and crews were well wrapped up against the cold! Inset: Film star Hans Albers about to leave in a LVG C VI of Deutsche Luft Reederei.

hours eighteen minutes that the AEG took to fly the 218 miles (350 km) to Weimar. It is no small wonder that the airline provided a leather coat, thick woollen blanket, flying helmet, fur gloves and goggles for all passengers and further fortified them with a stiff tot of brandy before take-off. Later, some of the JIIs had a small cabin hood fitted which allowed them to carry a further passenger, but they had to dispense with at least some of the personal insulation.

The Deutsche Luft Reederei added Frankfurt and Hamburg to their timetables and other lines joined them. Soon there were about thirty small companies operating in Germany, almost all inefficient and liable to go out of business at any moment. The same situation existed to a limited degree in other European countries, and the leading airlines soon realized that some sort of order was required in what was otherwise a chaotic situation. So, in 1919, the International Air Traffic Association

was formed, which evolved over the years to become the present-day IATA.

Among other companies to start operations in Germany was DELAG, who resumed their Friedrichshafen-Berlin airship service with the new LZ 120 *Bodensee (Lake Constance)*. It carried 2300 passengers in the summer and autumn of 1919 before the Allies stepped in and sequestered the ship as war reparations. Another promising German airplane suffered the same fate when the Allied Control Commission

refused to allow any further development of the Zeppelin-Staaken E4/20, a four-engined 100-ft (30-m) wingspan airliner for 18 passengers. More of a success was the smaller Junkers F13, a single-engined monoplane which introduced the famous Junkers practice of using corrugated duralumin for fuselage skinning. A handy little aircraft for four passengers, the F13 sold in quantity all over the world and was kept in service by Lufthansa on internal routes until 1938. A total of 322 were built.

Like other European countries, France was forced to use the converted bomber for her early post-war services, but the available aircraft were far more versatile and better suited for passenger-carrying. First into the air was the Breguet 14T – a sturdy aircraft which carried two passengers in an enclosed cabin and had a range of 290 miles (467 km). A Renault 300 hp engine produced a cruising speed of 78 mph (125 km/h), and the type was in use as early as December 1918, when the French businessman Pierre Latécoère used it on exploratory flights from Toulouse to Barcelona, Alicante and Rabat. Later the Breguet 14T was used in regular service with several French airlines.

The outstanding French airliner of this immediate post-war era was certainly the Farman F60, which had been modified for civil aviation from a bomber design of 1918. It was a large wooden biplane, fabric-covered and having a deep enclosed fuselage with two cabins, a four-seat arrangement forward and eight aft. The open cockpit was spaced between the cabins. In its time, the F60, a twin-engined machine, was fitted with pairs of engines from a variety of different suppliers, among whom were Salmson, Renault, Gnome-

Above: The 100-ft (30-m) span Zeppelin-Staaken E4/20 was a promising German design for a four-engine airliner which was test flown in September 1920. Then the Allied Control Commission stopped all further development and the machine was broken up in November 1922. Top left: The Junkers F13 had better luck. Professor Junkers developed it from his J1, the first all-metal aircraft.
Top right: The Breguet 14 was the first aircraft type to be used on pioneer French airline flights. Opposite page: An early poster of Air Union – an airline founded by a consortium of French airframe builders.

Pioneering days in Australia in the 1920s. The national carrier Qantas dates back to 1921 with the foundation of Northern Territory and Queensland Aerial Services Ltd. Right: Service aircraft pioneered many Australian routes. This BE2E is leaving Winston en route to Darwin in 1919. Bottom right: Qantas' first office at Duck Street, Longreach, Queensland, in 1921.

Aeroplane Passenger Services

Northern Territory and Queensland

Aerial Services, Ltd.

Will commence operations early in December as Passenger Carriers

Between the Railheads of Central-West Queensland.

The Machines to be employed in these Services are :

1 "Avro" Triplane Limousine (160 h.p. Beardmore Engine), with accommodation for 4 Passengers, with baggage.

2 "Avro" 3-Seater Biplanes (100 h.p. Sunbeam "Dyak" Engine).

For Passenger and Freight Rates apply —

Secretary, N. T. & Q. Aerial Services, Ltd.
Winton, Queensland.

We have the Sole Agency in Queensland for all

A. V. ROE & CO.'S Machines and Products.

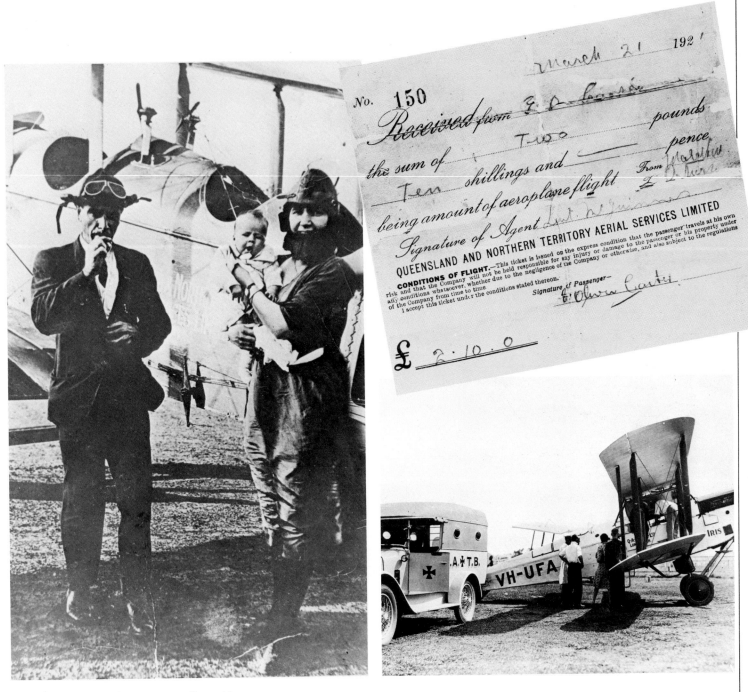

Above: Qantas' first infant passenger flew with her mother from Clonainry to Winston on 9 November 1922. The airline and the baby were about the same age! Top right: An early Qantas ticket. Right: The famous Australian Flying Doctor service dates from 1928 when it was founded by Rev Dr John Flynn, using aircraft supplied by Qantas.

Rhône and Maybach. The F60 was an impressive-looking airplane, and its long row of cabin windows made it look like an airliner. It was no surprise when pilots and ground crews alike named it the Goliath.

On 8 February 1919, a Farman F60 Goliath piloted by Lucien Bossoutrot made the first passenger airline flight from Paris to London. As civil flight was still not allowed in England, the passengers were all French officers and Britain steadfastly refused (and still does) to recognize the journey as a genuine airline flight. The following month, on 22 March, Bossoutrot opened the Paris-Brussels service with a Goliath that took two hours fifty minutes to complete the trip, which cost 365 francs. Thereafter the schedule was maintained on a once-weekly basis and regular customs examinations (the first on any airline) were carried out after the third flight.

The Goliath was one of the most advanced aircraft of its time, and its weatherproof cabin and forward observation window made it extremely popular with passengers. More than sixty of the type were completed and placed in service on European routes. When, later in 1919, a group of French airframe manufacturers, including Breguet, Blériot, Caudron, Farman and Morane, founded the Compagnie des Messageries Aériennes (CMA), the Goliath formed the better part of its fleet strength. Later, CMA would develop into Air Union and then become Air France.

While these events had been taking place in continental Europe, the day when civil flying was allowed to resume in Britain had been approaching. The Manchester-based company A V Roe was the first to introduce a regular civil air service in England. Services were legal again on 1 May 1919, and 10 days

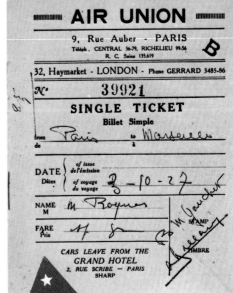

The Farman Goliath had originally been designed as a bomber in 1918, but after the war it was modified for civil use, and was converted with wicker chairs and curtains (top). It was operated by CMA and CGEA and Farman's own airline, Lignes Aeriens Farman. All of these companies later combined to form Air Union in 1923 and four of the aircraft were still operating as late as 1931. The poster reproduced (left) is the only one ever made to show a Farman Goliath. Above: A Goliath of CGEA arriving at Le Bourget in 1921.
Right: A ticket and baggage tag of Air Union for a flight from Paris-Marseille.

later, Roe used his Avro three-seaters, based on his famous 504K, to operate from Manchester to Blackpool and also to Southport. Roe charged a fare of £4 4s for the one-way trip and carried out 194 scheduled flights before he ceased operation in the following September.

However, Britain was a small country, which in 1919 possessed excellent railways, and so internal air services faced stiff competition. International routes to the continent were a different matter and the Royal Air Force (RAF) was already operating a regular mail and courier service between Kenley Air Force Station and British GHQ near Paris. This included the carriage of government ministers to the Peace Conference, and Winston Churchill used the service regularly. An early aviation enthusiast, he became the first British Prime Minister to fly the Atlantic during the Second World War, using a Boeing 314. On the resumption of civil flying, private firms were allowed to use Hounslow as a base, and the first recognized British commercial flight took off from there on 15 July 1919, when a DH9 belonging to Air Transport and Travel, piloted by Captain Jerry Shaw, flew to Paris with a single passenger. This was Major Pilkington of glass manufacturing fame, who had missed a boat train and had an important meeting in Paris. The company charged him £50, and he is reported to have been well satisfied with his journey.

The distinction of opening the first daily scheduled international airline flight anywhere in the world belongs to Air Transport and Travel Ltd. Using DH4s and DH9s, the airline operated between Hounslow and Le Bourget, Paris from 25 August 1919. In March 1920, the London terminal was moved to Croydon.

The de Havilland DH4 was a light

Handley Page Transport Ltd operated originally from the Cricklewood airfield of its parent company, the celebrated bomber specialists Handley Page Aircraft Ltd. The 0/400 formed the backbone of the fleet in its early days and, among other services, provided a regular Paris/London service during the 1919 Peace Treaty negotiations.

The triumph of Alcock and Brown in June 1919. The specially prepared Vickers Vimy was assembled in Newfoundland (bottom, far left) and lifted off in the early afternoon of 14 June (top). The flight ended ignominiously in a bog near Clifden, Co Galway, Ireland (bottom centre left) but the Atlantic was conquered and the flyers became world heroes (right).

bomber left over from the war, and it was easily convertible for passengers by placing a cabin roof over the rear cockpit. In this way two passengers were carried in relative comfort while a Rolls-Royce Eagle VIII provided a maximum speed of 121 mph (195 km/h). A larger model, the DH9, turned out to be less successful than the DH4, due partly to the unreliability of its Liberty engine. But these planes proved themselves on the routes to France and Holland and a DH9 was the first aircraft to be bought by Koninklijke Luchtvaart Maatschappij (KLM) when that great organization was founded on 7 October 1919.

Another early British airline company was Handley Page Air Transport, which naturally used its own 0/400 converted bomber for services between its factory aerodrome at Cricklewood and Paris. It was in one of these machines that the first in-flight food was provided for passengers in October 1919. Handley Page handed round a luncheon box, and from such small beginnings has grown the massive airline catering industry that exists today.

As 1919 drew to a close, aviation had been in existence as a practical reality for just 19 years. From its first hesitant steps at Kitty Hawk, the infant industry had grown into a lusty stripling with very obvious future potential. As if to emphasize the direction in which that potential could be best exploited, this same year saw the airplane (and also the airship) conquer one of the last great barriers left for it to cross.

The London newspaper *The Daily Mail* had offered a £10,000 prize for the first direct non-stop crossing of the Atlantic Ocean. By good fortune, when the war ended in 1918, Vickers Aviation found themselves with a suitable machine on their hands. It was a Vimy twin-engined bomber which had been

Opening the route to Australia. The brothers Keith and Ross Smith of the RAAF and their crew flew a Vickers Vimy from London to Darwin in 27 days during November and December 1919 to claim a £10,000 prize offered by the Australian government. The Vimy (top) was registered G-EAOU, which the crew interpreted as 'God 'elp all of us'! Refuelling (left) at Sourabaya appears to have been a tedious business. (Opposite) A souvenir postcard of the flight published in Australia.

designed to attack Germany, but it had not become operational before the end of hostilities.

Fitted with Rolls-Royce Eagle VIII engines, each of 360 hp, a production Vimy was specially modified for the Atlantic flight. Additional fuel tanks put the capacity up to 865 gals (3932 l) and so gave a theoretical range of nearly 2500 miles (4023 km). The crew was reduced to two and Captain John Alcock DSC was recruited as pilot, while a specialist in astro-navigation, Lieutenant Arthur Whitten Brown, became navigator. Alcock was 27 and Brown 33 at the time of the proposed flight. Prevailing winds over the Atlantic meant that a starting point in Newfoundland had to be found and the crew sailed out on the *Mauretania*, ahead of the crated Vimy, which finally arrived on 26 May.

It was now a race against time to assemble the aircraft, flight test it and begin ahead of several rivals. Finally, on Saturday 14 June 1919, Alcock taxied the Vimy, overweight and painted a dull buff, to the end of the temporary airstrip on Lester's Field, and started his take-off run. At 13.45 hours local time the Vimy was airborne and heading for Ireland. The flight was an incredible struggle against cold, icing, gales, fog and turbulence, in which at times Alcock lost all control. Nevertheless, due to the workmanship of Vickers and Rolls-Royce, the Vimy came through and eventually Alcock put her down on what appeared to be a friendly green field near Clifden in Galway. In fact it was a waterlogged peat bog and the Vimy nosed over as soon as her wheels ploughed into the ooze, but Alcock and Brown were safe and the Atlantic had been conquered. The way ahead for aviation was clear and the great days of the 1920s could begin.

Francouzsko Rumunská
Vzduchoplavební Společnost

AKCIOVÁ SPOLEČNOST-S KAPITÁLEM 10.000.000 FRANKŮ

TELEFON
ČÍS. 1273

TELEGR. ADRESSA:
AIREUROPIA PRAGUE

Denní Doprava Uzavřeným Létadlem
CESTUJÍCÍ · DOPISY · BALÍČKY

PRAHA → **ŠTRASBURK** za 3 HOD.
→ **PAŘÍŽ** za 6 HOD.
→ **VARŠAVA** za 3 HOD.

CHAPTER TWO

FOLLOW THE RAILWAY LINES

Produced in the spring of 1920, the Bristol Type 33 Pullman was very advanced for its time. It had a fully enclosed flight deck, and horn balanced ailerons for ease of control. The cabin (inset) was tastefully decorated in the post-war style. The Pullman also introduced the wicker passenger chair which became standard throughout the 1920s.

THE DECADE BETWEEN 1920 and 1929 is often said to contain the golden years of flying, and certainly they were among the most exciting in the history of air transport. Those who can still recall the 1920s remember the spirit of innovation that existed in those days, and the willingness of airline operators to be ever ready to go one step further than the next man, in the search for better performance and hence more business.

By 1920, aeronautical engineering had become an exact science and designers had already developed their thinking into certain fixed principles. But because the services available today, in terms of radio aids, computerized navigation systems and above all the turbine engine, did not exist, there was in flying a sense of adventure, of unknown dangers ahead and unique relief and satisfaction at the journey's end. The experience gained in the war allowed European aircraft companies to construct reliable airliners that were logical successors to the long-range bombers that were flying in 1918 at the war's end. The story of European air transport would be one of steady progress and the emergence of one dominant airline in each country, to become, often with government aid, the forerunners of the so-called flag carriers of today. There were difficulties in the early years of the decade, but by 1926

the major countries of Europe all possessed a national airline of some kind.

In the United States of America, the story was entirely different and took the form of an unregulated dash for wealth that rivalled the gold rushes of the nineteenth century, when aviators and financiers alike awoke to the realization that a fortune awaited the man who chose the right routes. By 1926, there were 420 operators of air services in the United States, all of them candidates for bankruptcy at any time. How these lines fared, and the story of aircraft types that formed their fleets, is the subject of this chapter, because in the contrast between American entrepreneurs and European state paternalism lies the main reason for the rise of the American industry to world pre-eminence.

In Europe, the airline industries of Germany, France and the United Kingdom grew along roughly similar lines, beginning with converted war-time airplanes and then developing the first of the new airliners. In Britain, in August 1920, Winston Churchill, then the Air Minister, announced that his department was to sponsor a competition to produce a large airliner. This was a new departure, and the start of the involvement of the British government in civil aviation which has continued ever since.

Three of Britain's largest aircraft concerns produced entrants for the contest — Vickers, Bristol and Handley Page. Two of the designs went on to serve on British airlines throughout the 1920s, but in some ways the third entrant, the Bristol Type Pullman, was the most remarkable of the three. It was produced in the spring of 1920 from the third of three large triplane bombers which had been ordered in 1918 by the Air Ministry but cancelled at the end of the war. The three massive wings spanned 81 ft 8 in (25 m) and four Siddeley Puma engines were mounted in pairs on the mid-plane. A very large slab-sided fuselage was fitted between the lower planes and this carried a heavy-duty undercarriage of four large wheels mounted in tandem pairs for support. Horn-balanced ailerons (another innovation) were fitted and the huge fuselage was counter-balanced with a tail unit that used biplane horizontal surfaces and triple fins and rudders. This allowed the Bristol design team to provide the crew and 14 passengers with the most luxurious cabin facilities available anywhere at that time. The crew flew the aircraft from a totally enclosed glass-fronted flight deck with excellent forward vision, and the cabin was well upholstered and decorated in the Art Nouveau style that suited the new post-war taste. Stout armchairs

"PERCY." BILLIARD MARKER SHEPHEARD'S HOTEL • MR. CORBY. (MECHANIC) • MAHAMMED SHEFIK PASHA UNDER-SEC. OF STATE • MR. WYATT (MECHANIC) • MR JEFFERIES DAILY MAIL • DR. CHALMERS MITCHELL (PASSENGER) • PILOTS CAPT. BROOME CAPT. COCKERELL • MR MERTON 'TIMES' CORRESP • H.E. AHMED PASHA ZIWA R. MINISTER OF COMMUNICATIONS • SIR G.B. MACAULEY MINI • SIR S. CL MINIST

supplied comfort that far outdid the somewhat spartan wicker chairs and railway-type luggage racks of the competing airplanes. When the Pullman proved more expensive and more difficult to handle in the air than its small and more economic competitors, the airline passenger lost the opportunity of luxury flight which would not fully return until the advent of the flying boats of the 1930s.

The Vickers entry was the civil version of the Vimy, the FB 27C, known as the Vimy Commercial. It marked the introduction of Vickers to civil airliners, and established a tradition which continues today in British Aerospace Corporation. The Commercial prototype first flew on 13 April 1919, which was before the Atlantic flight! The fuselage of the standard Vimy had been completely rebuilt to give an enclosed cabin with seating for 10 passengers and a lavatory. Company records appear to have been unusually discreet about mentioning this last very necessary facility, but the Vimy appears to hold the record for the first airborne toilet.

After modifications, the Vimy went into service with Instone Air Line Ltd from Croydon on 9 May 1920. It inaugurated the Instone service to Brussels and was in almost continuous service thereafter on the Brussels, Paris and Cologne routes. Carrying the name *City of London* and painted royal blue on the fuselage and with silver wings, the great bull-nosed airplane was one of the sights of Croydon for years. Wicker chairs and netted railway racks were the main features of the cabin, and the structure of the airframe was open to the view of all, albeit tastefully painted in cream. *City of London* was the first Vimy Commercial completed and remained the flagship of the Instone fleet until the company merged with others in 1924 to form Imperial Airways. By that time it had flown 107,931 miles (173,698 km) and carried nearly 30,000 passengers.

Opposite page: Egyptian government officials inspect the Vickers Vimy Commercial on a visit to Heliopolis. This was a civil version of the famous FB 27 Vimy bomber, immortalized as the first airplane to fly the Atlantic non-stop. A Sabena Handley Page W8f (top) on a route proving flight somewhere in Africa in 1925. The W8f was a standard W8b with a third engine added forward of the cockpit. The type was known as the Hamilton and built under licence in Belgium. The pilot, Leopold Roger, is third from the left. Bottom: An early Sabena poster shows the HPW8b.

The all-out winner of Churchill's competition was the Handley Page W8. When produced, it obviously outstripped its rivals and won the prize of £7,500. The Handley Page Company had more experience of the construction of large aircraft due to its wartime bomber programme, and it was these converted bombers that formed the fleet of the third British airline to fly out of Croydon — Handley Page Transport Ltd. They were also the first civil aircraft on the British register. No one was surprised therefore when Handley Page produced the winning W8, which carried over fifty percent more passengers than the Vimy for the same range, and used identical power plants — two Rolls-Royce Eagle VIIIs.

The W8 was an entirely new design and therefore needed a period for trial flights. It suffered a setback when the prototype crash-landed during one of these, due to a sudden change in the weather conditions. The type was eventually rebuilt as the W8b, with a smaller passenger capacity of 12. Three of these were built and named after members of the British Royal family — *Princess Mary*, *Prince George* and *Prince Henry*. During the 1920s other variants were introduced like the W9 and the W10. but two of the original aircraft served in the Imperial Airways fleet until the 1930s.

Therefore, in 1920, three airlines were operating regular services out of Croydon. The airfield itself was a military field built for the RAF, and so the new airlines settled down in the old hangar buildings that had been vacated by the service just a month before. When the airlines arrived there was simply no accommodation for offices or terminal buildings, and this was provided by setting up old wooden army huts along the edge of the airfield.

Conditions aloft were equally primitive. Despite the arrival of the W8 and the Vimy, in the early days the majority of the aircraft were the two- and four-seater converted de Havilland light bombers. They were very noisy internally and uncomfortable. There was no cabin heating, which meant that on most flights, passengers had to don flying suits for any hope of keeping warm. Even in the Vimy there was direct access from the cabin to the open cockpit, and any attempt to communicate with the flight crew resulted in a gale blasting its way through the aircraft. Really the best thing for a passenger to do was to keep quiet, hang on tight and concentrate on avoiding airsickness.

The arrival of machines like the Handley Page W8 altered all this. The enclosed and relatively comfortable cabin with its curtains and candlesticks (unused of course!) was a great improvement, and the W8 also carried a lavatory.

From now on, development was rapid and the hardships of the barnstorming days began to disappear. By 1922, the change of atmosphere from crude adventure to routine service was sufficient to make Instone become the first airline to provide uniforms for all its pilots. The blue serge and brass buttons were brought into use in 1922 and airline officers have worn almost the same outfit ever since. Instone's chief pilot was Captain Franklyn Barnard, an ex-RAF flyer who had first flown as a boy of 10 with Cody. Barnard recruited a number of his ex-service colleagues, but it is interesting to see that Sir Samuel Instone wrote to *The Times* in April 1922 about his company apprenticeship scheme for airline pilots. Parents were required to pay a premium of £500 to cover training fees and board

and lodging, and the boys got 10s per week pocket money. Captain Barnard was often in the news and not least for his habit of taking his dog Brownie with him on internal flights. Among others at Instone in these early days was Captain O P Jones, the celebrated 'million mile' pilot who was still flying for BOAC after the Second World War.

However, the going was never easy and there was a time in early 1921 when the British airlines nearly closed down altogether. In the autumn of 1920 it was becoming obvious that British airlines were being undercut on fare rates by their continental competitors, particularly the French, who enjoyed the benefits of heavy government subsidies. Commuters had the choice of two or three services and as supply greatly outstripped demand at the time, there was always a wasteful surplus of seats. Therefore, British lines cut back, and sadly in December 1920, Air Transport and Travel, the pioneer British line, went out of business altogether. Two months later, Handley Page were also forced to suspend their services, and Mr Frederick Handley Page (who would be the last independent British plane builder) asked his friend Winston Churchill for 'some sort of firm action by the government'. Never a man to let political dogma stand in the way of practical action, Churchill got his staff to set up a Cross Channel Subsidies Committee, which recommended a subsidy for both Instone and Handley Page of £25,000 each. This would allow flights to start again to Paris at fares of six guineas single and £12 for the round trip. There is a lesson here for present-day aviation administrators in that the whole exercise took less than four weeks, and both airlines were back in the air on 21 March 1921.

Churchill's intervention acted as a

necessary shot in the arm, and British aviation leapt ahead. The centre of all its international activity was the London Airport at Croydon, and it was here that the first air traffic control organization was set up, with its twin supporters, radio communications and meteorology. The Marconi Company had set up a wireless station at Croydon in 1920, by which simple communication could take place between the aircraft and the ground. The aircraft's communication with the ground involved the use of a trailing aerial which had to be wound in before landing, and pilots seldom placed great trust in the apparatus. One is said to have spent his time singing hymns all the way from mid-channel to Croydon, thus upsetting communications from base to all other aircraft. In any case, pilots preferred to rely on their own experience in bad weather, and the twin towers of the Crystal Palace were considered a more reliable guide to the location of Croydon than Signor Marconi's little box of tricks.

This all changed in 1922, when the first radio beacons were installed and direction-finding equipment was introduced. Pilots were able to get their position by calling up Croydon and then obtaining cross-bearings from Pulham in Norfolk and Lympne in Kent. This practical demonstration of the use of wireless-telegraphy made sense to pilots, and aircraft and radio have been inseparable technologies ever since. The first use of radio in emergency was the Croydon Station's directions to the runaway airship R33, which was guided safely home after drifting out over the North Sea with only a skeleton crew on board. It was also at Croydon that the International Distress Call *Mayday* was first concocted, from the French *m'aidez*, meaning *help*.

Along with the development of radio

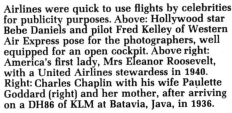

Airlines were quick to use flights by celebrities for publicity purposes. Above: Hollywood star Bebe Daniels and pilot Fred Kelley of Western Air Express pose for the photographers, well equipped for an open cockpit. Above right: America's first lady, Mrs Eleanor Roosevelt, with a United Airlines stewardess in 1940. Right: Charles Chaplin with his wife Paulette Goddard (right) and her mother, after arriving on a DH86 of KLM at Batavia, Java, in 1936.

came the setting up of a weather service. An agreement was made with the French and Belgian governments that hourly observations should be taken in each country and broadcast regularly to aircraft. A forecast was sent out hourly at differing intervals by each country, so that three messages an hour were available to air crews.

It is fascinating to note that while all these important technological innovations were going ahead, the grass field at Croydon was still being cut twice a year by a horse-drawn mower. This pleasant rural anachronism drew unfavourable comment from the press, who accused the Air Ministry of unnecessary parsimony and alleged that the grass was sometimes so long that it actually endangered the aircraft. The impatient journalist concerned had to wait until 1924, when the airport was at last equipped with a motor tractor. Even then there was a distinctly pastoral atmosphere at Croydon, and off-duty pilots were able to go after pheasant and partridge in the areas around the airfield.

Nevertheless, flying was always in the public eye. The press was always interested and publicity always available, especially when the film stars, the idols of the new age, began to use airlines. Chaplin's first flight in 1922 was on all the front pages.

The first airborne stewards also appeared at this time, and it is interesting that the airline companies thought it worthwhile losing the revenue of an extra passenger in order to provide inflight meals and drinks.

Other events should also be recorded as indicative of the way that flying began to be accepted into the social life of the time. An intended suicide was stopped by staff when he asked for a ticket on any plane, going anywhere.

'The First Air Cruise in History' was operated by a Junkers G31 of Lufthansa – a trimotor produced in 1928 (below). In May of that year, Lufthansa introduced the first air stewards (right). It is interesting to imagine the fate of the flowers and wine basket in any turbulence! Far right: The G31 in a Lufthansa poster of 1929.

Apparently he intended to leap from the aircraft when airborne. Several criminals were arrested at the steps of aircraft just as they were feeling that their escape attempts were about to succeed, and soon the name of Croydon was to become a symbol of romance and adventure that brightened the routine lives of thousands of Britons.

Sadly, as aviation became more widespread, the first accidents were inevitable. The world was long accustomed to accept the spectacular collisions that occasionally happened on the railways. Equally, it was no stranger to the perils of the sea; accidents to shipping, particularly to the well-known ocean liners, were accepted as part of the price man had to pay for access to other parts of the planet.

However, airplane accidents were another matter. In the first place, there was still a large segment of public opinion that looked upon flying as an unnecessary and dangerous pastime, and the popular quip that only birds and fools fly was still very much in vogue. Also, aircraft accidents, when they occurred, happened with such dramatic suddenness, and the whole machine disintegrated so quickly, that the prospect of survival was minimal for anyone unfortunate enough to be on board at the time. A morbid and critical interest was always taken, therefore, and there was more than a little of a 'told you so' attitude in much of the early newspaper reporting of accidents. The first fatal accident on a British scheduled commercial flight occurred on 14 December 1920, when a Handley Page 0/400 of Handley Page Transport Ltd crashed on take-off in fog at the company's field at Cricklewood near London. The pilot and flight engineer were killed, as were two passengers, but fortunately four others escaped.

Much more dramatic was the first mid-air collision between airliners, which took place over the French village of Thieuloy-Saint-Antoine, 18 miles (29 km) north of Beauvais, on 7 April 1922. It was not unusual for pilots in those days to use railway tracks as a guide to navigation. Occasionally, roads would also be used in the same fashion. On the day in question, visibility was poor and a Farman Goliath of Grands Express Aeriens from Le Bourget flew head-on into a DH18 of Daimler Airways on its way from Croydon to Paris. There were no survivors from either plane, and among the dead was a 16-year-old page boy called Hesterman who was part of the crew of the DH18. The accident highlighted, as nothing had before, the urgent need for proper international air navigation laws and hastened the negotiations then going on between European countries.

It was in these early years of the 1920s that all the major European airlines, or their direct predecessors, started operations. The French company CMA changed its name to Air Union in 1923 and eventually became the major part of Air France in 1933. Air Union operated the Farman Goliath on the London, Brussels and Berlin services, and added a variety of other aircraft types as the 1920s progressed.

In 1924, the Blériot company produced one of the first four-engined airliners with their Type 135, which went into service on the London-Paris line as a member of the Air Union Fleet on 8 August of the same year. Approximately the same size as the Goliath, it was 25 mph (40 km/h) faster and had an advantage in range of 125 miles (201 km) over the earlier machine. Four Salmson 9Ab radial engines were fitted – one pair on each of the mainplanes. The fuselage was built of wood, and 10 passengers were carried. The Blériot 135 was interesting in that it was claimed to be able to remain airborne on two engines. There was some substance to this claim but it is hard to believe that it could take-off on two engines as well. If so, the load must have been strictly controlled. The makers also claimed that the engines could be started in flight. These refinements apart, the Blériot 135 was a con-

ventional airplane for its day, and typical of the policy of the French industry to rely on proved designs.

It was not until 1928 that the next advance was made in French aircraft design with the Farman F180; an elegant, twin-engined biplane whose blue-painted hull immediately caused it to be named the *Oiseau Bleu*. The layout of this aircraft was eminently sensible and foreshadowed that of the big Imperial Airways biplanes of the 1930s. The twin engines were mounted in tandem above the top plane and this increased the comfort of the passengers and crew, who were far better insulated from engine noise as a result. The cabin was over 26 ft (8 m) long and 7 ft 8 in (2 m) wide, thereby allowing 24 passengers to be carried. The interior was light and spacious due to the seven windows on each side and a bar was fitted aft. On night flights, up to 17 passengers could be carried in couchettes, although there is no record of whether it was possible to sleep in such accommodation. The F180 went into service with Lignes Farman on their London-Paris service in February 1928, and in their publicity the line made much of the plane's ability to maintain altitude on one engine only with a load of 17,500 lbs (7938 kg).

The arrival of the F180 allowed Farman to beat off the challenge of Air Union, who had placed the Loiré et Olivier series of biplanes in service from 1926 onwards. The best of the series, the 213, was claimed to be the most luxurious passenger aircraft of its day. As the number of passengers had been reduced to twelve, and there were two bars and three stewards, this claim appears to have been substantiated. It was named *Rayon d'Or* and painted red, gold and white. Air Union put the 213 on its prestige London-Paris and

The Farman F180, *Oiseau Bleu*, was introduced on the London-Paris route in 1928. It was able to maintain height on one engine with a load of 17,500 lb (7938 kg) and was one of the first airliners to carry a bar.

The Loiré et Olivier 213 was used by Air Union for its luxury lunch-time London-Paris service. Painted in red, gold and white, it was named *Rayon d'Or* (The Golden Ray) (below) and its cabin was designed (right) after advice from the Wagons-Lits Company. Passengers were obviously pleased with the food and service (bottom right) which continued until 1931.

Menu

Hors-d'œuvre

—

Poulet poêlé aux Cèpes

—

Viande froide assortie

—

Salade verte

—

Entremets

—

Fromage

—

Corbeille de Fruits

(Voir la carte des vins du verso.
Wines as per list on other side.)

IV *bis*

Paris-Lyons-Marseilles services. The airline relied on high-quality service to attract passengers and even transformed one of the type into a complete flying restaurant in collaboration with the Compagnie des Wagons-Lits. The tables stretched all down one side of the fuselage and each could seat four people in comfort.

Although the British could fairly claim to have introduced the first in-flight meals, it was the French who brought their own splendid standards of haute cuisine to the airways. The following menu, served on Air Union's Paris-London service in 1927, is typical of the cross-channel meals that the company offered its patrons: hors d'oeuvres, crayfish à la Parisienne, chicken chasseur, York ham in gelatine, salade Nicoise, ice cream, cheese and fruit. The drinks available included champagne, red and white Bordeaux, spirits, soft drinks and coffee. As the flying time between the two capital cities was about two hours, there was a suitable period in which to serve this gourmet's delight. It is an interesting speculation to imagine the state of affairs on board during a gusty day, as all these early airliners flew through the weather rather than above it! Another point, not often remembered today, is that the actual time for travelling from central London to central Paris was only about twenty minutes longer in 1927 than it was in 1977!

Another national airline to start operations in the early 1920s was the Belgian flag carrier SABENA (le Société Anonyme Belge d'Exploitation · de la Navigation Aérienne), which operated the Farman Goliath between Brussels and Paris. It was founded on 23 May 1923 but did not fly into London until 1926. It is interesting that Sabena was route-proving to the Congo as early as

Souvenirs of Sabena's inaugural flight on its regular Congo service in February 1935 using Fokker FVIIs. Airliners on stamps have been firm favourites with philatelists and early items have attained considerable value.

1925, although it was ten years later that the first Brussels-Leopoldville (now Kinshasa) service was started.

On 1 January 1923, the first German aircraft to land in the United Kingdom touched down at Croydon. It was a Dornier Komet of Deutsche Aero Lloyd and had room for a crew of two and six passengers behind its Rolls-Royce Eagle IX 360 hp engine. The Komet had brought German airline officials to discuss the setting up of a London-Berlin service. It opened in April of the same year, operating jointly under the colours of Daimler Airways and the German company. In only three years, Deutsche Aero Lloyd merged with airlines operated by the giant Junkers company to form Deutsche Lufthansa, a name that has become one of the most famous in all airline history. When it was formed in 1926, Lufthansa inherited over 100 aircraft, most of them small, and a vast

Fliegen!

Deutsche Luft Hansa

Lufthansa started regular passenger services on 6 April 1926 between Berlin, Stuttgart and Zurich with this Dornier Komet III (below). Passengers board a Focke-Wulf A17a of Lufthansa in 1927 (top).

Top: Lufthansa pioneered the airport bus, starting about 1928 with a service between Berlin's Kurfurstendam and Templehof airport. The aircraft is a Junker G24. Above: A composite photograph of the Junkers W33 Bremen with the flight crew (left to right, Köhl, Fitzmaurice and von Hunefeld), who piloted it in the first east-west crossing of the Atlantic in April 1928. The flight took 37 hours and the aviators received the usual Broadway welcome (right).

There were two main reasons for Junkers' success during the inter-war years. Firstly, the durability of their all-metal aircraft, and secondly, the company's policy of encouraging civil aviation by making easy terms of purchase available and in some cases lending or giving away aircraft to small airlines.

network of German internal services.

In its early years, Lufthansa relied almost exclusively on the products of the Junker company. Following the successful F13, Junkers decided to build a larger and more powerful machine. This led to the decision to fit three engines, and it started a series of trimotors produced by Junkers, culminating in the classic Ju 52/3m, which made its maiden flight in 1930. The first aircraft of the series was the G24 of 1924, which holds the distinction of being the first multi-engine, all-metal monoplane in civil aviation. An earlier wooden version had been the G23. The same corrugated metal skinning that was pioneered in the F13 was retained, and three Junkers L5 liquid-cooled, in-line engines were provided. Nine passengers and a crew of three were carried and over sixty of the type were in service for Lufthansa by 1929. In July and August 1927, a G24 flew 12,000 miles (19,312 km) on a flight from Berlin to Peking, and a year later another of the type set up 11 world endurance and distance records.

The Junkers G24 was joined in the Lufthansa fleet in 1927 by the smaller W33 and its floatplane version, the W34. The W33 has the distinction of being the first aircraft to fly the Atlantic nonstop from east to west. This feat eluded airmen until 12-13 April 1928, due to the fact that the crossing had to be made into the prevailing winds. The W33 Bremen that made the flight was piloted by Captain Hermann Köhl and his crew was Gunther von Hunefeld and an Irishman, Commandant J Fitzmaurice. The crossing was made from the Irish Air Corps base at Baldonnel outside Dublin, to Greenly Island in Labrador. The journey took 37 hours! In all, nearly 300 W33s and W34s were built, and this rugged little machine served the German airline until the Second World War. It was also supplied overseas to Canada, South America and South Africa. In addition, some of them were used to train, in secret, the air crews of the new German air force.

In 1923 the British government turned to the well-tried method of reaching a political decision; it appointed a select committee, known as the Hambling committee, primarily as a result of subsidy problems which had arisen with the several airline companies then operating out of the United Kingdom. There was obviously a need to rationalize the situation then existing in the airline industry, and the committee recommended that there should be a single British commercial airline, which should receive a subsidy throughout its first decade of operations. These proposals were accepted by the government and on 1 April 1924 Imperial Airways came into being. It was formed from Daimler Airways, Handley Page, Instone and the British Marine Air Navigation Company and had a grand total of 15 aircraft with a total seating capacity of 119 – just about enough to fill one of today's medium-range jets. The general manager of the line was Woods Humphrey, who was said to have suggested the name of Imperial Airways, pointing out that the first suggested title of British Air Transport Service had initials that spelt BATS!

The new airline amalgamated just about all the commercial aviation expertise in Britain. To the technical ability of Handley Page and the style of Daimler was added Instone's flair for publicity – they once flew grouse across the channel to arrive in Paris in time for Lord Londonderry's lunch.

Imperial Airways has always been associated with the spread of an air travel network throughout the Empire.

It was obvious immediately that new aircraft types were required if this role was to be fulfilled, and orders were placed for two which would become famous. Meanwhile, the management had to deal with the first-ever pilots' strike, when they walked out after hearing that they were to be paid on a mileage basis. The dispute took a month to settle but after that things began to improve. However, there were still difficulties. In August 1924, a certain Francis Barry got his name into the record books by attempting unsuccessfully to prosecute Imperial Airways for excessive aircraft noise. The court informed him that it was a civil matter. Nevertheless, the young airline grew and continued to expand its services, despite the setback of a fatal accident on 24 December 1924 when a DH34 crashed on take-off at Croydon, killing all on board.

The new aircraft were ready by 1926 and both were powerful trimotors, specified for increased power and hence greater safety in the air. The first was the Argosy, built by Armstrong Whitworth at Coventry, and the company's first foray into the commercial arena after long experience with military aircraft. The Argosy was a large biplane with tubular steel structure and powered by three 385 hp engines built by the airframe manufacturers themselves. There was room for 20 passengers, but the cruising speed was still only about 90 mph (145 km/h). Nevertheless, the Argosy, with its 90-ft (27 m) wingspan, was the largest British airliner in service, and in August 1926 it commenced work on the Paris, Brussels and Cologne services. Seven Argosies were supplied in all and they flew for Imperial Airways until well into the 1930s. Named after British cities, they inaugurated the Silver Wing flights to Paris, during which the plane carried a

cocktail bar in place of two passenger seats.

The other machine introduced in 1926 was very different, although superficially the two airplanes were similar in appearance. The de Havilland DH66 Hercules was specified for operation in tropical climates, and its primary function was the carriage of mail and freight throughout the Empire. The seven passenger places were a secondary consideration. A pay-load of 620 cu ft (17.5 cu m) together with rugged strength and superb reliability, made the Hercules a success. The five aircraft Imperial Airways bought were stationed at Cairo and used to open up routes to Basra and on to Karachi. Eventually the service was extended to Delhi.

The Hercules was also ordered by West Australian Airways for its mail and passenger service between Perth and Adelaide. Four aircraft were delivered in 1929 and several improvements were added. The passenger complement was put up to 14 and the crew were placed in an enclosed cockpit. This latter refinement was later carried out on all Hercules. These fine airplanes also served Imperial Airways well and lasted in service into the 1930s. Together with the flying boats described in Chapter Six, these two aircraft formed the basic strength of Imperial Airways until the advent of the HP42s in 1930.

There is one other European airline of the 1920s that played an outstanding part in the story of the airlines. This is Koninklijke Luchtvaart Maatschappij Nv or, in English, Royal Dutch Airlines, known throughout the world as KLM. Founded in 1919 by a visionary Dutchman, Dr Albert Plesman, in October 1919, the new line was granted a royal charter by Queen Wilhelmina before it had ever flown an airplane. This royal

Top: Boarding an AW155 Argosy at Khartoum. The Imperial Airways airport bus looks distinctly uncomfortable. The interior of the Argosy (far left) shows the distinctive wicker chairs, which by this time were covered with padded cushions. Left: The de Havilland DH66 Hercules was used to provide postal and cargo services on British Empire routes east of Suez and inaugurated Imperial Airways routes to India.

The partnership between Dr Albert Plesman (right), the founder of KLM, and Antony Fokker (left), had started directly after the war and was to continue unbroken until 1934, when Plesman bought the DC-2. Fokker's chief designer Reinhold Platz's first project was the Fokker FII (top), which became the mainstay of the company in the early years. Most of these early aircraft were passed on to Lufthansa, where they remained in service until the mid-1930s. The FVII (above) became one of the most successful aircraft of its time, and the prototype demonstrated its endurance with a flight to Djakarta in 55 days.

Right: the FVIII first flew in March 1927, and was a twin-engined aircraft developed to give greater capacity than the FVII. It was designed to carry a crew of two and fifteen passengers, and there was generous space for mail and baggage in the nose section.

ROYAL DUTCH AIR LINES

SEE TWICE AS MUCH OF EUROPE IN HALF THE TIME

trust was not misplaced and Plesman would guide KLM to a pre-eminent place in world aviation before his death in 1930.

The first KLM services were made in a DH9 hired from the Air Transport and Travel Ltd. A British pilot flew on the opening service on 17 May 1920 from Croydon to Amsterdam. The Dutch terminal was at Schiphol, thus starting the career of one of the greatest airports in the world.

Plesman was not slow to buy his own aircraft and obtained them in his native Holland. The name of Antony Fokker dominates the story of Dutch aviation and he was already famous as the designer of Germany's best fighter aircraft when that country crashed to defeat in 1918. Fokker returned to Holland to set up an aircraft plant, and with him came Reinhold Platz, the brilliant engineer who had collaborated on some of Fokker's best designs. In 1919, work commenced on two types of single-engined high-wing monoplanes, the FII and FIII. These aircraft formed the basis of a whole series of successful Fokker designs, and started a partnership between Fokker and KLM which was unbroken until 1934 when Dr Plesman turned down the Fokker FXXXVI in favour of the Douglas DC2 – an historic and, as it turned out, correct decision.

When Plesman took delivery of his first Fokker FIIs in August 1920, he got an airplane that had actually been built in Germany and smuggled out, in spite of Allied Control Commission regulations. It was a neat, single-engine monoplane, and it flew the London service in September with a full load of four passengers. About twenty FIIs were built before being replaced on the line at Schiphol by the FIII – an enlarged version that could seat an

Travellers pass the flight time aboard a Fokker aircraft in the 1920s.

extra passenger. The FIII also sold well and KLM took 16 of them. All these early Fokker machines had an enclosed cockpit and were considered to be comfortable aircraft by the standards of the day. These new aircraft enabled Paris, Copenhagen-Malmö and Berlin to be added to the list of KLM destinations.

Then, in 1926, the Fokker team produced the most famous design it ever schemed. The Fokker FVII began life in 1924 as a logical extension of the typical Fokker single-engined high-wing monoplane. The idea was to offer a high-endurance, long-range transport, and the prototype proved itself by flying out to Batavia (now Djakarta), the capital of Dutch Java, in the summer of 1924. It reached Java after 55 days and many adventures. The first five FVIIs were sold to KLM and an improved version – the FVIIa – sold no less than 42 copies throughout Europe.

In May 1925 Fokker visited the United States to inspect his American factory (a Fokker T-2 had made the first non-stop coast-to-coast trip in May 1923) and here he learned of a contest set up by Henry Ford, the automobile magnate, around a 2000-mile (3218-km) circuit. Fokker hastily telegraphed instructions to Platz back in Holland to add two engines to the FVII in order to enter the race, and the result was the Fokker FVIIa-3m – a vastly improved machine. Speed went up by thirty percent to 118 mph (190 km/h) and the range doubled to 1600 miles (2575 km). The actual contest aircraft, the *Josephine Ford*, was used for Admiral Byrd's successful flight over the North Pole on 9 May 1926. An FVII was also used for the transpacific flight by Sir Charles Kingsford-Smith and C P Ulm from San Francisco to Brisbane between 31 May and 9 June 1928. The airplane was a FVIIb-3m called *South-*

The first crossing of the Pacific by air was carried out by a crew led by Sir Charles Kingsford-Smith (second from right), using a Fokker FVIIb–3m Southern Cross on a flight which began on 31 May 1928 and ended in Brisbane on 9 June.

ern Cross, and it became world-famous overnight.

The FVIIb-3m was probably the most successful civil airplane of the 1920s, and over 200 were sold. It was built in seven other European countries, and an American version was known as the F10. Among airlines to buy this splendid machine besides KLM were Ala Littoria, Swissair and Air France. In America, it was one of the first aircraft to be operated by the Eastern Airways fleet.

The present air-transport system in the United States is the largest and most successful ever devised by man. Millions of Americans use it every year and unless they have experienced it, Europeans have little conception of its size and all-embracing integration into the industrial and commercial life of America. Aviation was, incredibly, a late developer in the United States, despite its early beginnings there, and it was as late as 1925 that the Department of Commerce formed a Joint Civil Aviation Committee which pointed out how seriously the nation lagged behind Europe in aviation development. This led President Coolidge to separate civil aviation control from the Defence Department and set it up under the Department of Commerce. At the same time, legislation went through Congress which allowed all mail contracts to be awarded to airlines if the price was right. This led to the foundation of a large number of small airlines. Many of these early mail services were flown by an American-produced version of the DH4, powered by a Liberty engine. It was not used for passengers, but then passenger-carrying was not important to companies seeking mail contracts. Western Air Express was among the first concerns to fly people, and did so on its routes between Salt Lake City and Los Angeles.

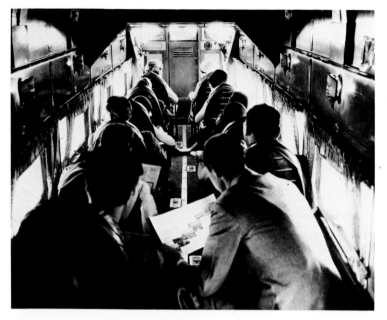

Top: On board a Ford Trimotor. The *Tin Goose* as it was known had an unenviable reputation for discomfort, but cabin service was provided by the co-pilot (above). A typical meal included cold chicken, tongue and ham or salad, with coffee, tea or milk, and fruit salad for desert. Right: A poster for Colonial Air Transport showing a *Tin Goose.*

Top: The Ford Trimotor was one of the strongest aircraft structures produced, and thrived in rugged conditions. Bottom: The Trimotor *City of Indianapolis* was used by TWA in 1930 for the first United States coast-to-coast service, taking 36 hours for the trip. Refuelling is taking place at Harrisburg, Pennsylvania, with the engines running due to the wintry conditions!

American aviation received a tremendous boost from Lindbergh's transatlantic flight in 1927. It aroused great interest across the nation and from this point on, the story is one of new companies, development and take-overs, until there emerged in 1930 the big four airlines; American Airlines, which was put together from 15 smaller outfits; United Air Lines, a fusion of six; Eastern Airlines, and Transcontinental and Western Air, known as TWA. To these must be added Pan American whose inception is described in Chapter Six. Pan Am eventually became the largest international airline. By 1930 the total number of companies had been reduced to 40, although there were 500 aircraft, with a route mileage of 30,000 miles (48,280 km). That same year, the American lines carried 170,000 passengers, which was nearly double the total carried elsewhere.

The aircraft that lay at the centre of all this success was a tough all-metal trimotor that had a formidable reputation for reliability and profit-making, and yet by all accounts was as uncomfortable a method of transportation as any airplane yet flying. This was the Ford 4AT Trimotor, known throughout the flying world as the *Tin Goose*.

The Ford Trimotor originated in the offices of the Stout Metal Airplane Company, which was bought out by Henry Ford in 1925. Stout had a design for an Air Pullman and Ford encouraged the development of this into a three-motor transport plane. The initial results were not good, and so Ford fired Stout and brought in a new engineer, called Harold Hicks. He redesigned the Air Pullman, and there is no doubt that the Fokker FVII was much in his mind as he did so. The first flight was in June 1926, and over 200 of the aircraft were built before production ended in 1933.

Speeding the mail! Postal authorities quickly realized the potential of aircraft as mail carriers, but progress in the early years was slow. Top left: The first mail flight in Germany took place on 10 June 1912 using an Euler biplane. Top right: One of the first letters ever carried to Australia by a Handley Page aircraft. Centre left: Delivering mail to a Rumpler RuC biplane of Rumpler Luftverkehr. Bottom left: An All-American Aviation mail pick-up experiment which did not prove successful.

Flying the mail produced pilots of a tough pioneering character (above). They were usually armed as forced landings due to weather or mechanical failure were a regular occurrence.
Top right: Mail being loaded on a National Air Transport machine at Hadley, New Jersey in 1927. It is interesting to note that the guard wore a rifle. Right: A postal cover from a mail flight piloted by Charles A Lindbergh from St Louis to Chicago in February 1928.

The fifteenth production example of the Trimotor, named *Floyd Bennett*, flew Rear Admiral Richard Byrd and three companions over the South Pole on 29 November 1929. He had already flown across the North Pole in 1926.

Both the Wright and Pratt & Whitney plants supplied power units for the Trimotor and it was put into service by all the major American airlines. Pan American alone took 28, and it flew in their fleet alongside the Fokker F10. Its superiority over the Dutch design lay in its all-metal construction, which included an extremely thin corrugated skin. Then a Fokker crashed with the American Notre Dame football team coach Knute Rockne on board, and the all-metal Ford's reputation for safety rocketed. It also heralded the end of any wooden aircraft being used in America.

The Ford *Tin Goose* established the American domestic airlines and turned them into multi-million dollar businesses.

It also convinced American designers that all-metal construction was obligatory in any future airliner, and it stimulated a demand for ever-increasing availability of seats.

These three achievements led to immense consequences. At the beginning of 1930, in faraway Santa Monica, Southern California, a team of aircraft engineers working for the Douglas Aircraft Company started tentative schemes for an airplane which Donald Douglas provisionally called the DC-1.

Three years would pass before the plans would bear fruit, but when they did, things would never be the same again. In only 10 short years, America would change from being aviation's backward boy into a veritable giant – a stature which the United States industry has been able to retain to this day.

CHAPTER THREE

LUXURIOUS LEVIATHANS

ON A COOL AUTUMN MORNING in the year 1900, a young German economist left his home in Friedrichshafen and set out for the shores of the nearby Bodensee (Lake Constance). In his pocket was a commission from the prestigious *Frankfurter Zeitung* to be present at a trial flight of the airship LZ 1, the invention of a retired general who had been kicked out of the Army on the direct orders of *Kaiser* Wilhelm II.

The young man was Hugo Eckener and this 17 October 1900 proved to be an important day. His subsequent article on the performance of LZ 1 was hardly complimentary. He pointed out, quite correctly, that a speed of 16 mph (26 km/h) – the maximum that LZ 1 could manage – was too slow to provide headway against even a moderate breeze. This criticism angered the general, *Graf* Ferdinand von Zeppelin. Naturally, neither he or Eckener realized the vital role that fate had in store for the part-time journalist. The journey that Eckener started that October day was to take him around the world, make him the most famous airshipman in history, and destroy his dreams when his marvellous *Hindenburg* was blown up in New Jersey, USA, just 37 years later.

The vision of ships in the sky is a dream as old as man himself. The idea persisted with thinkers in all early civilizations, and the Chinese attempted to produce man-lifting kites several thousand years before Christ.

The Greeks and Romans added more legend to the record of flight than they achieved in scientific thought and it was left to the English philosopher Roger Bacon to first advance the idea of lighter-than-air aeronautics in 1267. Progress remained slow, however, until the isolation of the gas hydrogen, first named by the French scientist Lavoisier in 1790, although it was in use some years earlier. The problems of hydrogen were manifold. It was difficult to contain in bags using traditional materials such as silk or paper. Furthermore, it was one of the most inflammable materials known to man, and throughout the history of hydrogen-filled airships, it was said that on every flight 'death was the passenger without a ticket'. In the event, the problem of leak-proof gas-bags was solved in 1783 by two French scientists, the Robert brothers, and the first manned flights were made in November of that year by a Montgolfier hot air balloon, closely followed by a hydrogen balloon built by Jacques Charles. It flew on 1 December 1783 with Charles himself and Aîné Robert as passenger.

Balloon development continued throughout the nineteenth century, but the apparently simple step of applying motive force eluded aeronauts throughout the whole hundred years. Hydrogen became the standard floatation material, and hot air was not used widely until it made a dramatic comeback with sporting balloons in the 1970s. But efficient propulsion giving confident manoeuvrability had to wait until Gottlieb Daimler produced the internal combustion engine at the end of the century. Then airships built by the Lebaudy brothers and the Brazilian Santos-Dumont began making controlled flights of increasing duration in France.

As the twentieth century dawned, however, it was in Germany that an airship flew and first drew the world's attention to the name of Count Ferdinand von Zeppelin. In the years that followed, his name became interchangeable with the word airship in the mind of the general public. More importantly, Zeppelin airships were the first flying machines to provide mass air-travel for the German public, and did so several years before the First World War. Zeppelin airships hold the distinction of being the world's first airliners.

Born in 1838, Ferdinand von Zeppelin was a professional soldier who first interested himself in air cruisers as a potential military weapon. He was also a capable engineer, and when he left the Army in 1890 after a quarrel with the Kaiser, he turned his attention to airship design.

Zeppelin soon realized that airships had no future unless the unwieldy gas-bags were contained inside a structure which gave them rigidity in the air. This was the birth of the rigid airship, and the design of all future large airships followed Zeppelin's ideas.

Zeppelin began the construction of his first airship in 1899. He had raised finance from various sources in Germany for this LZ 1 (*Luftschiff Zeppelin 1*). The machine was built in a huge floating shed on Lake Constance and was the largest contrivance ever planned to go up in the air at that time. The monster was 420 ft (128 m) long and 38 ft (11 m) in diameter and its framework was made of aluminium, covered with fabric, and divided into 17 compartments for the gas-bags.

The airship carried two gondolas which were mounted beneath the hull and in total it held 400,000 cu ft (11,327 cu m) of hydrogen. To power LZ 1, Zeppelin provided two Daimler engines, each of 15 hp. These were to be the airship's undoing, because it was considerably under-powered for the weight, which was a little over 10 tons.

Zeppelin had his airship ready by July 1900 and it first took-off from Lake Constance with five people on board on 2 July. The contraption lumbered somewhat unsteadily to about 1000 ft (305 m)

LZ 1, Zeppelin's first rigid airship rises above the Bodensee (Lake Constance) in the autumn of 1900 (left). The Count (top left) piloted the ship himself, but three trial flights proved that LZ 1 was dangerously under-powered. The second flight was witnessed by Hugo Eckener (top right) and awoke the interest in airships which led to his life's work in their development. The picture of Graf Zeppelin dates from 1912 and that of Eckener from 1929, at the time of LZ 127s world voyage. Above: Graf Zeppelin writes of 'harnessing the forces of nature' in May 1914.

and remained aloft for an hour and a quarter. At no time during the flight was the ship really under control, but Zeppelin was encouraged by even this small success and the ship was taken back into the hangar, where improvements were made. It flew again on 17 October 1900, and it was on this occasion that Hugo Eckener first saw an airship. LZ 1 made only one other short flight two days later, and then, with the Zeppelin funds almost at an end, it was scrapped soon afterwards.

It was not until five years later that Count Zeppelin began the construction of a second airship, called LZ 2. Although the ship was only approximately the same size as LZ 1, it carried a great deal more power. The two engines provided 85 hp each, and the hull was very much stronger than the earlier ship. Unfortunately, the maiden flight was a disaster, due to engine failure at take-off, and the ship drifted helplessly over Lake Constance before being caught by a motorboat which was following it, and brought down to the surface of the lake. Once again Hugo Eckener was present to record the occasion, and he also saw the second attempt to fly LZ 2 in January 1906. Despite cold weather conditions and a buffeting wind, the airship was launched and it rapidly gained height to 1500 ft (457 m) and cruised at speeds up to 33 mph (53 km/h) over the lake. Then, for no apparent reason, the forward engine stopped, control was lost, and the ship was blown 20 miles (32 km) away, to land ignominiously in the branches of a tree. High winds completed the damage begun by the stalled engine, and by dawn of the following day, the ship was completely wrecked.

For Count Zeppelin, this latest crash appeared to be the end of his schemes, but he mortgaged the remains of his

Zeppelin became a national hero in Germany as a result of his persistence in airship development. The popular postcard (above), when unfolded, revealed the slogan 'Hats off to Count Zeppelin'.

Top: Count Zeppelin raised much of the finance for his airships by public subscription. This satirical cartoon is captioned 'We've put all our money into it and all we get back is the ballast!'. Above: LZ 3 made a series of successful flights, beginning in October 1906 and was later handed over to the German army. Right: The control car of LZ 3. The ballast bags are hung alongside, and the propellor drive is prominent.

fortune, raised money from friends and produced LZ 3 in 1906. This time his efforts were successful, and the ship went on to make a number of uneventful flights. In September 1907 it remained airborne for over eight hours and at last the world began to take note.

LZ 4 followed soon afterwards. It was longer and the engines were more powerful, each producing 105 hp. By July 1908, it was carrying passengers for 12-hour flights, some of which covered a distance of nearly 200 miles (322 km). Even the King and Queen of Württemberg made a short flight in the LZ 4, and so became the first royalty to leave the ground in a flying machine.

However, trouble loomed ahead. During an attempt to make a 24-hour flight around a number of German cities, LZ 4 suffered the now-familiar engine trouble. It force-landed near the Daimler plant at Echterdingen, so that the manufacturer's experts could sort out the problem. While the work went on, a violent storm blew up, the airship became impossible to control, and during one particularly strong squall a gasbag exploded. LZ 4 was reduced to a charred wreck within seconds.

It was at this point that Hugo Eckener stepped in to the rescue of the Zeppelin airships. He had been employed as a part-time public relations man (an innovation in those days) by Zeppelin, and now he placed articles about Zeppelin and his airships in every major newspaper in the Reich. These were the years of ultra-patriotism in Europe, and no appeal to nationalist sentiment went unheeded. Within hours of the story's appearance, Zeppelin received offers of money from every corner of Germany, from rich and poor alike, and soon the Count had six million marks at his disposal. With this astonishing sum to hand, the old general formed a new

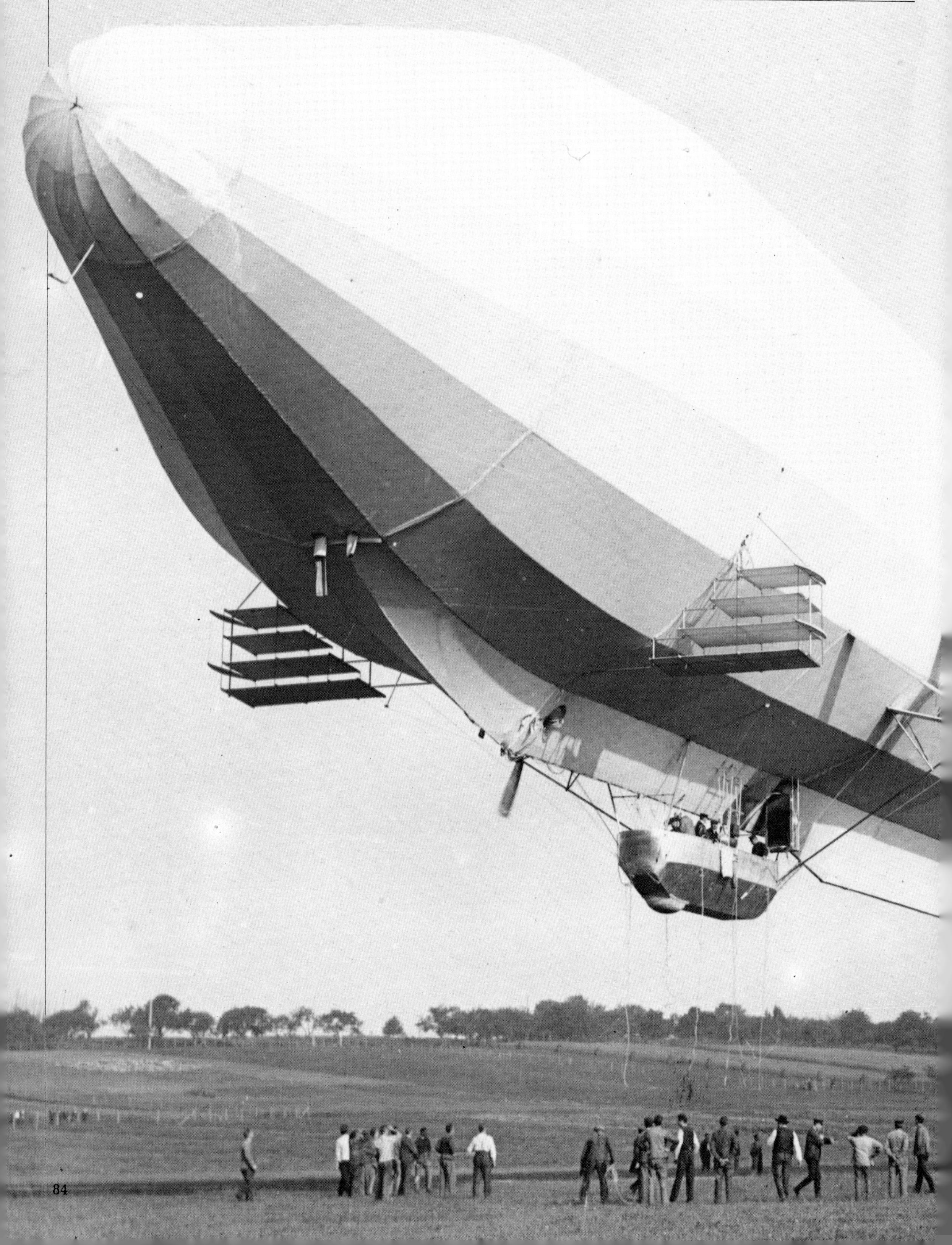

LZ 7 *Deutschland* rises gracefully aloft on the maiden flight on 19 June 1910 when Count Zeppelin himself piloted it from Friedrichshafen to Düsseldorf. The passenger cabin (right) was located amidships. The active career of LZ 7 lasted just nine days and ended on 28 June with a crash in the Teutoburger Forest.

company, and Hugo Eckener joined as a full-time employee. Soon LZ 5 flew for the first time. It was larger than LZ 4 and had increased engine power.

The new ship went aloft for the first time on 26 May 1909, and three days later Zeppelin set out to fly to Berlin. Once over the capital, he planned to circle the imperial palace at Potsdam (a tart reminder to the *Kaiser* of his dismissal of Zeppelin from the army!) and then fly back to his base at Friedrichshafen. The plan turned out to be more difficult than anticipated. Strong head winds forced him to turn round 100 miles (161 km) from Berlin, and even then the airship ran out of fuel 95 miles (153 km) from base. The crew were forced to make an emergency landing, during the course of which LZ 5 buried its nose 16 ft (5 m) into the only tree in the field! It was typical of the bad luck that dogged Zeppelin throughout his airship career, although the damage to LZ 5 was repairable.

Zeppelin followed on with LZ 6 – a ship that was destroyed during a hangar fire in Baden Baden in September 1910. The tale of accidents and disasters did not encourage the German General Staff to believe that Zeppelin's air cruisers were anything more than the crazy dreams of an eccentric old soldier. Eckener therefore was persuaded, somewhat reluctantly, to consider the use of airships as civilian transports. Count Zeppelin was equally unenthusiastic but nevertheless authorized the plan.

So, on 16 November 1909, the Deutsche - Luftschiffahrt - Aktien - Gesellschaft, the German Airship Transport Co Ltd, was formed. Under its shortened name of DELAG, the company was the first in the world to carry passengers in large numbers by air for commercial profit, and was the first economically successful air transport operation.

A number of large German cities, including Cologne and Munich, invested substantial sums of public money in the company and city councillors were nominated to the Board, while the construction of hangars went ahead, thus pioneering a long tradition of civic involvement in airport management.

The assembly of the world's first passenger-carrying airship LZ 7 began immediately, and it was ready by May 1910. The maiden voyage was made on 19 June and, with 32 people on board, Count Zeppelin piloted the ship to Düsseldorf himself. Here it was handed over to DELAG and named *Deutschland*. In the week that followed, the airship made several flights to Frankfurt am Main and Baden Baden.

Then Zeppelin's bad luck struck again. On the morning of 28 June, *Deutschland* took-off with twenty passengers, mostly reporters, for a publicity trip. Once again, engine failure proved to be the airship's undoing and a forced landing was planned for Münster where a Zeppelin back-up force was based. LZ 7 failed to make it and came down in the Teutoburger Forest, completely smashing its rear section in the crash. Incredibly, there was no loss of life.

DELAG had to wait until March 1911 for a replacement airship. This was the *Ersatz Deutschland* or *Deutschland II*, which was put together quickly, using some of the parts salvaged from LZ 7.

At the same time, Hugo Eckener was appointed Director for Flight Operations and immediately began training for his airship captain's certificate. He received it on 6 February 1911 and so was ready to take *Deutschland II* into the air on 11 March. From then until the following May, it operated without incident. On 16 May 1912, Eckener was engaged to take aloft a party of VIPs, and for once made an error in that cautious judgement for which he would later become famous. He ordered the airship out of its hangar in a strong crosswind, with disastrous results. LZ 8 struck the entrance pillars with vicious force, and the damage was so great that the ship had to be completely rebuilt.

Even so, an increasing number of people continued to get their first taste of air travel in DELAG airships, and cruises were available on a daily basis. While it must be admitted that nothing approaching a regular schedule was available, the service was good enough to attract the interest of the German shipping magnate Albert Ballinn, and his Hamburg America Line began to act as booking agents for DELAG throughout the country. Another travel luminary, the ubiquitous Herr Baedeker, was also quick to realize the potential of safe air travel. Soon, bookstalls in every city on the DELAG route were full of guides to the sights of the district from the air, presented in the true Baedeker style. To all this, Eckener added a proficient crew-training school and set up an embryo weather-forecasting service, which not only served the flight crews but gave early warning of cancellations to intending passengers if weather conditions looked adverse.

New ships were now added to increase the DELAG strength. First came the *Schwaben* (LZ 10). Between July 1911 and June 1912, it made 218 flights and carried 1553 passengers. Then, after safely landing all her compliment, it broke up on the ground during a storm at Düsseldorf and burnt out. By the time of this disaster, another airship called the *Viktoria Luise* was in commission and DELAG's route pattern had been extended to take in Potsdam,

LZ 8 *Deutschland II* ends up wrecked across the roof of the Düsseldorfer Halle airship shed on 16 May 1911. The accident happened when, with uncharacteristic lack of caution, Dr Eckener ordered the ship undocked in a strong crosswind.

In 1909, during the International Air Fair at
Frankfurt (right), Count Zeppelin met an ex-
soldier turned butcher named Stephan Weiss,
who had served under the Count's command in
an Unlan regiment. Weiss had produced a liver
sausage using his own recipe and gave the
airship pioneer a sample, asking his permission
to call it 'Zeppelinwurst' in the Count's honour.
The Count agreed and 'Zeppelinwurst' has been
a registered trade mark ever since.

Fuhlsbüttel and Hamburg. Two more airships, the *Sachsen* and the *Hansa*, were added to the fleet.

The *Hansa* was probably the most efficient and safest of all Zeppelin's pioneer airships. Dr Eckener took it aloft for the first time in July 1912, and stationed it first at Potsdam and later at Hamburg. By the end of October 1913, the *Hansa* had flown 632 hours for a total distance of 21,230 miles (34,166 km) and had carried 6217 passengers. In September 1912 it had pioneered the first international airship flight with a passage from Hamburg to Copenhagen. After a stop in the Danish city, it flew over Malmö in Sweden before returning to Hamburg. As usual, Eckener was in command for this flight, and with him on board was Count Zeppelin, who was now 76. The Count appeared to enjoy every moment of the 450-mile (724-km) journey.

When the First World War broke out between the European powers in August 1914, the DELAG operations came to an end. In the four years of the company's life, it had carried 10,197 passengers in a total of 1599 flights which had covered 107,231 miles (172, 571 km).

Ironically, the success of DELAG's civilian operations re-awakened the interest of the German military authorities in the war-potential of airships. In particular, the Imperial Navy, under Admiral von Tirpitz, was looking for a large airship that could act in the twin role of scouting for the High Seas Fleet and also carry a useful pay-load of bombs to English naval bases. Naval experts joined the staff of the Zeppelin company and once again the old Count turned his thoughts to the air cruisers that he had first conceived so many years before. Meanwhile, naval aircrews began to train with DELAG air-

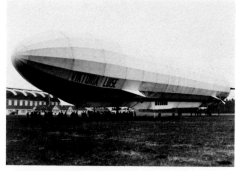

Top: The passenger cabin on board the LZ 13 *Hansa,* the most successful of all the pre-1914 Zeppelins. *Hansa* operated with her sister ship LZ 11 *Viktoria Luise* (above) for the DELAG company, which carried over 10,000 passengers before the advent of the war in August 1914. The Hamburg-Amerika shipping company had a financial interest in DELAG and acted as its booking agents (left).

ships and were allowed to fly on passenger trips.

The partnership proved to be an uneasy one. The naval designer planned heavy weapon loads for the proposed ships, for which the Zeppelins were unable to provide sufficient lift. This conflict between naval staff demands and aeronautical efficiency was to lead directly to the loss of the L 1 and L 2, which were the first pair of naval airships. L 1 crashed into the North Sea off Helgoland in September 1913. Then on 10 October, L 2 blew up on a test flight and 25 lives were lost, including that of the designer, Felix Pietzher of the naval staff. These two disasters destroyed the complete airship expertise of the German Navy. Furthermore, critical comments by Eckener on the cause of the crashes led to a worsening of the relationship between the Zeppelin works and the Berlin Admiralty.

The new commander of the Naval Airship Division, *Korvetten Kapitän* Peter Strasser, stepped into the breach. To combat low morale, Strasser realized that the Navy needed a replacement airship quickly, and so the reliable old *Sachsen* was hired on a temporary basis, and new crews began training. It was not a moment too soon, for the opportunity to train on peace-time flights would prove short. On 28 July 1914, Germany mobilized her naval reserves and the High Seas Fleet assembled at Kiel. Three days later she was at war.

Airship development, in particular, went ahead in Germany, and Zeppelin's faith in the rigid airship was now justified. The size of ships doubled in a year, and soon a fleet of the silver-grey monsters was ready to launch attacks across the North Sea. On the night of 19 January 1915, the first bombs fell on England at Great Yarmouth and Kings Lynn. Operations continued throughout the spring of that year and on 31 May, LZ 38 got through to London, where it unloaded 3000 lbs (1361 kg) of bombs and killed seven people.

The impact on British public opinion of these early raids was out of all proportion to the damage caused or the casualties sustained. British propoganda concentrated on the damage to civilian property and the loss of innocent lives, and soon the word Zeppelin was synonymous in the British mind with dead babies, wrecked homes and a terror-stricken population.

The reality was somewhat different. Although by the end of 1916, sixty Zeppelins had been completed (LZ 60 first flew on 1 January 1916) and they were now of vastly improved power and speed, they relied to a great extent on fair weather, and airship captains avoided stormy conditions. Several raids planned in 1915 ended in fiasco as the big ships were blown miles off-course and bombs were unloaded into the sea or onto empty fields.

The wartime experience of the Zeppelin company determined the future pattern of all rigid airship development in the two decades that remained of airship life. Three countries built rigid airships after the war – Germany, the United Kingdom and the United States of America, but both the United Kingdom and the United States relied on German design experience for the construction of their machines.

Two airships from the 1914-1918 period stand out. One was German and the other British, and they pointed the way ahead.

The German LZ 104 (L 59 in the Navy list) was built in 1917 as the fore-runner of a new, enlarged class of Zeppelin, the so-called V-type. L 59 was re-built from the earlier W-type L 57 with the addition of two extra gas-bags. It measured 743 ft (226 m) and was 78 ft 7 ins (24 m) in diameter.

After two false starts, L 59 set out from Jamboli in Bulgaria on 21 November 1917. It crossed Turkey, passed over the Mediterranean and passed down the Nile Valley to Wadi Halfa. There the crew received a recall message by radio from Germany and L 59 retraced its tracks. It arrived back at Jamboli on 25 November, having been in the air for 95 hours and travelled 4040 miles (6502 km). The long-range flight potential of large airships demonstrated by the African journey of L 59 was confirmed in dramatic style only twenty months later by the British airship R 34.

British airship design was unashamedly based on German designs copied from Zeppelins LZ 76 and LZ 96 shot down during the war. The two rigids, R 33 and R 34, completed in 1919, followed the German pattern closely.

R 34 gained world fame when it made a double crossing of the Atlantic in July 1919 under the command of Major C H Scott, RAF, with a crew of thirty. It took off from East Fortune, Scotland on 2 July, and despite headwind and buoyancy problems, landed at Roosevelt Field, Long Island, New York, having taken 108 hours 12 minutes' flying time. It returned to England in 75 hours with a tail-wind, and so became the first aircraft to cross the Atlantic in both directions.

The success of L 59 and R 34 inspired Germany and the United Kingdom to persist in the search for safe civilian travel by airship while the United States turned to the military role. However, she had indifferent success, and only the German-built *Los Angeles* had a useful life. The safe, non-flammable but expensive, helium gas was now available from United States sources and, while American airships were spared the horror of hydrogen fires, no less than three vessels – *Shenandoah, Akron* and *Macon* – broke up in flight.

After the war, the prospects for airship construction in Germany looked anything but bright. Work continued in the Zeppelin factory on the LZ 126, which was sent to the United States as *Los Angeles.*

Count Ferdinand von Zeppelin did not live to see the post-war revival of civil airships. He died on 8 March 1917 at the age of 79 and, having turned his attention to the bomber airplane, is said to have remarked that airships no longer interested him in the slightest. His company carried on in the post-war years under Eckener's guidance.

The first three ships went to France, Italy and the United States, and the successful delivery flight of LZ 126 *Los Angeles* to New York meant that plans for a larger transoceanic airship could go ahead. Eckener raised 2½ million marks, and the German government added a further 1½ million marks. The new craft was planned for a volume of 3,700,000 cu ft (104,773 cu m) with a length of 776 ft (236 m) and 100 ft (30 m) diameter, making it the same size as the largest ocean liner. On 8 July 1928, the completed ship was named *Graf Zeppelin.* Eckener had chosen the name, which was given to the ship by the Count's daughter.

The *Graf Zeppelin* was the most successful airship ever built, both in operational and commercial terms, and in the nine years of active life, it caught the imagination of the public as no aircraft had done before. The first flight, under Dr Eckener's command, was made on 18 September 1928 and lasted

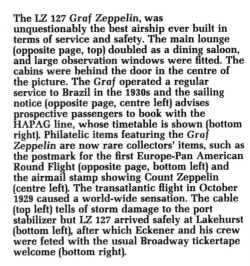

The LZ 127 *Graf Zeppelin*, was unquestionably the best airship ever built in terms of service and safety. The main lounge (opposite page, top) doubled as a dining saloon, and large observation windows were fitted. The cabins were behind the door in the centre of the picture. The *Graf* operated a regular service to Brazil in the 1930s and the sailing notice (opposite page, centre left) advises prospective passengers to book with the HAPAG line, whose timetable is shown (bottom right). Philatelic items featuring the *Graf Zeppelin* are now rare collectors' items, such as the postmark for the first Europe-Pan American Round Flight (opposite page, bottom left) and the airmail stamp showing Count Zeppelin (centre left). The transatlantic flight in October 1929 caused a world-wide sensation. The cable (top left) tells of storm damage to the port stabilizer but LZ 127 arrived safely at Lakehurst (bottom left), after which Eckener and his crew were feted with the usual Broadway tickertape welcome (bottom right).

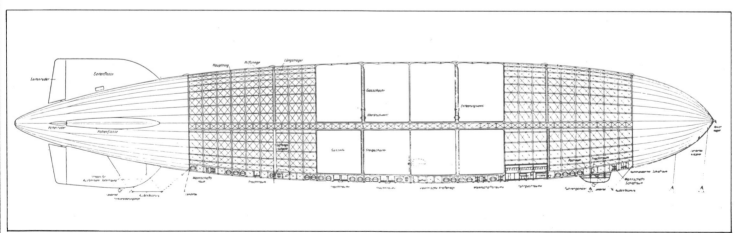

Airship designers had to fight a battle
for strength without undue weight. Top
left: Zeppelin engineers test a model airship in
the wind tunnel at Friedrichshafen. Top right:
The simple triangular girders designed by
Barnes Wallis stand out clearly in this picture
of R100 under construction at Howden,
Yorkshire, in 1928. Wallis used only 11 different
girder lengths to build his ship. Bottom: The
complete structure of LZ 129, the *Hindenburg*.

Gas bags fitted into LZ 127 *Graf Zeppelin* await inflation with cheap but inflammable hydrogen gas (top). The picture shows clearly the ship's complex structure. Bottom left: LZ 126, which was supplied to the United States Navy as ZR III *Los Angeles* receives its canvas covering at the Zeppelin works in early 1923. Bottom right: The control cabin of LZ 127. The helmsman of the horizontal control stands in the nose while the helmsman of the vertical control is on the port side of the cabin. Note the perforated girders for lightness.

35 hours – an incredible feat for a new ship.

Eckener was very pleased with the performance of the *Graf*, and he arranged a transatlantic trip for the following 10 October, – the anniversary of Columbus' discovery of the New World. Bad weather over the Atlantic, always the final master of airship navigation, delayed Eckener's plans, and finally he got away on 11 October, flying around central Atlantic storms by dipping south to the Azores. Then, in mid-ocean, the *Graf* passed through a storm that caused it to pitch violently, and most of the fabric tore from the port vertical fin surface. Crew members, including Dr Eckener's son Knut, clambered outside the airship and replaced the fabric, clinging to the structure, with the ocean 800 ft (244 m) below. The giant airship weathered the storm and headed on for Washington, DC and the safety of the airship base at Lakehurst, New Jersey. The flight had lasted 11 hours 43 minutes. Dr Eckener and his crew had safely delivered twenty passengers and 62,000 pieces of mail, and they received the customary ticker-tape welcome that New Yorkers reserve for their heroes.

Americans flocked to Lakehurst to inspect the new German monster. They were astonished to learn that, despite its size, the hull weighed a mere 57 tons and that it was capable of flying 6214 miles (10,000 km) at a speed of 68 mph (109 km/h) with a pay-load of 33,069 lb (15,000 kg). The control gondola and the passenger cabins were joined and streamlined into the hull. The ship was controlled from the pilot's bridge, aft of which was the radio and navigation room. Then there followed an electric galley and a pleasant lounge which also served as dining saloon. Large windows looked down on the scene below, and

Left: Passengers look down on the world passing below from the promenade deck of LZ 129 *Hindenburg* before dining in comfort in the most spacious dining saloon ever to leave the ground (below centre). After dinner, they gathered round the famous aluminium piano (below). On arrival in the United States, American Airlines ran a connecting service to other cities using a DC-3 (bottom left).

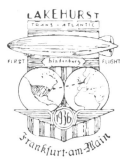

IN 3 TAGEN NACH SÜD-AMERIKA!
DEUTSCHE ZEPPELIN-REEDEREI

aft again were two rows of five twin-berth cabins. The crew of forty had their quarters in the hull above.

It is not an exaggeration to say that, in the nine years that followed, this great airship dominated world aviation as a true 'queen of the skies'. Its size and reliability gave it something of the aura that surrounds the giant ocean liners, and this was at a time when size counted for a great deal. In a Germany that had yet to see Hitler in power, Hugo Eckener and his great airship symbolized for Germans their national recovery from the defeat of 1918, and the economist-turned-pilot was even asked to run for *Reichspresident!*

In the years that followed, the *Graf Zeppelin* was seen all over the globe, from the icy wastes north of Spitsbergen to the jungles along the Amazon. Under Eckener's guidance, it circumnavigated the world from Lakehurst via Berlin, Tobol'sk, Tokyo and Los Angeles in 21 days in August 1929. World confidence in airship travel soared, and Eckener began to prepare plans for his vision of a fleet of passenger-carrying *Zeppelins*.

Then, in October 1931, the airship world received the first of two giant blows from which it was never to recover. Earlier, in 1924, Ramsay MacDonald's government in Britain had launched a programme to build two large civil airships for the so-called Empire routes, at a cost of £1,350,000 spread over three years. The programme was bedevilled throughout by politics, and what followed remains the saddest chapter in the history of aviation.

The contract was let in two parts. The first, for a ship to be called R 100, went to a subsidiary of the giant Vickers combine, the Airship Guarantee Company. The second airship, R 101, was to be built by the state-owned govern-

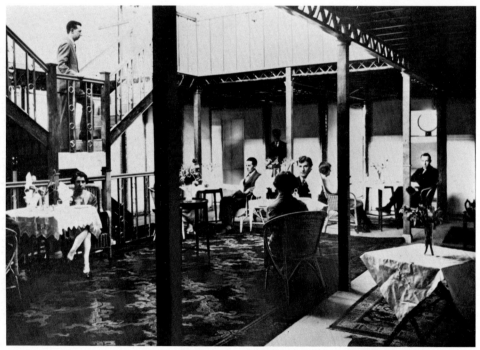

ment airship works at Cardington in Bedfordshire. Immediately, the press nicknamed them the 'capitalist' and 'socialist' airships.

The contract for R 100 was a very tight one, and money was always short. But Vickers had the great advantage of the services of Barnes Wallis, the brilliant innovator who became one of the all-time great names in aviation. Wallis designed a structure that was at once brilliantly simple but of enormous strength. In all, he used only 11 different components to build the hull, and yet the result was an efficient and attractive-looking vessel.

At Cardington, it was a very different story. The design team, headed by Lieutenant Colonel V C Richmond, soon ran into trouble with bureaucratic officials and endless interference at all levels. Eventually R 101 made its maiden trip on 14 October 1929, but it was obvious that there was something dangerously wrong. No one could fault the excellent workmanship of the Cardington fitters and riggers, and the passenger accommodation buried in the hull was far ahead of the *Graf Zeppelin*. But the 777-ft (237-m) ship was clearly overweight and underpowered, and after only 10 short flights it was decided to lengthen it by 46 ft (14 m) in order to add more gas-bags and so increase the capacity.

Meanwhile the R 100 was ready, and from the day of the maiden flight on 16 December 1929, it proved to be the best airship ever built in Britain. The trials went without a hitch and on 29 July 1930, it set out from Cardington for Montreal with a crew of 42, and 13 passengers. The commander was Captain R S Booth and he guided it across to Canada without incident, apart from a short thunderstorm along the St Lawrence River. After several demonstra-

Top: The brilliant R 100, designed by Barnes Wallis and built by Vickers, performed exactly to specified requirements, but was broken up after the R 101 disaster. Centre: The main lounge of the R 100. On the stairway left is the late Neville Shute Norway, chief draughtsman under Wallis on the project, who later found fame as a novelist. Bottom: The main frame of R 100. Wallis later used the same geodetic construction principles in his *Wellesby* and *Wellington* bombers for Vickers.

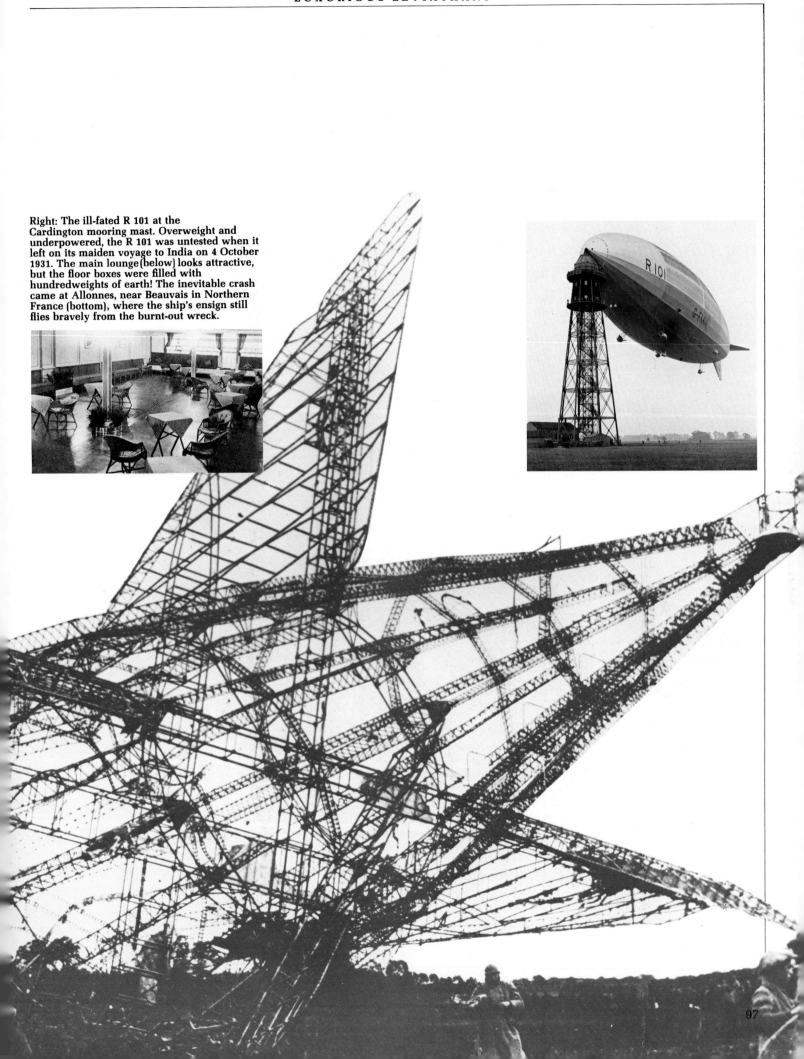

Right: The ill-fated R 101 at the
Cardington mooring mast. Overweight and
underpowered, the R 101 was untested when it
left on its maiden voyage to India on 4 October
1931. The main lounge (below) looks attractive,
but the floor boxes were filled with
hundredweights of earth! The inevitable crash
came at Allonnes, near Beauvais in Northern
France (bottom), where the ship's ensign still
flies bravely from the burnt-out wreck.

tion flights in Canada, including one over Niagara Falls, the R 100 returned safely to England.

Meanwhile, the alterations to the R 101 were going ahead and now political expediency began to dominate good engineering sense. The American depression was causing problems in England and it was rumoured that the least successful airship would be scrapped. Under this threat work rushed ahead, and then the Air Minister, Lord Thompson, insisted that an inaugural flight to India, scheduled for 4 October 1931, must go ahead. Under this kind of pressure, the engineers at Cardington reluctantly, and against their better judgement, reported the R 101 ready. Even so, they knew that all the ship's gas-bags leaked appallingly and that the proper speed trials had not been carried out.

The day of the flight dawned with a rising gale in the English Channel and the forecast of worse weather. Yet R 101 flew according to plan with a fatigued crew, the ship as yet unfinished and untried, and no real plans for the impossible journey ahead. The result was inevitable. At the height of the gale, at 0200 hours on Sunday 5 October, R 101 plunged into a hillside at Beauvais in Northern France and blew up. Of the 54 people on board, only 6 survived, and Lord Thompson was not among them. It was the end of airship development in Britain and it is fair to say that the difficulties of handling these huge monsters in adverse weather was as important a factor in their demise as the explosive qualities of hydrogen. The R 100, potential rival of the great *Graf Zeppelin*, was cut up for scrap and sold for £450!

However, the *Graf Zeppelin* flew on and in 1933 began scheduled services between Germany and Rio de Janeiro.

The final Zeppelin, the LZ 130, also named after the firm's founder, *Graf Zeppelin*. It never entered commercial service and was broken up in the Second World War.

Leitwerkfläche
Fin

Höhenruder
Elevator

Längsträger
Longitudinal girder

Leitwerkfläche
Fin

Seitenruder
Rudder

Landerad
Landing wheel

D-LZ 130

Motorgondel
Engine car

NEW YORK
LAKEHURST

RECIFE
(PERNAMBUCO)

RIO DE JANEIRO

BUENOS
AIRES

LZ 130 wurde von dem Luftschiffbau Zeppelin, G. m. b. H. in Friedrichshafen a. B. erbaut. Seine Länge beträgt 245 m, bei einem größten Durchmesser von 41,2 m. Das Gerippe besteht nach der bewährten, bereits vom Grafen Zeppelin angewandten Bauweise aus Längsträgern, Ringen und aus der Drahtverspannung. Die Außenhaut bildet ein starkes wasserdichtes Stoffgewebe. Das Traggas wird in 16 voneinander unabhängigen Gaszellen im Schiffskörper mitgeführt. Zum Vortrieb des Schiffes werden 4 Daimler-Benz-Dieselmotore von je 1000 PS Höchstleistung verwendet. Alle für die Schiffsführung erforderlichen Einrichtungen und Geräte sind in der unter dem Bug angeordneten Führergondel vereint.

LZ 130
„Graf Zeppelin"

Hilfsring
Intermediate ring

Hauptring
Main ring

Entlüftungslutzen
Ventilation hoods

Entlüftungsschacht
Ventilating shaft

Gaszelle
Gas cell

Achssteg
Axial corridor

Küche
Kitchen

Speisesaal
Dining room

Fracht
Freight

Mannschaftsräume
Crew's quarters

Halle
Lounge

Kabinen
Cabins

Navigationsraum
Navigating room

Führergondel
Control car

Anker-Kouis
Bow mooring cone

FRANKFURT a. M.
HALLE 1
HALLE 2
RHEIN-MAIN

Once again an airship was back on the routes and the *Graf* averaged about 16 round flights a year. In 1936 it was joined by the *Hindenburg*, probably the largest man-made object ever to rise in the air, and this behemoth inaugurated the first regular transatlantic air service.

Eckener had hoped to fill the *Hindenburg* with helium, the inert and safe gas that was only obtainable in the United States. But by 1936, the Americans had realized the true nature of the Nazi regime in Germany and refused to grant export licences for the gas. There was a touch of irony in this as Eckener remained an opponent of the Nazis throughout the Hitler period. Nevertheless, the *Hindenberg* was filled with hydrogen.

This latest airship was a great step forward. She carried 60 passengers and a crew of 55 and cruised at 78 mph (125

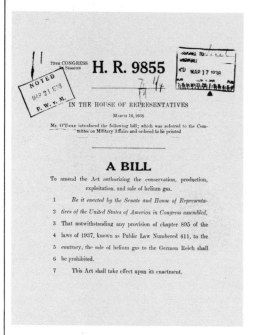

Seven million cubic feet (198,219 cu m) of hydrogen blow up as LZ 129 *Hindenburg* explodes at Lakehurst, New Jersey on 6 May 1937. Thirteen passengers and twenty two crew died but the United States remained adamant that she would not supply the safe helium gas to a Germany dominated by the anti-semetic Nazi regime (above).

km/h). Two passenger decks crossed the interior of her hull and provided a luxury which was only to be found elsewhere on passenger liners. There was even a special lightweight piano and a small isolated smoking room.

In 1936, the *Hindenburg* successfully completed ten round trips to the United States and six to Brazil. Eckener's plans appeared to have been vindicated, as on 4 May 1937 the *Hindenburg* lifted off from Frankfurt am Main airfield to open the new transatlantic season. It arrived at Lakehurst three days later. Then, on an American spring evening as Captain Max Pruss prepared the ship for landing, the *Hindenburg* blew up astern and plunged to the earth, a raging inferno of burning hydrogen in which 35 people died. Miraculously, 62 survivors got out alive, including Captain Pruss.

The *Hindenburg* disaster remains the world's most publicized aircrash and has never been satisfactorily explained. Eckener blamed a fractured staywire which punctured a gas-bag, but stories of sabotage have persisted down the years. But the main reason was the use of hydrogen, and the crash meant the end of the large civil airship. Ever since, plans have been advanced from time to time for the construction of latter-day designs. The Goodyear Company successfully built a series of small non-rigid airships, called blimps, which served the United States Navy well on anti-submarine duties until the 1950s. Goodyear still maintain a small fleet of advertising airships.

In the skies today, the airplane reigns supreme as a passenger carrier, and it is likely to remain unchallenged for the future. Airships, if they have any role at all, must have potential as mass freight carriers. This hypothesis is discussed further in Chapter Eleven.

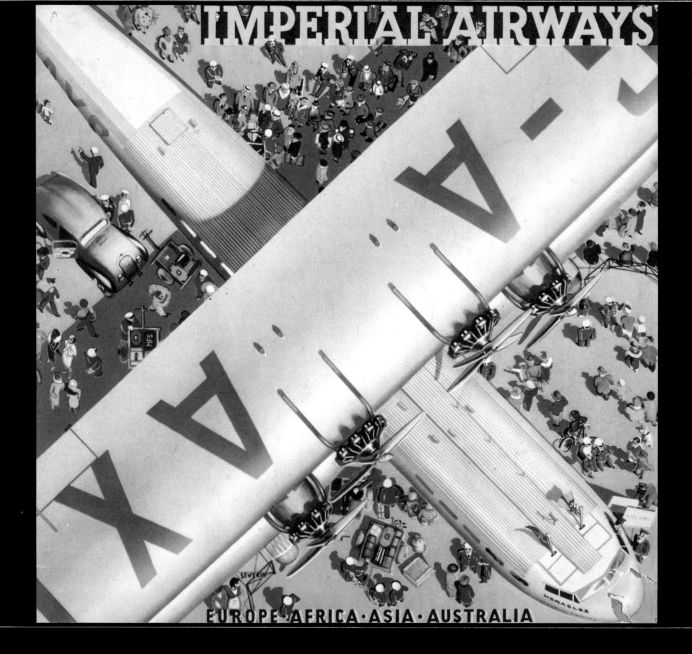

CHAPTER FOUR

HALCYON DAYS

THE AIRLINES CAME OF AGE in the 1930s. In the years that followed 1930, the airliner would change from a lumbering biplane, capable of perhaps 90 mph (145 km/h), into a streamlined metal giant that would carry twice the number of passengers and do so using about two-thirds of the power. It was in the United States that this revolution took place, and it meant a complete reversal of the position of the airline industries of that country and Europe.

The reasons for the American domination of aviation in the 1930s are not hard to find. The story is one of conservatism and complacency in Europe, particularly on the part of Imperial Airways, and a vigorous story of American enterprise. Perhaps one of the main reasons for the decline of British civil aviation in the 1930s was the death of Sir Sefton Brancker, the first Director of Civil Aviation, in the R101 disaster in 1931. Sir Sefton was the outstanding British aviation visionary of his day, and no one ever really replaced him. He was responsible for encouraging Imperial Airways to place an order for eight new large machines from the Handley Page Company in late 1929, and the first of these made its maiden flight on 17 November 1930. The aircraft which took-off that day from the Handley Page airfield at Radlett, north of London, was considered the ultimate in airliners, and it was certainly an imposing machine. Named the HP42, the aircraft was a giant biplane, its upper wing measuring 130 ft (40m). The structure was all-metal. A corrugated metal skin covered the front and centre fuselage, while the wings and rear fuselage had fabric skins. The upper and lower wings were joined with diagonal Warren struts which eliminated the need for bracing wires. Four Bristol Jupiter

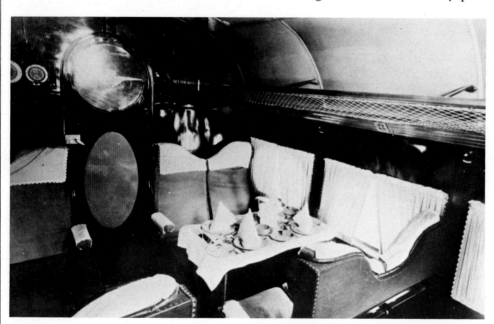

The ultimate in style is shown (above) on board the HP42 with elegant drawing room chairs and lace-edged curtains contrasting with railway carriage luggage racks. Right: Passengers boarding an HP42 at Croydon for the Silver Wing service to Paris. The journey took just over a leisurely two hours. Next page: The Imperial Airways fleet in 1935.

IMPERIAL AIRWAYS

THE GREATEST AIR SERVICE IN THE WORLD

Rudder

Rudder Balance

Elevator

Fin

Tail Plane

Fixed Wireless Aerial

G AAXD

Registration Marking

Royal Mail Insignia

Aft. Luggage and Freight Compartment

Entrance Door for Passengers

Bath Cabin fitted with Heating Apparatus

Ventilators

Engine cut away to show Cabin

4 Air-cooled Bristol Jupiter Engines; each of 555 b.h.p. (equipped with superchargers) in the Heracles class and 490 b.h.p. each in the Hannibal class

Amidship Mail Luggage and Freight Compartment

Automatic Safety Slot

Standard Navigation Light

Captain

Wind Driven Generator

Steward

2 Lavatories

Connecting Passage between Cabins

Kitchen

Aileron

First Officer

Navigation Light

Forward Cabin with seating accommodation for 20 passengers in the Heracles class and 10 in the Hannibal class

HERACLES and HANNIBAL CLASSES

These Air Liners differ only in details of their equipment

HERACLES Used on the European Services	Heracles G-AAXC	Horatius G-AAXD
HANNIBAL Used on the Africa and India Services	Hannibal G-AAGX	Horsa G-AAUC
	Hanno G-AAUD	Hadrian G-AAUE
	Helena G-AAXF	Hengist G-AAXE

Span, 130ft. 0in.; Length, 89ft. 9in.; Height, 27ft. 3in.; Weight fully loaded, 13.4 tons; Speed, 130 m.p.h.

Air Liner built by Handley Page Ltd. Engines built by The Bristol Aeroplane Co. Ltd.

SCYLLA CLASS

Scylla G-ACJJ Syrinx G-ACJK

Span, 113ft. 0in.; Length, 86ft. 3in.; Height, 29ft. 6in.; Weight fully loaded, 14.3 tons; Speed, 130 m.p.h.

Air Liner built by Short Bros. (Rochester and Bedford) Ltd. Engines built by The Bristol Aeroplane Co. Ltd.

4 Air-cooled Bristol Jupiter Engines each of 555 b.h.p. equipped with superchargers

Servo Rudder

Main Rudder

Elevator

Aft Navigation Light

Rudder

Fixed Wireless Aerial

Main Petrol Tanks

Ventilators

Forward Cabin with seating accommodation for 10 passengers

First Officer

Captain

ATALANTA CLASS

Used on the South Africa and India and Eastern Services

Atalanta G-ABTI Athena G-ABTK
Amalthea G-ABTG Astraea G-ABTL
Andromeda G-ABTH •Aurora VT-AEG
Artemis G-ABTJ •Arethusa VT-AEF

Span, 90ft. 0in.; Length 71ft. 11in.; Height, 16ft. 4in.; Speed, 155 m.p.h.; Weight fully loaded, 8.9 tons)

•The property of Indian Trans-Continental Airways, an associated company of Imperial Airways.

Air Liner built by Sir W. G. Armstrong Whitworth Aircraft Ltd. Engines built by Armstrong Siddeley Motors Ltd.

SCIPIO CLASS FLYING-BOATS

Used on the Mediterranean section of the Africa, India and Australian Services

Scipio G-ABFA Sylvanus G-ABFB
Satyrus G-ABFC

Span, 113ft. 0in.; Length, 78ft. 5in.; Height, 23ft. 0in.; Weight, fully loaded, 14.3 tons; Speed, 135 m.p.h.

Air Liner built by Short Bros. (Rochester and Bedford) Ltd. Engines built by The Bristol Aeroplane Co. Ltd.

engines, each of 550 hp, moved the HP42 through the air at a steady 100 mph (161 km/h). This low speed meant that passenger comfort and safety had been placed first and foremost, and a very advanced standard of comfort was certainly achieved. Twenty four passengers were carried, and a glance at the cabin almost gave one the impression of being in the drawing room of an English country house. Chintz curtains hung at each window, and large comfortable armchairs were provided for the passengers. They were carried in two cabins, and the noisiest part of the fuselage, the section next to the engines, was set aside as the baggage hold. High-quality meals were served in-flight. By any standard, these meals were excellent when compared to the packaged food on airlines today. Most of the preparation of the food took place in-flight, and it was the boast of Imperial Airways' catering staff that no tinned food was used on any of their services.

The prototype HP42, which was the first of eight to be built, was called *Hannibal*, and registered G-AAGX. This great all-silver biplane became one of the most famous aircraft in all civil aviation, and photographs of the type in service have come to epitomize Imperial Airways to generations of aviation enthusiasts.

The HP42 was supplied in two versions. The first four were classified the E type (because they flew East), and were called *Hannibal*, followed by *Horsa*, *Hanno*, and *Hadrian*. The remaining four were designated HP42Ws (because they flew West routes in Europe), and were called *Heracles*, *Horatius*, *Hengist* and *Helena*. All eight aircraft had been delivered to Imperial Airways by February 1932.

These much-loved machines soon established a reputation for efficiency

and safety, flying millions of miles and carrying hundreds of thousands of passengers. The first W airplane, the *Heracles*, operated on European routes and by September 1938 (that is, seven years of service), had flown over 1 million miles (1,610,000 km) and carried 95,000 passengers.

Although there were a number of incidents involving the HP42, its safety record was outstanding. In August 1931, the *Hannibal* had left Croydon with a full load of passengers when an air screw came loose and damaged two other air screws as it fell away from the aircraft. Captain F Dismore was in charge, and he managed to land the great machine using the one remaining engine, in a field near Tonbridge in Kent. His superb handling of the airplane, and the rugged structure built by Handley Page, saved all the passengers and crew. The reputation of the HP42 soared, and the *Hannibal* was taken back to Croydon, repaired and replaced in service. There were no fatal accidents of any kind with the HP42 until 1940, when the *Hannibal* disappeared without trace over the Indian Ocean. The last HP42 in service was the *Helena*, which was finally dismantled in 1941.

Imperial Airways, unlike its American counterparts, adhered to a policy in the 1930s of using a few exceptionally large and luxurious aircraft, rather than attempting to exploit the market by increasing the size of its fleet. So it was in 1935, when the DC-3 was already in service, that it added two large S17 biplanes built by Short Brothers to its fleet. These were the famous Scylla and her sister, the Syrinx. These luxury craft actually provided more space than the HP42, which they somewhat resembled.

The next machine to go into service with Imperial Airways was the Arms-

Airline propaganda in the 1930s laid stress on the normality of life in the skies (top). Passengers on an HP42 of Imperial Airways observe the two minutes' silence on Armistice Day, commemorating the dead of the First World War. Above: The galley aboard the Short S17 Scylla. Most of the meals were prepared in flight and Imperial Airways boasted that no tinned food was ever served!
Opposite page: The world grows smaller as the airlines speed up. An Imperial Airways poster of 1937. The speedbird symbol overprinted on the map is still in use today on British Airways' intercontinental aircraft.

trong Whitworth AW15, the Atalanta. The airline ordered the Atalanta in 1931 for its Nairobi-Cape Town and Karachi-Singapore routes. These flights had to be made in tropical conditions and provision was needed for landing at airfields which, in some cases, were more than 6000 ft (1829 m) above sea level. Contemporary records seem to indicate that the Atalanta never quite achieved the performance required, because although it had seats for 17 passengers, it usually operated with only 11 or 12. It was a high wing monoplane with a span of 90 ft (27 m), a total weight of 9 tons, and was powered by four Armstrong Siddeley Serval engines which were rated at 340 hp each. The Atalanta was used entirely on the Empire routes of Imperial Airways and remained in service until 1941. Specially equipped Atalantas were used on pioneering flights to Aus-

tralia. Of the eight aircraft constructed from 1932 onwards, only one was lost in an accident. Of the remaining seven, three continued to fly until 1942 and the last two were used by the Royal Indian Air Force for anti-submarine duties in 1944. By 1932, Imperial Airways had opened routes which were 11,767 miles (18,937 km) in total, and were carrying 34,000 passengers a year.

By 1934, the Imperial Airways fleet was formed mainly of the HP42s, the Atalantas, the two big Short S17s and the Short Scipio flying boats which maintained the Mediterranean leg of the route to India. In May of that year, the airline took delivery of the first of twelve de Havilland DH86 four-engined biplanes. Known as the Diana class, this was the first four-engined airplane to come from the Hatfield-based company. It had been produced at the request of the Australian govern-

ment, who wanted a commercial airliner for the Singapore-Brisbane route. This meant that it had to operate in tropical climates and fly long hours over water. The resulting airplane was a highly-developed version of the company's popular Dragon. Powered by four Gipsy Six in-line air-cooled engines of 200 hp each, it had a crew of two and seating for ten passengers. Imperial Airways used it on its European routes to Paris and Vienna and also on African and Far East lines. Other airlines to use the DH86 included Railway Air Service Limited, the Australian carrier Qantas, and Jersey Airways. The latter company brought six DH86s in 1935 and one was still flying at the end of the 1950s. Production of the DH86 stopped in 1937, but a twin-engined version, somewhat smaller and called the Dragon Rapide, became another classic airplane.

An Imperial Airways poster showing aircraft types used on their shorthaul routes in the mid-1930s. Passenger interest in aircraft details was much greater then and airlines responded by issuing attractive cut-away drawings.
The Art Deco style so beloved in the 1930s emerges from this Imperial Airways poster (opposite page). The emphasis was clearly on service and comfort.

The Dragon Rapide was not a true airliner in the modern sense of the word, but it enjoyed a remarkable success as a short-range feeder-line aircraft. A number continue in service even today, and in all some 728 machines were produced. In addition, a military version known as the Dominie was used for training and communications by the RAF, and a total of 532 were produced. BEA used Dragon Rapides for a number of years after the Second World War on its flights to Scotland and the Channel Islands.

The years that followed 1930 were a time of growth for Imperial Airways, but the pace was leisurely. Most of the services of the Imperial routes to South Africa and the Far East were on a weekly basis, while there were two flights a day to Paris and one daily to most of the other European capitals. In 1933, the journey to India started on a Saturday and ended on the following Friday, with stops at Athens, Gaza, Basra and Sharjah. The flight from London-Cape Town departed on a Wednesday and took 10 days to complete. Although these journeys seem never-ending by modern standards, they compared very favourably with the time for a passage by sea.

Although the company had an excellent safety record, there appears to have been a 'press on regardless' approach by its pilots. On one occasion, a passenger was sitting in a wicker chair aboard the *Heracles* when the big biplane entered a patch of violent turbulence. The seat broke away from its mounting brackets, but on landing, the pilot dismissed the affair as 'quite normal' for the route. It was only when the passenger noticed that part of the wing had also broken off that the pilot realized the serious nature of the incident.

Checking-in time was two hours

before departure, and the total weight allowed on any one ticket was 220 lbs (100 kg). This included the passenger, who was solemnly weighed together with the baggage! Very little baggage ever appeared to be lost, unlike today, and the passenger's overnight bag arrived at the hotel without any further action on his part. Because the aircraft cabin was not pressurized, careful attention was given to advice on clothing for the journey. Cabin heating had also not been supplied, and therefore passengers were recommended to dress in woollen clothes and reminded that the early mornings could be very cold. Imperial Airways always issued a blanket to passengers who felt in need of protection from the early morning nip. Another problem was the very detailed customs check which went on at all terminals. This could often take up to two hours after arrival and was a considerable irritation. On the credit side, however, the food provided throughout the flight was impressive. By the mid-1930s, a five-course meal, fully prepared and cooked on board, was standard on Imperial Airways and proved to be one of the company's major advantages over its competitors.

The flight to the East must have been a great adventure. It was carried out at heights which allowed the passenger to see the details of the ground below, and the machines seldom operated in cloud. Overnight, the amenities ranged from luxury hotels in Athens to a native rest house on Lombok Island, where passengers were expected to share beds, and the lavatory consisted of a wooden box with two holes drilled in the ground!

By 1936, Imperial Airways were moving 68,000 passengers each year and flying a total of 4,560,000 miles (7,339000 km). It was time to expand.

To the board of Imperial Airways,

any extension of its services appeared most profitable if carried out on the Empire routes. The decision to build and operate the Short Empire flying boats is recorded in the next chapter. It was typical of the narrow outlook of Imperial Airways that during the years of Imperial expansion, the routes to Europe were almost neglected and, while other airlines flew modern American equipment, Imperial Airways soldiered on with the HP42. This led a number of British private operators to set up European services, and these largely used the small de Havilland airliners, such as the DH86 and the Dragon Rapide. Eventually, in 1935,

Above: The Lufthansa network of the 1930s compares favourably with that of today! The aircraft is a Ju52/3m.

several of the smaller companies, Hillman Airways, Spartan Airlines, United Airways and British Continental Airways, joined together to form British Airways.

From 1936 onwards, Imperial Airways had to face the competition of British Airways on European routes. British Airways set up its operational base at Gatwick, East Sussex, and commenced services with Fokker FXII airplanes and DH86As. Then, in 1937, the airline obtained licences to operate to Croydon and introduced two very significant aircraft types. The first was the Junkers Ju52/3m. The other was the Lockheed Electra.

The two aircraft demonstrated the advances made by the American industry, compared to European practice, in the short time that had elapsed since 1930. The Junkers was a traditional slow, safe European design, whereas the Lockheed was a modern stress-skinned, fast American product flying at half the speed again and using considerably less power.

The Junkers Company had intervened in airliner design for a second time with the huge G38, a four-engined monster which made its maiden flight on 6 November 1929 and was delivered to Lufthansa in June of the following year. The aircraft had the typical appearance of the Junkers design – an all-metal structure and corrugated dur-alumin skinning. It was designed around a very large wing and 6 of the 34 passengers were actually seated inside the leading edge, where they had a panoramic view from the large windows there. In addition, another observation cabin was available in the nose. The aircraft had a range of 2100 miles (3380 km) and two were placed in airline service. Among the routes flown by the two Lufthansa G38s was Berlin-

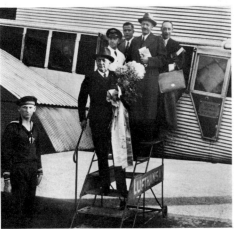

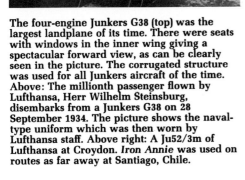

The four-engine Junkers G38 (top) was the largest landplane of its time. There were seats with windows in the inner wing giving a spectacular forward view, as can be clearly seen in the picture. The corrugated structure was used for all Junkers aircraft of the time. Above: The millionth passenger flown by Lufthansa, Herr Wilhelm Steinsburg, disembarks from a Junkers G38 on 28 September 1934. The picture shows the naval-type uniform which was then worn by Lufthansa staff. Above right: A Ju52/3m of Lufthansa at Croydon. *Iron Annie* was used on routes as far away at Santiago, Chile.

Rome via Vienna and Berlin-Copenhagen and Stockholm.

The G38 was an aircraft ahead of its time and Junkers were far more successful with their next machine, the Ju52, which first flew on 13 October 1930. It was powered by a single engine and found to be lacking in performance. Therefore, the seventh aircraft off the production line was equipped with two extra engines, one on each wing, and this three-motored version took to the air for the first time in April 1932. It then became one of the best civil airliners operating in the 1930s, and was Germany's leading transport of the Second World War. Between 1932 and 1939, some 200 Ju52/3ms were built and sold to over 30 different airlines. The total production in peace- and wartime amounted to 4835 airplanes.

A low-wing monoplane, all-metal and covered in the characteristic Jun-

kers corrugated sheet duralumin, the Ju52/3m carried seventeen passengers and a crew of two. It was one of the most rugged airplanes ever built, and used for just about every purpose, including bombing. A number of military versions were used in the infamous Guernica raid during the Spanish Civil War. During the Second World War, Luftwaffe air crews nicknamed the type *Iron Annie*, and it became a firm favourite with its operators.

The next Junkers airliner was the Ju86 of 1934, which originally appeared with Rolls-Royce Kestrel engines, each of 745 hp. Eventually, however, it was fitted with the Junkers Jumo 205, which was the only diesel engine ever to be loaded into a land plane airliner. Compared with a petrol engine it was, of course, heavier, but it consumed less fuel, therefore making it cheaper to run. The Ju86 was really a converted bomber

German airliner design advanced rapidly in the 1930s, spurred on by the military ambitions of the Nazi regime. Top: The Junkers Ju86, a medium-range machine, remains the only landplane airliner to be diesel-powered. In reality, it was a converted bomber. Above: The Junkers Ju90 – a four-engined long-range airliner which was the largest European aircraft at the start of the Second World War. Below: Kurt Tank's outstanding Focke-Wulf Fw200 Condor at Floyd Bennett Field, New York, after its 24-hour, non-stop flight from Berlin on 10-11 August 1938.

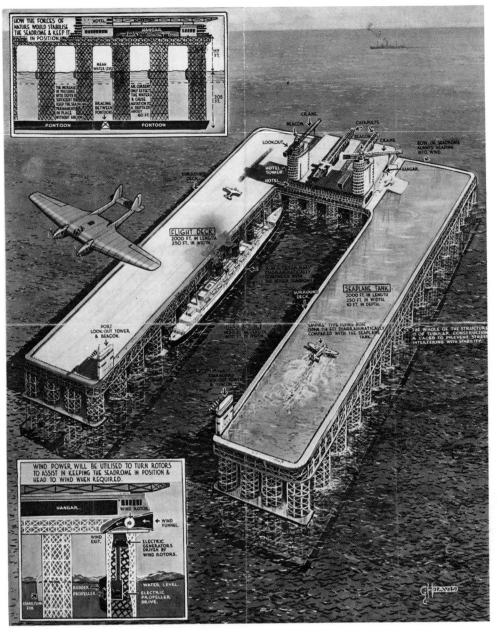

The Heiser Seadrome was a proposal by an Australian engineer to surmount the range problems anticipated by designers in the 1930s. The cost would have been prohibitive, but the principle of flotation has been extensively used in the North Sea oil industry.

and it did not prove altogether successful, with only 10 being ordered for Lufthansa, although a few other aircraft were sold to South America and South Africa.

Two other significant airliner designs came from Germany in the years between the wars. The first was a large four-engined transcontinental airliner designed by Dr Kurt Tank of the Focke-Wulf Company, who proposed to Lufthansa his famous Fw200 Condor which flew in July 1937. The Condor was designed as a direct replacement of the Ju52, and to counter the success of the Douglas DC-3, which was going into service in large numbers. The result was an elegant, low-winged, four-engined airliner of very modern appearance and built entirely of metal. Like the DC-3, it had a retractable undercarriage, and fulfilled expectations when the first prototype, named *Brandenburg*, flew from Berlin direct to New York, a distance of more than 4000 miles (6437 km), on 10 August 1938. The journey took 24 hours 55 minutes at an average speed of 164 mph (264 km/h). The Condor was bought by the Danish airline DDL and was also used in Brazil. Lufthansa bought 10 altogether. These were placed in service in 1938 and continued to serve during the Second World War. Another Fw200 became Adolf Hitler's personal aircraft. The type was also developed as a maritime patrol and anti-shipping aircraft, and as such became notorious during the war, particularly among allied merchant seamen.

At about the same time that the Condor was appearing, the Junkers Company also produced a large four-engined airliner which had a capacity for forty passengers. This was the Ju90 – yet another airliner to be developed from a bomber. The first prototype flew

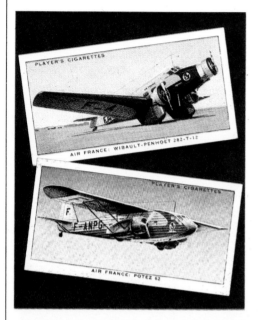

only a month after the Condor but this machine was lost in a crash early in 1938. The Ju90 is important in that it was the largest airliner flying in Europe at the outbreak of the Second World War, although only 12 examples were ever completed for civil use.

The rest of Europe during the 1930s concentrated largely on producing aircraft for its own national needs. In France, the national airline Air France had been founded on 30 August 1933 by the merger of the four largest airlines operating in that country. The new airline found itself with about 23,000 miles (37,015 km) of routes and a fleet of 259 aircraft of many different types, most of them out of date. Therefore, a plan was formed to standardize the equipment, and the French industry produced a number of good designs which served Air France well until the outbreak of war. Routes were pioneered in Europe,

and in 1937 experimental transatlantic flights were undertaken. Another advance was the eastern route which reached China in 1938. Between 1930 and 1939 the airline had doubled its passenger totals to just over 100,000.

Between 1933 and 1938, Air France used the Wibault-Penhoët 283, a fast three-engined plane, on most of its European routes. Not unlike the Ju52 in appearance, the Wibault was somewhat smaller but had a useful cruising speed of 150 mph (91 km/h). It was powered by three Gnome-Rhône Titan Major seven-cylinder radial engines of 350 hp each. It was of all-metal construction and its main characteristic was the large fairings around the undercarriage to reduce drag. The new airline ordered 10 Wibault 283s in 1934 and kept them in service until 1938, by which time the Dewoitine D338 had been developed.

The D338 was introduced in 1936,

Top: Two well known Air France machines were the Wibault-Penhoët 282-T-12 and the Potez 62. Both were familiar visitors to Croydon and were suitable subjects for cigarette card advertising. Above: The Bloch 220 was an all-metal transport which Air France introduced in 1937 and operated throughout the Second World War and the post-war years. Opposite: An Air France poster from 1938, showing their Far Eastern route and the Dewoitine D338.

AIR FRANCE
THE FRENCH AIR LINE

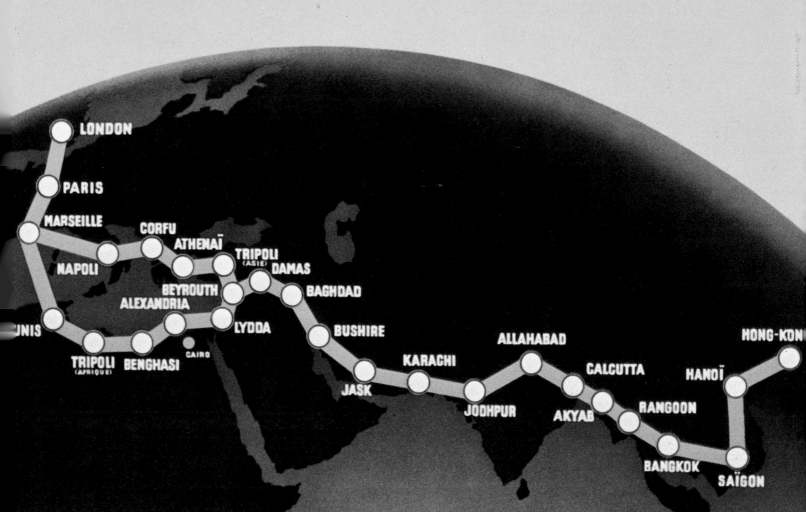

The Dewoitine D338 allowed Air France to reduce its Le Bourget-Croydon time to 1½ hours, a fact which the Air France publicists were quick to advertise.

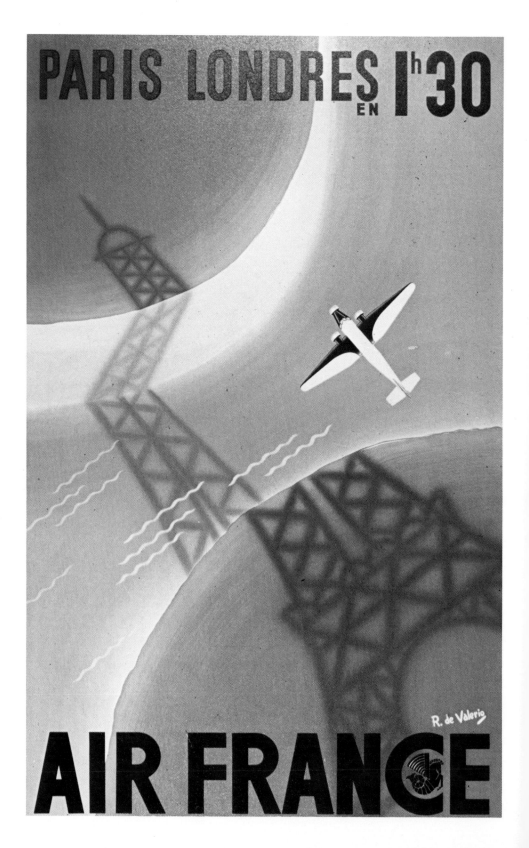

and could carry 22 passengers on European routes. Thirty were built for Air France, and it was the first of the company's machines to possess retractable landing gear. The company used it on all its services, including African and Far Eastern runs, and on the latter services six passengers could be carried in sleeping berths. The Dewoitines were supported in Air France service by the Potez 62, a high-wing, twin-engined monoplane which became the workhorse of the company from 1936 onwards. Finally in 1937, Air France introduced the Bloch 220, an all-metal transport which looked remarkably like the DC-2. Only 16 examples of the Bloch 220 were built, but this robust and safe commercial twin-engined aircraft was in service right through the Second World War, and helped to rebuild the Air France European routes in the years immediately after 1945.

Italy in the 1930s concentrated on the development of a series of airliners produced by the Savoia-Marchetti concern, which had produced earlier a very successful series of flying boats. The first of the SM liners was the ten-seat, three-engined S71 of 1930 and this was followed by the S73, an eighteen-seat trimotor which was used by Ala Littoria and sold abroad to the Belgian airline Sabena. All these Italian airplanes were similar in appearance, and the largest of the series was the thirty-seat SM75, on which a retractable undercarriage was introduced for the first time. This group of machines was equipped with either Fiat or Alfa Romeo engines and the final version was the SM83, developed from the famous SM79 Sparviero bomber.

The Soviet Union covers the largest area of a continent in the world, and it has, therefore, a direct interest in efficient airline services. From as far back

The trimotor layout of the Savoia-Marchetti series of airliners was the trade mark of Ala Littoria and Sabena between the wars. Left: A local resident poses before a Sabena SM73 of the Brussels-Elizabethville service. Below: A cabin scene aboard a Sabena SM73. Bottom: The SM83 was a civil version of the famous SM79 Sparviero bomber. Ala Littoria used it mainly on its South Atlantic services between Rome and Natal.

as 1932, when it had been set up as the
state airline, Aeroflot has shown itself
to be capable of almost continuous progress. In that year it managed to transport 27,000 passengers, and by 1935 the
number had risen to 111,000. In addition, a network of services extended
across the entire Soviet Union from
Leningrad and Odessa to Moscow and
then right across the Ural Mountains to
Vladivostok. By 1940, the year before
the German invasion, the network of
services had reached 90,000 miles
(144,840 km), and 395,000 passengers
were being carried annually. Russia
had possessed air services since the
1920s, and the country was unique in
that a railway ticket was completely
interchangeable with a seat on an airliner. People who had wanted to fly
simply bought a railway ticket and then
turned up at the local airport to see if
they could get a seat. If a plane had to
abandon its journey for any reason,
passengers were automatically
refunded the cost of the railway ticket.

Throughout the 1930s, Russian
designers produced a series of different
airliner types. The Russian government
gave strong backing to the development
of aviation and soon world-famous
names began to appear like Tupolev
and Yakovlev. In its early years Aeroflot expanded its operations with 260
Kalinin K5 monoplanes and the Tupolev ANT 9 trimotor. These aircraft
formed the backbone of Aeroflot services during the 1930s, but mention
must be made of the gigantic ANT 20
which first flew in July 1934, and was
the largest aircraft in the world at the
time. It was named after the Soviet
writer Maxim Gorki, and had a wing
span of 206 ft (63 m). Eight in-line
AM34 RN engines of 900 hp each were
provided. Six were mounted on the
large single wing and two more in a cell

PLAYER'S CIGARETTE

Above: The Tupolev ANT9 depicted on a
cigarette card of the period. This particular
model has been fitted with skis and is in the
colours of Deruluft. From the
same factory in 1934 came the huge Maxim
Gorki (left). It had been ordered as a
propaganda aircraft with electrically
illuminated writings under the wings, which
also housed a printing press and photographic
darkroom with a telephone office and
broadcasting station in the fuselage. It survived
for only a year, being lost in a mid-air collision,
but later 16 improved versions were produced,
some lasting until 1945.

perched high above the fuselage. Despite its size, the ANT 20 carried only 72 people and it was used largely for propaganda purposes. On board there was a small printing shop, a photographic studio, a cinema and a radio transmitting station. Unfortunately, the big machine was lost in an air collision with a military aircraft in May 1935, but Tupolev followed it with at least sixteen of the type, and eight were reported to be still flying in 1945.

In the United States, the decade had begun with a drastic reorganization of air services, carried out by Walter Brown who was Post Master General under President Herbert Hoover. Brown saw clearly that the existing chaos of small airlines in the United States could not continue, and he set about forcing mergers with a ruthlessness that had seldom been seen in United States government policy. Small operators were forced out of business as the United States Post Office awarded the bulk of the airmail to a relative handful of airlines which were considered to be well run and financially sound. In May 1930, Brown invited the heads of the large airlines to Washington for a meeting which came to be called the Spoils Conference. It was an appropriate name because the spoils literally went to those airlines which supported Brown's plans to establish three main mail routes across America. United Airways got the northern route, the newly-formed American Airlines were allocated the southern route, and the central route went to a new airline called Transcontinental and Western Air Express, which later became the legendary TWA.

Brown's plans seemed to be successful until 1934, when a scandal blew up in Washington. Senator Hugo Black of Alabama presided over a Congressional

Sleeping facilities have been a preoccupation with airlines from the early services. Reclining seats were introduced (top) by Lufthansa on the Albatross L73, an eight-seat airliner biplane of 1926, nicknamed the *Flying Sleeping Car*. 'Togetherness' (bottom) aboard a Pan Am Stratocruiser on the North Atlantic run in 1950.

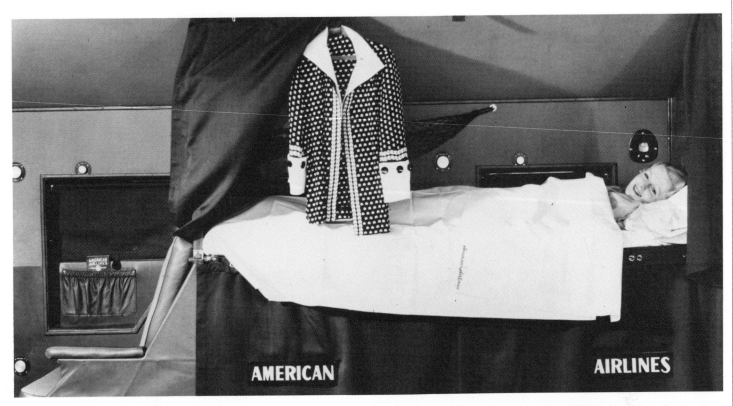

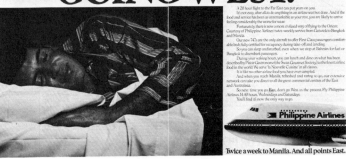

American Airlines introduced the first full sleeping berths on their Curtiss Condors in 1933 (top and left). Sleepers in the 1980s (above)! Philippine Airways offer bed certified for landing and take-off. Previously, passengers were roused for these events!

United Airlines introduced the Boeing 247 in March 1933 (left), and things were never the same again. The all-metal, fast monoplane with retractable undercarriage (top) drove all its competitors like the Curtiss Condor (above) from the airways. But United's monopoly of the 247 led other airlines to order the Douglas DC-2, which led in turn to the demise of the Boeing.

enquiry which eventually found Brown guilty of malpractice, although he was cleared of fraud. After a disastrous decision to make the United States Air-force carry the mail, President Roosevelt decided to begin again and award fresh mail contracts. A conference of 45 operators took place and only airlines without connections with aircraft manufacturers were allowed to participate. So Boeing had to break its link with United, and other aircraft builders sold their interests in TWA, Eastern and American Airlines. So it was that the big four airlines in America became independent, and other large concerns involved, such as Braniff and Delta, have prospered to this day. It was this decision which ended the connection between airline and manufacturer, so that both had to exist independently, that led to the design of the marvellous Douglas DC-3.

The depression had forced the motor industry to withdraw from airplane construction in the United States, and this left the field clear for three new companies, of which Boeing were the most experienced. They were joined by Douglas and Lockheed, and such was the development of these three concerns that they have dominated the airline business ever since. In the early 1930s, the best American airliner was the Curtiss Condor, a fat biplane produced for American Airlines, which entered service in 1933. The Condor was the first airliner with a retractable undercarriage and it was also capable of being converted into sleeper accommodation. More significantly, it was the first airliner to use the Wright Cyclone – a nine-cylinder radial which would eventually power the early DC-3s. This large biplane had much in common with European practice but it was soon overtaken by a dramatic new develop-

ment from Boeing. Having won the coast-to-coast mail order, United Airlines required a machine which could operate over that distance. It placed an order with Boeing and the result was the Model 247.

This was an all-metal construction and it is rightly regarded as the first modern airliner. It cruised at 160 mph (257 km/h) and could carry a full load of passengers from coast-to-coast in just under twenty hours. The machine was not a success, however, due to two factors. Boeing had specified the Pratt & Whitney Hornet engine, but United Airways asked instead for the trusted but low-powered Wasp. Consequently,

The immortal Douglas DC-3 was developed from the DC-2, one of which was entered by KLM in the London-Melbourne Air Race of 1934 and was second overall (top left). The first DC-3 to be delivered to TWA (right). The type had been developed for American Airlines, who put it into service in June 1936 between New York and Chicago. In all, 11,000 aircraft were built, making the DC-3 the most successful aircraft ever. Opposite page: A Douglas DC-3 features in this poster for Air Vietnam.

the 247 could carry only 10 passengers. Secondly, the President of United Airways, William A Patterson, placed a huge order for sixty machines at a cost of $4 million. This was the largest single order in airplane history at the time, and it was more than Boeing could handle with comfort. The order tied up the assembly lines at Seattle for a year and forced TWA and American Airlines to look elsewhere. Unfortunately for Boeing, they went to Douglas.

In 1932, Jack Frye, the boss of TWA, had asked Douglas to build him a trimotor airplane. At the time, Douglas was designing something he considered to be very much better. The result was

the DC-1 and for Douglas it was the gamble of a lifetime. The DC-1 could carry four more passengers than the Boeing for the same operated cost. It first flew in 1933, but was quickly developed into the DC-2 – a larger machine which appeared a year later. Then the gamble of Donald Douglas paid off, when TWA placed an order for twenty aircraft. Eventually, he went on to build 220 DC-2s while developing the famous DC-3. So successful was the Douglas series of airliners that only 75 of the Boeing 247 were built. United Airlines also ordered Douglas machines but the Boeing 247 had earned its place in airline history, being the first big trans-

port with an ability to climb away with a full load on one engine.

The DC-2 was successful in Europe as well. It was bought by KLM, and in October 1934 the Dutch company entered it in the London-Melbourne air race. It came second overall and KLM promptly ordered a total of 14 aircraft. Other airlines in Europe followed their lead. The decision of the President of KLM, Dr Arnold Plesman, to order the DC-2 led to a break in that company's long relationship with the Fokker concern, whose factory was located alongside KLM's headquarters at Schiphol. At that time, Fokker were offering KLM their FXXXVI. This was a large machine with a wing span of 108 ft (33 m), but it was of a wood and fabric skin with a metal frame, and so was years behind the all-metal DC-2. In addition, it required four Wright Cyclone engines, as opposed to the two mounted in the DC-2, and it had a fixed undercarriage. The machine did not fly until 22 June 1934, by which time Douglas had announced their forthcoming DC-3 which could carry up to 32 passengers; the same as the FXXXVI but at a cruising speed of at least 30 mph (48 km/h) more than the Dutch machine's 150 mph (241 km/h).

KLM therefore cancelled its orders for the FXXXVI but Anthony Fokker cut his losses by acquiring the Dutch rights for building the DC-2, and sold these machines to KLM.

The DC-3 first flew on 17 December 1935, and in all about 11,000 aircraft were eventually built. American Airways were the first to receive quantities of the new machine and it was placed in service on the New York-Chicago non-stop run in June 1936.

Looking very similar to its predecessor, the DC-3 was an all-metal, low-winged monoplane with a wing span of

95 ft (29 m) and a length of 64 ft 6ins (19 m). The maximum weight was 25,200 lbs (11,430 kg), and the range extended to 1300 miles (2092 km). Between 1936 and the entry of the United States into the Second World War, more than 800 aircraft had been built and sold. Every airline in America used the DC-3 and it could be found in most of the leading European airlines as well. More than 10 times that number were built during the war and the Dakota, as the RAF called their DC-3s, was seen in the airforces of every allied nation. It was built under licence in the Soviet Union and saw service throughout the Vietnam War. Today, in the 1980s, there are still over 500 DC-3s serving in airlines throughout the world.

As well as the rise of Donald Douglas' series of DC aircraft, the 1930s also witnessed the beginnings of what was to become an institution – that of the air hostess. In the 1920s, the cabin staff was invariably male, and BEA maintained that practice right up to the Second World War. It was in America that there appeared for the first time that peculiar creation identified only with the twentieth century – the airline stewardess. The first air stewardesses actually flew with Boeing Air Transport (BAT), who were later part of United Airlines. They were led by a trained

In 1930, the world's first stewardesses flew with United Airlines (top left). All trained nurses, their founder and leader Ellen Church is standing on the aircraft steps, third from the left. An innovation in 1932 to pass the long flight hours was the presentation of election results to passengers by a stewardess of United Airlines (top right). Right: The all-American girl! A stewardess of TWA in the war years.

nurse, Ellen Church, and eight of them were recruited to fly on the route from Chicago to San Francisco. The girls were all nurses and were only taken on a three-month trial basis. The scheme was the brainchild of the San Francisco office manager of BAT, Steve Stimpson, who noticed that passengers were often airsick and in need of attention. This was in 1930, and in those days, the co-pilot handed out lunch boxes and served coffee from a thermos flask. Stimpson thought that the airline would prove more attractive to passengers if an in-flight service was available, and he persuaded the redoubtable W A Patterson, later to become Eastern's president, to let him try out the scheme.

The first flight with Ellen Church on board as stewardess took-off on 15 May 1930. Although even then the job had an air of glamour and daring about it, the duties were often far beyond the tasks fulfilled by the flight attendants of today. These included assistance in refuelling the aircraft, transferring baggage when passengers changed planes at the mid-point of the journey at Cheyenne, and mopping up cabin floors. In addition, there were the normal tasks of attending to the passengers' needs, serving meals (usually cold chicken sandwiches), and seeing to the safety and comfort of travellers. This even meant

ensuring that passengers going to the toilets actually used the correct door, and not the adjacent one, which led outside to a quick trip to eternity!

When a flight was grounded through bad weather, the stewardess was expected to find hotel accommodation for her passengers. She had to keep the travellers entertained in-flight, and Ellen Church recalled the boxer who was so scared at the thought of flying that she spent the whole trip holding his hand. Not to be forgotten also was the job of checking that the seats were all bolted to the floor, and if a passenger wanted to read, the stewardess had to put a towel round the light in order to direct the beam onto the page.

The stewardess scheme proved a winner from the first, and today the stewardess is very much part of the mystique of air travel. She is, after all, the member of the staff that actually sees more of the passenger than any other, and her appearance and bearing can do more good (or bad!) for the line's reputation than anything else, other than lost baggage. Companies spend much money and effort on recruitment and training (Eastern has recruited and trained 22,000 stewardesses over the years), and a lot of emphasis is put on appearance. Intensive instruction on passenger relations is only rivalled by attention to emergency procedures.

The United Airlines class of 1940 graduates line up before a DC-3 to receive their wings (top left) Top right: The early stewardess uniform closely resembled nurses outfits, and passengers were served from silver coffee pots. Next page: The de Havilland DH91 Albatross remains for many people the most beautiful aircraft ever built. This poster was used for advertising by Imperial Airways in Germany – a difficult task in 1938.

Steuerbord Positionslicht

Vier luftgekühlte *Gipsy Twelve* Motore
von je 525 PS

Mittlere Kabine fü

Vordere Kabine für 8 Fluggäste

Landescheinwerfer

Festantenne

Antennenmast

Verstellbare Luftschrauben mit
Eisschutzmittel

Flugzeugfunker

Flugkapitän

Flugzeugführer

Navigations-Instrumente, Blindflugausrü-
stung und vollautomatisches Selbststeuer-
gerät

Gepäckraum

Steward

Küche

Eingang für Besatzung

Einlass für
Motorkühlung

Auslass für Motorkühlung

Elektrisch erwärmte Düsen für
Fahrtmesser

Verstellbare Luftschrauben mit
Eisschutzmittel

Bakenanflug-Gerät

IMPERIAL AIRWAYS

EUROPA · AFRIKA · INDIEN · DER FERNE OSTEN · AUSTRALIEN · VEREINIGTE STAATEN VON AMERIKA - BERMUDA

Achtere Kabine für
6 Fluggäste

Postladeraum

Waschraum

gäste

G-AEDI

Internationale Zulassung

Eingang zur Kabine

Fahrgestell, das unterhalb der Kabine
eingezogen werden kann

Landeklappen unterhalb der
Tragflächen-Hinterkante

Landescheinwerfer

DIE FROBISHER KLASSE

DIE SCHNELLSTEN ENGLISCHEN VERKEHRSFLUGZEUGE

4 MOTORE · SCHNELL UND BEQUEM

Printed in England by Ben Johnson & Co. Ltd., York, and published in England by Imperial Airways Ltd., Airway Terminus, London. IA/P/321/14m/3/39 Stuarts

NAME OF CARRIER
OR CARRIERS
NOM DU OU DES
TRANSPORTEURS } BRITISH AIRWAYS LTD No. BA/ WS 18249

For Addresses see page 2. Adresses en 2e page.

Passenger's Name
Nom du Voyageur } THE RT HON NEVILLE CHAMBERLAIN

FARE
PRIX
SPECIAL
FLIGHT
R

From
De LONDON to MUNICH
AND RETURN

Leaving on
Partant le } 29/9/38 at 08.30
Time. Heure.

From } HESTON Airport {Via Line} {Via Ligne} No(s)

The newly formed British Airways used the Lockheed Super Electra to fly British Prime Minister Neville Chamberlain to the infamous Munich Conference in September 1938. This is the scene at Hendon, BA's headquarters, as Chamberlain promises 'peace in our time'.

Although the job is demanding and offers plenty of hard work, there are always plenty of recruits who consider the excitement and glamour of air travel to be well worth the effort and standard required.

Such was the domination of American aviation by the DC-3 that few other aircraft were developed as airliners in the United States during the 1930s. One exception was the Lockheed Company's Electra, which came out in 1934 as a small, fast, all-metal, twin-engined medium-range airliner with a capacity for 12 passengers. The Electra sold very well, particularly to the smaller airlines, and the first production version was delivered to North West Airlines in July 1934. It was put into service between St Paul and Chicago, and altogether 148 airplanes were supplied to such companies as Braniff and Pan Am. Lockheed followed with their Model 14, which they called the Super Electra. This featured more powerful Pratt & Whitney engines and enjoyed considerable export sales. It was purchased by KLM, followed by British Airways and Aer Lingus. Orders were also received from Japan and Canada. It was a Super Electra that carried the British Prime Minister Neville Chamberlain to Germany in September 1938, for the historic Munich Conference.

From Boeing in 1939, just before the outbreak of the war, came the next significant development in the civil airliner. It had been known for many years that aeroengines operated at their best performance at high altitudes. However, above 10,000 ft (3048 m), the human body has to be supplied with additional oxygen if it is to remain efficient and not suffer altitude sickness. To overcome this problem, engineers had long proposed that the cabin of an airplane should be pressurized and the

Stratoliner was the forerunner of a completely new generation of civil aircraft with pressurized cabins. The cabin pressurization was derived from turbocharged Wright R-1820 engines and the fuselage of the new airplane was circular in section. This allowed the pressurization to be adequately contained, and the resulting cabin accommodated forty passengers who could be carried at a cruising height of 20,000 ft (6096 m). This was well above normal bad weather conditions, and resulted in a much more comfortable flight. The Boeing 307 Stratoliner first flew on 31 December 1938, and went into service with TWA in mid-1940. Although only 10 production Stratoliners were built, the design pointed the way for the great piston-engined airliners that were to follow.

By the end of the decade, America had left Europe far behind in airliner development. The old HP42s and the Ju52s still flew on for Imperial Airways and Lufthansa, although the latter company had introduced some interesting new designs during 1938. The United Kingdom's first large aircraft of all-metal, stressed-skin construction was the Armstrong Whitworth AW27 Ensign, a forty-seat airliner developed from the Atalanta, with the same high wing but with a retractable undercarriage. A large machine for its time, the Ensign was powered by four Armstrong Siddeley Tiger radial engines and had a wing span of 123 ft (37 m). Fourteen aircraft were supplied and the first went into service in October 1938. Hardly had the Ensign proved itself on European and Empire routes when war broke out in September 1939, and by May 1945, only seven of the original forty survived. By then they were hopelessly out of date and were broken up.

In May 1937, the de Havilland Com-

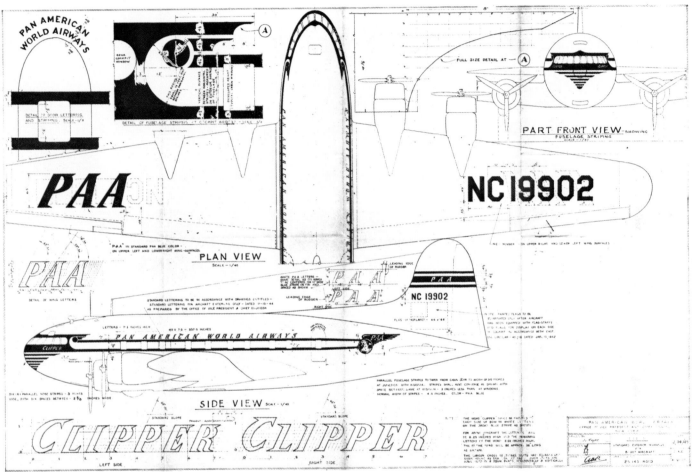

The Boeing Model 307 Statoliner, first of the modern pressurized mass transports, was introduced (top left) in 1940. Far left: The cabin provided ample space and comfort. Fifty three seats were provided and the forward cabin made up into sleeping berths (left). The Stratocruiser had an imposing appearance, as the livery scheme blue print for Pan Am (above) clearly shows.

Imperial Airways introduced the Armstrong Whitworth AW27 Ensign in 1938 (right). Seen here at Croydon is the prototype aircraft, registered G-ADSR. The cabin (below) was spacious but did not compare with contemporary American practice. The de Havilland DH95 (bottom) was a civil project of 1938 that was not developed due to the outbreak of war, but 23 aircraft served the RAF and the Royal Navy.

pany produced what to many people remains the most beautiful-looking aircraft ever to be manufactured. The DH91 Albatross possessed an elegance that has seldom been exceeded and the clean lines gave the machine an exceptional performance, particularly where range was concerned. Incredibly, the DH91 was built entirely of wood and was full of advanced features. The four Gipsy engines were air-cooled by an ingenious series of intakes in the leading edge of the wing. Seven models of the Albatross were produced, and it entered airline service in October 1938. Initially, it operated the London-Paris service and considerably reduced the flight times, as the cruising speed was 210 mph (338 km/h).

This put an end to the leisurely five-course meals which used to be served to passengers, and light snacks became the order of the day.

Another airliner of pre-war years from de Havilland was the DH95 Flamingo – a high-wing aircraft which was compared to the Super Electra, but was considerably slower.

From 1936 onwards, Imperial Airways came under considerable political criticism due to its alleged lack of enterprise in developing British air services. Under the chairmanship of Lord Cadman, a committee was set up to report on airline development, and it reported back in February 1938. Briefly, Cadman proposed that Imperial Airways should become Britain's long-distance carrier, while British Airways should operate in Europe. Argument raged about the proposals and they were not adopted.

Then, in 1939, an Act of Parliament was passed which nationalized both airlines and in 1940 they amalgamated to become British Overseas Airways Corporation (BOAC). But by then the world was at war.

CLIPPERS
IN
THE SKY

THE EARLY YEARS of aviation saw the rise of another method of air transport – the intercontinental flying boat. It had its heyday in the late 1920s and throughout the 1930s and, in military versions, it made a substantial contribution to the Allied victory at sea, particularly in anti-submarine work. After the war, it quickly fell victim to the all-conquering land-based airliners.

The reasons for the popularity of flying boats in the inter-war period are not hard to define. Despite the progress made in the design and development of large landplanes by 1930, many people in aviation firmly believed that the runway lengths necessary would place unacceptable economic restraints on them in terms of construction costs.

The airship was considered in the 1920s to offer the best prospects for long-distance travel. After the cycle of British and American airship disasters, the airlines in both countries turned with relief to the big flying boats. The type had its greatest success in the years 1931-39, and if the Second World War had not intervened, with the subsequent demand for long-range land-based bombers, the flying boat may well have developed further than it actually did. Even so, British and American designers developed the type into the most sophisticated aircraft of its time.

Those who made the case for the flying boat argued that it did not need a long runway – only a clear stretch of water free of obstacles. In an emergency, it could always put down in the sea, because most international routes overflowed oceans, as they still do today. In 1935, the Martin Aircraft Company designed the hull of their famous *China Clipper* so that it could make a skid-landing on a grass field if ever forced to do so.

Two other important advantages were

The promenade deck of a Short C class Empire flying boat in 1937. Travel operators still thought in terms of luxury liners and this Imperial Airways publicity picture has the object of tempting prospective travellers to India away from P & O Lines. The picture has obviously been posed by professional models, but because the C class boats were unpressurized and usually flew at 5000-6000 ft (1524-1829 m), the use of the promenade deck was possible, in theory.

This Curtiss NC-4 flying boat (top), made the first transatlantic crossing from Newfoundland to Plymouth, via the Azores and Lisbon, from 19–31 May 1919. The pilot was Captain Albert Read. Left: The first airline in Africa was operated by this three-seat Levy-Lepen Type R flying boat, which was built for the French Navy in 1917. The service started on the Congo River on 1 July 1920, but tropical heat and humidity wrought havoc with the wood and fabric structure of the aircraft. The rare picture (above), shows a Benoist flying boat built at St Louis, Missouri. A similar machine, the Benoist XIV, opened the world's first regular passenger air service in Florida on 21 January 1914 from Tampa to St Petersburg.

argued in favour of flying boats. They did not require the complicated, expensive and heavy landing gear fitted to airplanes and were therefore cheaper to build. Additionally, the unlimited take-off length available allowed flying boats to be larger than an equivalent land plane. Therefore, flying boats could offer far more comfortable passenger facilities (the Short Empire boats of 1936 even had a promenade deck) and extra fuel capacity meant the long-range requirements for transoceanic crossings could be met. On the other hand, it was difficult to illuminate the landing channels and pilots hated night flights.

The flying boat, like the seaplane, was a development of the early float-planes, but differed in having a hull which floated in the water and acted as an undercarriage. The earliest pioneer of the type was the American Glenn

Curtiss, who built his first flying boat in 1912. In the United Kingdom, the three Short brothers had formed a company at Rochester, Kent, and showed early interest in waterborne craft. Both the Shorts and Curtiss supplied floatplanes to the RAF during the First World War.

Before the war began, however, a flying boat featured in an attempt to set up the first scheduled airline service in America. The aircraft was a long-forgotten type – the Benoist XIV – the brainchild of St Louis motor manufacturer Tom Benoist. In December 1913, he signed a contract with the city authorities of St Petersburg, Florida, undertaking to set up a regular service to Tampa, 22 miles (35 km) away. Benoist's small flying boat, a single-engined 45-ft (13-m) span biplane, carried a sole passenger and although Mr A C Pheil, Manager of St Petersburg, paid $400 (an enormous sum in those days) for the

first passage across, the regular fare was set at $5. At this price, the line could hardly have been profitable and it went out of existence in a few months.

Like every other modern war, the 1914 conflict accelerated technical innovation and when it ended in 1918, the flying boat had evolved into a potential global transport. This was demonstrated in May 1919, less than a month before Alcock and Brown's non-stop Atlantic crossing, when three large four-engined Curtiss flying boats of the NC-4 type set out from Rockaway, Long Island to fly to Lisbon via Newfoundland and the Azores.

The Curtiss NC-4 was one of the largest aircraft of its day. It spanned 126 ft (38 m) – nearly twice that of Alcock and Brown's Vickers Vimy – and was fourth in a series of boats designed for convoy protection. NC-1 was a large three-engined biplane with a central

This weird triple triplane is the Caproni Ca 60 Transaereo, which was the first airliner designed to carry 100 passengers across the Atlantic. Unfortunately, the giant machine was a complete failure and crashed on its maiden flight over Lake Maggiore on 4 March 1921. The Ca 60 is a good example of design imagination being ahead of technical research!

hull and rear-suspended tail surfaces. It first flew in October 1918 and six weeks later established a record (and displayed its capabilities!) by taking 51 people aloft. Curtiss decided that a further engine was required, and the NC-4 received three tractor engines plus a fourth pusher engine in the centre engine nacelle, midway between the upper and lower planes.

The war ended before the aircraft could be sent on their intended convoy duties and so it was decided to attempt an Atlantic crossing instead. On 16 May 1919 three boats set out on the largest stretch of the crossing from Newfoundland to the Azores. NC-1 and NC-3 came down in the sea (the crews were safely recovered) but NC-4 made it and passed on to Lisbon and eventually to Plymouth in England, where it arrived on 31 May to be greeted by a large crowd and a civic reception. After the

crossing, NC-4 was given to the Smithsonian Institution in Washington, DC, where it is still to be seen as a relic of man's first flight across the Atlantic. The success of NC-4 publicized the flying boat type, and France, Germany and Italy all showed interest. In Britain, the Felixstowe Seaplane Experimental Station designed the F5, which was built by Shorts, and had the first metal hull of any aircraft.

In 1920, the first embryo air services operated by flying boats began. The first was in the unlikely surroundings of Cental Africa on a run between Leopoldville (now Kinshasa) and N'Gombe in the Belgian Congo. It was operated by Sabena, the Belgian state airline, and used the Levy-Lepen Type R – a French boat with space for a pilot and two passengers. It was powered by a single 12-cylinder Renault engine of 300 hp.

Conditions in the Congo were not the

best in which to operate an airline. It is certainly true that the great river made an excellent take-off surface once logs and crocodiles had been cleared away, but the heat and humidity wrought havoc with the fabric covering of the aircraft and a close inspection was needed after each flight.

The other service established America's first international scheduled airline when Aeromarine West Indies Airways used one of their own products, the Aeromarine Model 75, to open a service for passengers, mail and freight between Key West in Florida and Havana in Cuba. The south east coast of the United States therefore saw the beginnings of flying-boat-operated airlines and, because this area and the beautiful Caribbean Islands are so suited to the type, the last flying boat line in the world still operates there.

With these embryo airlines in

existence, it was to be expected that development would progress along conventional lines. In Germany, Britain and the United States of America, designers were content to move cautiously. This was not so in Italy, however, where in 1921, the Caproni Company made a giant leap forward when it produced the strangest looking aircraft that ever lumbered into the air.

The Caproni Ca 60 Transaereo earns its place in airliner history from the fact that it was the first aircraft designed to carry 100 passengers across the Atlantic. Unfortunately, the scheme was too ambitious and completed without the necessary research, which would have told the designers that a nine-wing airplane with three sets of triple wings had a drag and stability problem which made it impossible to fly.

When complete, the huge aircraft was the largest plane yet built. The hull was

The Savoia-Marchetti SM66 (above), was the successor to the famous SM55. Italian airlines used the type from 1934–40, and it did war service on air-sea rescue. A tunnel in the wings allowed access to passenger cabins in the twin hulls. Its predecessor, the SM55 (bottom), first appeared in 1924 and is most famous for the two mass transatlantic flights in 1930 and 1933 led by General Italo Balbo.

made of wood, with metal reinforcing, and the three sets of wings were spaced equidistant along the deep ship-like hull with its banks of promenade-type windows and spacious accommodation. Eight American-made 400 hp Liberty engines were fitted, four ahead in a three-tractor, one-pusher configuration, and the reverse combination astern.

This impossible contrivance weighed 24½ tons and it is a miracle that it ever got into the air at all, yet it did. On 4 March 1921, Caproni chief test pilot Semprini taxied the Ca 60 out across the waters of Lake Maggiore. The airplane carried ballast to represent sixty passengers as Semprini opened up all eight engines to full power. After a long run over the surface of the lake, the Ca 60 rose in the air, but at about 60 ft (18 m), it suddenly pitched forward and nosed down before Semprini could take any action. He scrambled out as the wreck plunged to the bed of the lake. It was salvaged, but while under repair, an accidental fire destroyed the remains.

Elsewhere in Italy, the Savoia concern had started to produce the first of its long line of commercial flying boats. In 1923 it flew the type S16ter for the first time. It was based on a design which dated back to 1919. By 1926, six of these handy little aircraft were flying the Rome-Sanremo route for the Società Incremento Turismo Aereo (SITA).

The Savoia Company followed the S16 with one of its most successful airplanes which was to be in constant use for the next decade. In 1924 Chief Engineer Alessandro Marchetti (he gave his name to form Savoia-Marchetti) produced the SM55, the twin-hulled boat that became a familiar sight in Europe and across the Atlantic.

Conceived as a military machine in the torpedo bomber role, the SM55 was

considered too advanced by the Italian Airforce (Reggia Aeronautica) and it took some years before the type appeared in squadron service. However, with the military hardware removed, the twin hulls provided two comfortable cabins for 10 passengers, and Società Aerea Mediterranea (SAM) used it on a network of Mediterranean routes until 1937.

The SM55 retains its place in flying boat history for the famous mass flights it made to North and South America in 1931 and 1933 under the command of Italo Balbo. Designed to show off the emergent power of *Duce* Benito Mussolini's Fascist state, 14 SM55s arrived in Rio de Janeiro on 15 January 1931 after a 6500-mile (10,461-km) journey from Italy. The 1933 flight allegedly commemorated the tenth anniversary of the Reggia Aeronautica and this time Balbo led 25 SM55Xs from Orbetello to

New York and back to Rome. Pictures of the massed SM55Xs in the world's press did indeed give a sense of power and speed, and must have given Il Duce great comfort!

So successful was the SM55X that Marchetti used the same twin-hull layout for the SM66 – an enlarged version for 14 to 18 passengers with a 108-ft (33-m) wingspan and three Fiat 12-cylinder V-type liquid-cooled engines rated at 750 hp each. The type came out in 1932 and the new Italian state airline Ala Littoria (it absorbed SISA and SAM) took 23 machines, using them with success up to the outbreak of war with Britain and France in June 1940. Routes operated included Rome-Tripoli-Tunis and Brindisi-Athens-Rhodes-Alexandria. Tough and resilient, the SM66 was used on air-sea rescue up until 1943.

1928 was a significant year for the flying boats, and more importantly for

A Short S17 Kent (above) at anchor alongside the company's Rochester works, while the harbour crew clean the passenger cabin windows. The four Bristol Jupiter XFBM engines stand out well in the picture, as does the enclosed cockpit, considered a great luxury by aircrews in 1930. Three Kents were built and operated in the Mediterranean for Imperial Airways.

civil aviation. First, the British airline Imperial Airways completed its plans for an airlink with India. This ambitious project used three different aircraft and seven days in transit. The aircraft that made the project feasible was the Short S8 Calcutta, a large biplane flying boat using three Bristol Jupiter nine-cylinder radial engines.

Passengers took the train at Victoria Station, London for the coast and then boarded an Armstrong Whitworth Argosy bound for Genoa. At Genoa, the passengers got on the Short Calcutta for the leg to Alexandria. The final stage on to Karachi was then made in a DH66 Hercules, although two aircraft were needed if the Calcutta arrived with a full load of 15 people. These passengers were accommodated in an all-metal hull, and facilities were available for the serving of hot meals in flight. This was very necessary as the cruising speed was only 92 mph (148 km/hr) and the flight stages were very long. The Mediterranean service was inaugurated on 16 April 1929 and meanwhile the Short Brothers' design offices had been working on plans for an improved version of the Calcutta. These added 14 ft (4 m) to the wingspan and provided a fourth engine. This increase in power was largely used in adding to passenger comfort. The cabin was enlarged and passengers were seated in four rows with folding tables. The crew benefitted from an enclosed flight deck in place of the open cockpit fitted on the Calcutta. The new boat was christened Kent and three of them joined the five Calcuttas already in service. After a running-in period, the Kents took over the Genoa-Alexandria service and the Calcuttas were put on the run to South Africa.

Elsewhere, great events were taking place. In the spring of 1927, the United States Post Office announced that it was seeking tenders for a contract to carry mail between Havana and Key West on the tip of the Florida Keys. This announcement caught the attention of Juan Trippe – a remarkable American who was then only 28 years old. The story of Trippe's visit to Havana which led to the foundation of Pan American Airways has been told in Chapter Five. Pan American services from Key West to Havana opened on a mail-only basis on 28 October 1927 and the first fare-paying passengers were carried on the following 16 January.

In the meantime, Juan Trippe had leased a Sikorsky S-36 amphibian flying boat on a two-month loan from the manufacturers. It was the start of a partnership between Igor Sikorsky and Pan Am that was to last until the Second World War, and place a series of attractive and profit-making flying boats on routes across the Caribbean to South American cities, and eventually on transpacific and Atlantic flights as well.

Sikorsky built only one S-36 and Pan Am returned it to him when the two months were up. But the *Pan America*, as the S-36 was called, showed that the type was ideal for the Caribbean routes, and in all Pan Am bought 39 of the S-38 – the enlarged version with which Sikorsky followed the S-36. The lay-out was basically the same – the wings were supported by the tough stream-lined hull and the empennage (tail assembly) was fixed aft on four connecting rods. A retractable undercarriage made it amphibious.

The S-38 went into service in October 1928 and many of the boats lasted until 1934, and one or two even until 1938. Some were transferred to China under the flag of Pan Am's subsidiary, the China National Airline Company (CNAC).

The growth of Pan American Airways

in the next three years was astonishing even by American business standards. Contracts were won for flying mail on six major international routes which led as far south as Santos in Brazil, and Santiago in Chile on the opposite side of the South American continent. Early route proving was carried out by no less a figure than Charles A Lindbergh, whom Trippe had signed up on the strength of his solo Atlantic flight in May 1927. Lindbergh demonstrated that the proposed Pan Am network was feasible and it was obvious that orders must be placed for new equipment immediately. Meanwhile, in 1928, Pan Am carried 9500 passengers and flew 129,335 miles (208,144 km), earning nearly $300,000.

In August 1930, Pan American Airways acquired a second flying boat fleet when it bought out the holding of one of its rivals on the South American

The Sikorsky S-40 (top), of which three examples were built for Pan Am in the early 1930s, when it was the largest aircraft then built in the United States, could carry 40 passengers in comfort. The luxurious surroundings included wall-to-wall carpeting and wood veneers (right). Above: The Consolidated Commodore was supplied in 1929 to NYRBA (New York, Rio and Buenos Aires Line Inc) which was absorbed into Pan Am in 1930. Left: Juan Trippe, President of Pan Am (right), talking to Charles A Lindbergh in 1928.

routes – the New York, Rio and Buenos Aires Line Inc (NYRBA). Pan Am obtained from them a modern fleet of the elegant Consolidated Commodore. This flying boat was larger than anything that the line had possessed before, seating 22 passengers and cruising at 102 mph (164 km/h) using two Pratt & Whitney 575 hp Hornet engines. In addition there was a boat base in Miami, Florida and the route network was extended to Argentina, ending at Buenos Aires. The Commodores brought the total aircraft strength of the Pan Am fleet to 97.

The Consolidated Commodore was a large monoplane flying boat. The airframe was all-metal and the skin partially metal and fabric. It had a range of 1000 miles (1609 km) and carried its passengers in three spacious cabins. The two forward cabins usually seated eight passengers each and four more were placed in the rear cabin. There

was plentiful thick carpeting throughout and a lounge atmosphere was created by the thick padded upholstery that was evident everywhere, including the separate window seats for promenading passengers. When Pan Am absorbed the NYRBA, the line obtained one of the most advanced airplanes of the day and added to its route network which now extended over 8900 miles (14,323 km) through 15 different countries.

The Commodores became part of the Pan American fleet on 15 September 1930 and only remained the largest boats in company ownership for just one month. On 10 October, the first of the new Sikorsky S-40s, ordered the previous year, arrived at Miami. In this design Sikorsky followed the basic layout used in the S-38, but the wingspan was increased to 114 ft (34 m), and four Pratt & Whitney Hornets were used. Again, landing gear was provided, but the attraction of the aircraft was a deep

The historic Sikorsky S-42 (bottom) of 1935 went
into service on the San Francisco-Hawaii line,
and was subsequently used by Pan Am on
flights to South America and the Far East. One
of the type, Clipper III, was used on
transatlantic trial flights in 1937. Top left: A Pan
Am poster showing the S-42 routes in the
Caribbean. The spacious elegance of the S-42's
cabin (top centre), shows the standards which
disappeared after the Second World War. Top
right: The flight deck of the S-42, with Captain
Ed Musick (above), who pioneered Pan Am's
Pacific services. This S-42 was fitted with one of
the first Sperry Automatic pilots.

boat-shaped hull which could seat up to forty people in even better conditions than the Commodore.

The S-40 was by far the largest American commercial aircraft when it was introduced, and in many ways it was almost an airborne ocean liner. Watertight doors and bulkheads formed an integral part of the superstructure and the cabin was teak-panelled in the style so beloved of the 1930s. Ships lifebelts were even hung on the walls. In flight, the S-40 made a tremendous impression of grace and power. Juan Trippe had always considered his fleet to be merchantmen of the air, and saw his airliners as the twentieth-century version of the old sailing clippers. It was natural then that when the first S-40 was christened at Washington on 12 October 1930 by Mrs Herbert Hoover, wife of the President of the United States, it received the name *American Clipper*. It was a happy choice, and one that has stood Pan Am well over the years. The remaining two S-40s were to be called *Caribbean Clipper* and *Southern Clipper*, and from then until the Second World War, all Pan Am four-engined flying boats were allotted a Clipper name and the term was used throughout the company's publicity.

For a while Trippe and his colleagues turned their attention away from the Caribbean and South America and began an expansion of their domestic United States routes. A line was developed up the West Coast from Seattle, Washington, to Fairbanks, Alaska, with the object of island hopping around the perimeter of the Pacific to Japan and China. This route was obviously long and expensive, and political reasons also made Japan an unpromising market in the 1930s. China was a different matter however, so Trippe put his con-

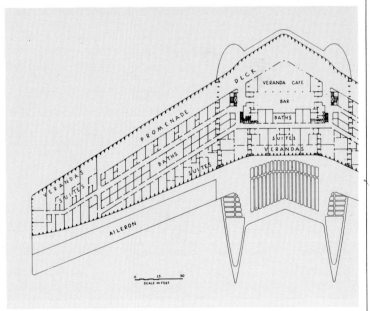

The unfulfilled dream – the dining saloon
(above) of a proposed 100-ton Sikorsky
transoceanic flying boat offered to Pan Am in
1938. The giant machine (centre right) had twin
decks and the upper of these carried two rows
of individual staterooms. The design study (top
right) proposed a cruising speed of 300mph (483
km/h) and a capacity of 100 passengers.
Another design from the 1930s by Norman Bel
Geddes (bottom right), was inspired by the
Dornier Do X. It was intended to carry 451
passengers and 155 crew, and provided all the
facilities usually found on ocean liners, in the
wings.

siderable technical team on the twin problems of drawing a specification for a suitable aircraft – a range of 2500 miles (4023 km) was demanded – and surveying suitable islands for mid-Pacific touchdown points. These would not only have to provide fuel and technical backup for the flying boats, but also have hotels and weather forecasting bureaux. In these years Pan Am ran its own very efficient meteorological service.

Two companies responded to the tender documents when they were issued, and at the end of 1932 orders were placed which led to the construction of two famous types of boat – the Sikorsky S-42 and the Martin M-130. While the construction of three of each type went ahead, Pan Am prepared the ground in Asia by prudently acquiring a forty percent interest in the China National Aircraft Corporation. The latter was in poor financial shape and Pan Am set about putting it back on its feet. Meanwhile, Hong Kong and San Francisco were selected as the termini for the transpacific route. Eight thousand miles (12,875 km) separated the two, and the first stop was Hawaii. The next stage was 1380 miles (2220 km) northwest to Midway Island, before flying a further 1260 miles (2028 km) on to the uninhabited Wake Island. Trippe had some difficulty in discovering if Wake was indeed United States sovereign territory! Finally, the route dipped down to Guam (certainly an American island), and eventually to Hong Kong. Later Manila and Macao were added and a Hawaii–Auckland, New Zealand branch was opened, with calls at Canton Island and Fiji.

The Sikorsky was ready first and made its maiden flight on 29 March 1934. It was a large, all-metal high-wing monoplane and carried four Pratt &

Whitney Hornets – by now a well-proven power plant. An innovation was the use of three-bladed variable-pitch propellers. The prototype proved its potential with a number of impressive height records with varying loads, but the S-42 never met the range asked for in the specification, even with a reduced passenger load. Nevertheless, it went into scheduled service between San Francisco and Hawaii in April 1935 and the golden age of the Pacific clippers began. Pan Am ordered a further seven of the S-42s and used them mostly on South American routes. The usual load was 35 passengers and a crew of 5, while on night flights sleeping berths could be fitted for 14.

The limited range of the Sikorsky having restricted it to medium-range routes, the long stages were taken over by the Martin M-130 which was delivered to the company in October 1935. It

was not unusual to find the two aircraft operating together, and Pan Am still used the S-42 for light-laden route-proving flights, keeping the Martins for revenue earning.

The Martin M-130 is inseparable in aviation history from the name China Clipper. Although officially the three aircraft were called China Clipper, Philippine Clipper and Hawaii Clipper, all three were generally referred to by the public as the China Clippers. Large, all-metal flying boats, the Martins were altogether better boats than the Sikorskys and they possessed the range of 3200 miles (5150 km) required for the all-important long Pacific stages. The engines were four Pratt & Whitney Twin Wasps – the first appearance of this classic of aeronautical machinery. Thirty two passengers were carried, and the luxury and space provided for them far exceeded anything available on air-

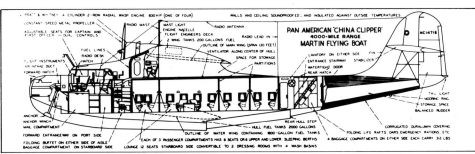

Opposite page: Dinner aboard the *China Clipper!* The big Martin M-130s opened the transpacific route in October 1936. The flight took five days with sixty hours in the air. Overnight stops (above) were made at bases specially built on remote Pacific islands like Wake and Midway. The M-130 was fully equipped for the journey, and proved ideal for the job.

Fliegt in die Bäder

The Dornier Do J Wal features in this poster
from the 1920s preserved in the Lufthansa
archives. The Wal was originally built in Italy
to avoid restrictions imposed on German
aircraft construction by the Treaty of Versailles.

lines today, even in the first class category. An attractive colour scheme in silver and pale green added a functional note. Full restaurant service was available and passengers sat six at a table – repeat, *table.* (The ludicrous interseat flap which passes for a table in modern aircraft was as yet unknown.) An additional comfort was a self-service pantry where passengers could get soft drinks and in-flight necessities on unpressurized aircraft, such as ear plugs and air sickness bags.

The *China Clipper* lifted off from San Francisco on 22 November 1935 to open the Pacific service. Watched by 125,000 people and commanded by Captain Ed Musick, Pan Am's senior pilot, she headed west with a full load of mail but no passengers. Scheduled flights began on 21 October 1936 and continued without interruption until the Japanese attack on Pearl Harbor in December 1941. The only setback was the loss of the *Hawaii Clipper* at sea between Manila and Guam in July 1938.

While the spectacular successes of the Americans undoubtedly dominated the flying boat scene in the early 1930s, European interest in the type was as keen as ever. The German Dornier concern had set up in Italy after the First World War because the peace treaty terms prohibited construction of these craft in Germany until 1926. In 1923 Dornier launched the Wal, a twin-engined high-wing monoplane that was to appear in several variations and have a production run of 300, over half of which were built in Italy. The Wal was eventually produced in Germany, and also in the Netherlands and Spain under licence. The type carried from eight to ten passengers and operated on many Mediterranean services. However, its chief claim to fame is the use made of it by Deutsche Lufthansa in its

DEUTSCHER
SCHLEUDERFLUG
D. „EUROPA"—NEW·YORK
2. JUNI 1931

DEUTSCHER
SCHLEUDERFLUG
D. „EUROPA"—
NEW YORK
15.–16. JULI 1932

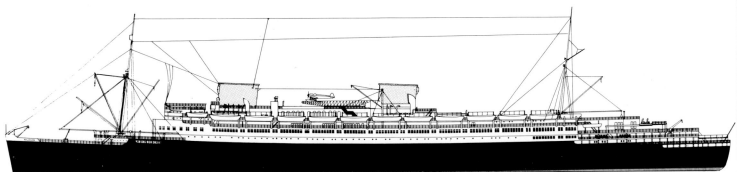

The Junkers W 34 seaplane was used to speed
up the transatlantic mail by a day. It was
catapulted from the Norddeutscher Lloyd
liners Bremen and Europa when the big ships
were 24 hours away from journey's end. The
catapult was placed amidships on the sports
deck (bottom).

Flying boat
is catapulted
at 93 mph
(150 km/h)

Catapult sled

Repair shop and
spare parts stores

Rotating crane
to hoist flying
boats on board

Flying boat
moves onto
reinforced
floating sail

Lufthansa opened a Europe-South America mail service in 1933 using the converted freight *Westfalen* (5400 tons) as a floating mid-ocean base for its Dornier Wals. After landing, the flying boats taxied on to a drag sail (left) which was towed behind the ship, and, as speed increased, lifted the aircraft out of the water. The crane then took over (above) and the refuelled aircraft catapulted on its way (right).

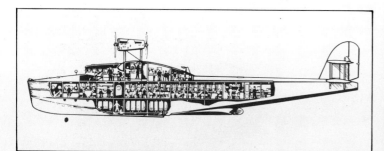

The Do X Dornier was an ambitious project, planned to carry 150 passengers on regular transatlantic flights. The machine had three decks (above) and luxurious passenger accommodation (right), but performance was poor. The machine seldom attained an altitude of 1500 ft (457 m). It was destroyed in a Berlin museum during an air raid in the Second World War.

mail service to South America in the 1930s. Lufthansa got over the range problem by stationing a ship in mid-ocean, which was then used as a floating base. The Wal alighted alongside the ship – a converted freighter called *Westfalen* – and was then hauled on board, refuelled and catapulted back into the air to complete the journey. The transocean stage of the flight was from Bathurst in the British Gambia to Pernambuco in Brazil, and the first experimental runs were made in May 1933. A weekly service was inaugurated and by August 1935 the first 100 runs had been completed. A total of 328 crossings were carried out in all.

Germany also fitted catapults in her two record-breaking ocean liners *Bremen* and *Europa*. The ships carried a Junkers 33 seaplane and the craft carried mail ashore while the ship was 600 miles (966 km) from either Southampton or New York. In this way a full day was saved from the time taken to deliver the transatlantic mails.

No description of Germany's contribution to the history of the flying boat is complete without some reference to the Dornier Do X – the giant craft with which Claude Dornier hoped to carry 150 passengers in comfort on regular transatlantic flights. Work on the design of this twelve-engined goliath was started in 1926 and, after continual structural difficulties, the first flight was eventually carried out in October 1929. It was the largest aircraft in the world at the time, but never lived up to expectations although on the maiden flight the Do X took 169 people into the air, including 10 crew and 9 stowaways. These crowded the three decks, although the passenger deck was designed initially for 75. The lower deck contained the fuel tanks and bag-

gage, while the flight deck also contained the crew's sleeping quarters. Experience showed that the Do X was badly underpowered, and even after a complete engine change when 12 Curtiss Conquerors of 600 hp each were fitted, the huge aircraft could only struggle up to 1600 ft (488m). Even a flight to New York via the Canary Islands and Brazil could not hide the inefficiencies of the Do X and it flew infrequently after returning to Europe in 1932, and eventually was broken up.

France also experimented with large flying boats, mainly through the designs of the Latécoère company. Their Type 300, of which a single example was produced and named *Croix du Sud*, had pioneered French mail services on the South Atlantic until it was lost with all hands in December 1936 after three years on the route. Air France ordered three more of the type, which had four

The Latécoère 300 (above) made several Atlantic crossings on the southern route from Dakar to Natal, Brazil, from December 1933 onwards, but it was lost at sea in December 1936 with its crew, including the Captain Jean Mermoz, one of the best known French pilots of the day.

The huge Latécoère 521 (below) was begun in 1933 but was badly damaged by a hurricane during its maiden flight to the United States via the Caribbean in January 1936. When it was rebuilt the machine proved to be a good performer but it did not enter commercial service due to the Second World War.

engines mounted in twin pods over the
wing, but one of these also crashed.

Latécoère followed the Type 300 with
a very large boat – the Type 521.
Although it had approximately the same
dimensions as the Do X, it weighed
considerably less and was an excellent
performer. It used six Hispano-Suiza
liquid-cooled engines and cruised with
70 passengers at 130 mph (209 km/h).
The first aircraft was named *Lieutenant
de Vaisseau Paris*, and from 1936
onwards it carried out a number of
development flights which culminated
in a trip to New York via Lisbon and
the Azores in August 1938. Unfortunately plans to open a French Atlantic
service were stopped by the outbreak of
war in September 1939.

Despite these efforts from France and
Germany, it was left to the United
Kingdom to celebrate the apotheosis of
the flying boat with the Short S23 C

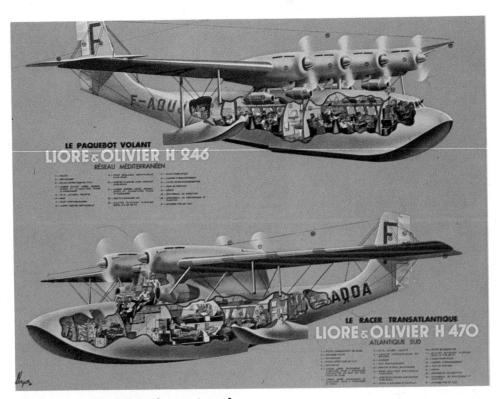

Above are two French flying boat projects of
the 1930s from the Loiré et Olivier factory. The
H 470 was specifically ordered by the French
government for South Atlantic mail services. It
first flew in 1936 but was sunk in an accident in
1937 and this incident delayed the programme
until it was abandoned on the outbreak of war
in September 1939.

class of 1936, which became known as the Empire boat and remains today one of the great classic designs of aviation history. By 1935 Imperial Airways had established a network of routes through the African and Asian possessions of the British Empire, which was at the height of its power. Weekly services were available as far as Cape Town and Singapore, and although by today's standards the seven-day schedules seem something of an endurance test, the pace was leisurely, jet-lag was unknown and timesaving over seaborne transport was substantial. Then, in 1935, the British government announced the Empire Air Mail Scheme, with the proposal that all mail dispatched from the United Kingdom for delivery along the Empire air routes should be carried by air without surcharge as far as was practical. This task was beyond the capability of the current

Imperial Airways fleet of HP42s, Atlantas and Kents, so a new aircraft would have to be ordered for the service. It would have to be capable of carrying 24 passengers in luxurious surroundings and have space for a minimum of 1 ton of mail. A cruising speed of not less than 155 mph (249 km/h) and a range of 650 miles (1046 km) minimum was expected. In the event, the contract went to Short Brothers, a name synonymous with the flying boat, and work began. The resulting aircraft was a large, all-metal, flying boat with a deep twin-decked hull and wing-mounted stabilizing floats. The Bristol Aeroplane engine works at Patchway produced a new robust radial known as the Pegasus, and four of these 950 hp powerplants were provided. Considerable aerodynamic research went into the wing design and Chief Designer Arthur Gouge produced an innovation – a type

of flap which increased lift by a third without alteration of trim and with a speed reduction of only 12 mph (19 km/h).

The first Empire boat flew on 4 July 1936 with Short's chief test pilot John Parker at the controls. It was the first major airliner to be ordered straight from the drawing board and so there were some fears about its performance. Named *Canopus* (all the S23s received names beginning with C), it triumphantly fulfilled all the predictions of its designers and it was in service for Imperial Airways over the Mediterranean by October. Twenty seven more aircraft included in the first order were delivered from Rochester up to February 1938, and a further eleven with the up-rated Pegasus engine were ordered in late 1937.

The first regular service opened in February 1937, and the S23 was soon a

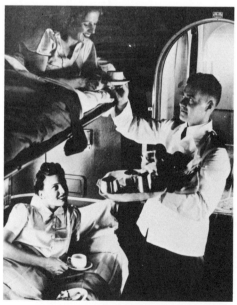

Ancient and modern worlds meet as Palestinian Arabs (left) watch a Short S23 C class Empire boat alight on the waters of the Sea of Galilee. The Empire boats (above) carried 24 passengers in great comfort and this picture shows part of the night-time cabin arrangement. The picture is probably posed by professional models – in practice, service in unpressurized aircraft was sometimes difficult due to sudden turbulence!

Empire boat *Circe* taxies in Southampton Water, alongside the Union Castle motor liner *Capetown Castle*. The Empire boats cut the surface time to the Cape by a third, although Union Castle ran a passenger service by sea until 1977.

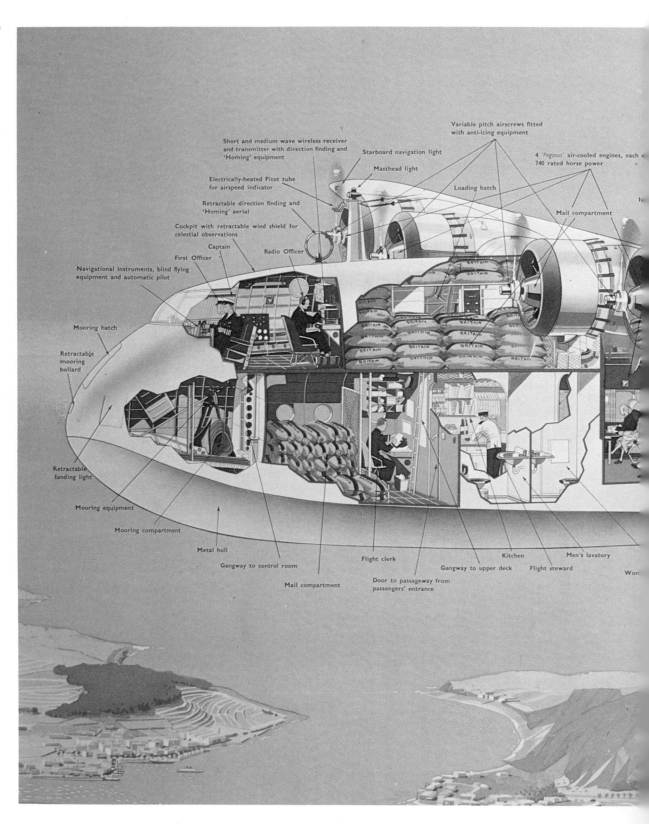

This Imperial Airways publicity poster shows the interior of the C class Empire flying boat. The type was the most successful machine ever operated by the airline and became a British prestige symbol from 1936–39.

Short and medium wave wireless receiver and transmitter with direction finding and 'Homing' equipment

Variable pitch airscrews fitted with anti-icing equipment

Starboard navigation light

Masthead light

4 'Pegasus' air-cooled engines, each 740 rated horse power

Electrically-heated Pitot tube for airspeed indicator

Loading hatch

Retractable direction finding and 'Homing' aerial

Mail compartment

Cockpit with retractable wind shield for celestial observations

Captain

Radio Officer

First Officer

Navigational instruments, blind flying equipment and automatic pilot

Mooring hatch

Retractable mooring bollard

Retractable landing light

Mooring equipment

Mooring compartment

Metal hull

Gangway to control room

Mail compartment

Flight clerk

Door to passageway from passengers' entrance

Gangway to upper deck

Kitchen

Men's lavatory

Flight steward

Fixed aerials

Controllable cooling gills

All-metal wing

Port navigation light

Freight hatch

ntilators

International registration marking

Mail, freight and baggage hold

Adjustable chairs

Aft cabin

Flaps fitted to trailing edges of the wing

Midship cabin

Main gangway

Wing tip float

Promenade cabin

ry

familiar sight on the Empire routes. From the Imperial Airways base at Hythe on Southampton Water, the great boats flew to Egypt, India, East and South Africa, Malaya, Hong Kong and Australia. In the latter country, the new airline Qantas Empire Airways operated the Singapore-Darwin-Brisbane stages of the routes.

The highest standards for passengers was offered by the Empire boats, and many travel experts believe that comparable conditions have never been available since. The cabin was roomy, the seating consisted of large armchairs, and there was a promenade area especially provided, with windows that gave a clear view of the scenery passing below. A separate smoking room was available and the food, mostly cooked on board, consisted of such items as fricassee of chicken, roast fillet of veal, poached salmon écosse, and even crêpes suzette prepared at the table! In an age which expected this kind of service in its ocean liners, the airlines were determined not to be left behind, and Imperial Airways in the 1930s set standards that have never been surpassed.

A spectacular experiment in the battle for increased range. The Short-Mayo composite S20/S21 Composite aircraft was the brainchild of R H Mayo, technical chief of Imperial Airways. The carrier was a greatly modified S23, renumbered S21, and the S20 Mercury was the long-range component of the duo. The combination was successfully used to break a number of long distance records but the war in 1939 ended the project.

With the Empire services soundly established, it was time to demolish the last great obstacle to transglobal travel – the scheduled transatlantic flight for mail and passengers. No aircraft other than the German airships could make the crossing non-stop, so the first commercial surveys were made via Foynes in Ireland and Botwood in Newfoundland. These were made in July 1937 jointly with Pan American Airways using the S23 Caledonia and a Sikorsky S-42 Pan American Clipper III. The trials were successful but, throughout 1938, Imperial Airways experimented with the object of improving range capability. In-flight refuelling was attempted for the first time on a civil aircraft and the seaplane *Mercury* made several record distance flights after being lifted into the air on the back of its parent machine, a converted S23 named *Maia*, which formed the lower component of the unusual Short-Mayo composite aircraft. In fact, the Empire boats were prevented from establishing a regular service to New York by the Second World War but at least a mail service opened in August of that year.

The prize for the first transatlantic mail service went to America, when Pan American Airways opened a New York–Southampton service on 28 June 1939, operating via Newfoundland. Pan Am were allowed to do this by the use of the Boeing 314, a giant flying boat which they had been developing with Boeing from as long ago as 1935. A contract was placed for six aircraft with a transoceanic range, and the first model took off on 7 June 1938. It was big, the wing span was 158 ft (48m) and it could travel a route stage of 3500 miles (5633 km) with 77 passengers. Here at last was the true global airliner, and the first aircraft of the type to be

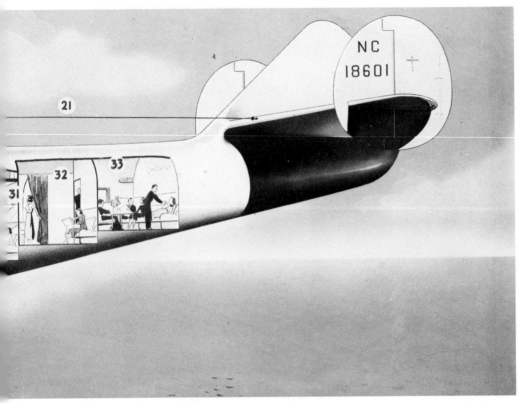

The Boeing 314 *Yankee Clipper* was probably the best of the pre-war flying boats. It was the first aircraft to go into regular transatlantic service and possessed wonderful facilities for both crew (below) and passengers (bottom). The flight deck remains the largest ever fitted to a modern airliner. The type is famous as the personal transport of Britain's war-time premier Winston Churchill.

The ultimate in flying boats! The enormous Hughes H2 Hercules (above) was built by the eccentric American millionaire and aviation pioneer Howard Hughes. Conceived as a wartime freight project to avoid enemy submarine activity, the wooden Hercules was completed by Hughes long after the need for such aircraft had disappeared. They flew it just once at a height of 50 ft (15 m) for 1 mile (1.6 km)! It remains one of the largest aircraft ever to fly and is preserved in California. The British Saunders-Roe Princess (below) was the last of the great commercial flying boats. Built as a transatlantic airliner for BOAC, it suffered many technical setbacks, and the airline announced its abandonment of flying boat services even before the flight of the first prototype in 1952.

made went to the Pacific to replace the loss of the tragic *Hawaii Clipper*. The second aircraft was to find fame as *Yankee Clipper*, and it was this ship that carried the Atlantic proving flights.

A dream was fulfilled for Juan Trippe on 28 June 1939, when another 314 *Dixie Clipper* carried the first fare-paying passengers from America to Europe. The fare was $375 single or $675 return. The service was made weekly until it ended abruptly in September when war broke out. However, until then, seven drawing-room-style compartments were available for passengers, one of which was set aside as a promenade, while another was used as a formal dining room with 14 places. Berths were provided for all passengers at night.

So the flying boats went to war. The Sunderlands and Catalinas of the RAF and USAF played a formidable part in the air war that raged across Europe and Asia. But as peace returned, land plane development had progressed so much that the return of the flying boat proved to be uneconomic. Passengers preferred to take-off as near to their homes as possible, and airports sprang up in every major city. The DC-4s, Stratocruisers and Constellations had killed the flying boat by 1950, even though schemes for giant boats were still in progress. The eccentric multimillionaire Howard Hughes (who has a genuine record of aviation success), produced his mammoth wooden Hughes H2 Hercules for the first and only time in November 1947. Fifty thousand people watched the largest airplane ever (nicknamed the *Spruce Goose*) fly for 1 mile (1.6 km) at about 50 ft (15m) with Hughes himself at the controls. The age of the commercial flying boat ended in Europe in November 1950, when BOAC took its last boats out of commission.

Today, flying boats are rarities in the airlines of the world. Nevertheless Antilles Air Boats Inc, a company based in the Virgin Islands, maintains 120 daily services in the Caribbean using Grumman flying boats, and it also operates two Short Sandringhams on charter and sightseeing trips. These two venerable aircraft are today the sole surviving reminders of the golden age of the flying boat, and of its pioneering of the great air routes which today are taken so much for granted.

CHAPTER SIX

WINGS ACROSS THE WORLD

THE WAR WHICH BROKE OUT IN EUROPE in the autumn of 1939 soon spread to the rest of the world and stopped civilian air transport everywhere except the Americas. The airlines were faced with the requisition of their aircraft by the military services and, in many cases, they closed down altogether. An example of this was Swissair, which stopped flying for the duration of the war.

The war had a radical effect on air passenger transport. It brought about major technical advances in the design of aircraft and, equally importantly, it gave millions of people their first experience of flying. But it was a very different kind of flying to that experienced by airline passengers before 1939. Although many people failed to realize it at the time, the days of high living were over. When the airlines returned in 1945, the experience gained in moving troops by air was soon applied to the airliner. Passengers found themselves packed tightly together, with very little space, and set out in rows which gave no opportunity of moving about in-flight other than a hurried dash to the toilet. The pre-war luxury was quickly forgotten. It had fallen victim to the increased operating costs of the large piston-engined aircraft developed during the war, and increased speed made the serving of meals, other than those which were pre-cooked, a very difficult process.

When the war started, all British services to the Continent were suspended, but a few weeks later it was found to be possible to run jointly with Air France a daily service between London and Paris. Flying boat operations on the North Atlantic stopped, but they continued in the Mediterranean, and British Airways even managed flights to Stockholm. This period of truce ended in the West when Germany invaded Denmark and Norway. Then France fell, and the new British national airline BOAC, formed on 1 April 1940 from Imperial Airways and British Airways, set up its headquarters in Durban, South Africa. From Durban, a new service was operated from the east coast of Africa to Egypt and thence to India, the Far East and Australia. Services from Bristol to Lisbon were planned and a restricted flying boat service across the Atlantic operated throughout the war using the Boeing 314. But all this was a limited operation, with BOAC carrying only 29,000 passengers in 1941 compared with the total of 72,700 carried in 1939. Even so, throughout the war, BOAC was operating a route mileage which was more than ninety percent of the pre-war figure of Imperial Airways.

The war practically extinguished Air France and Lufthansa, but KLM managed to survive. When Germany occupied Holland, Dr Plesman was arrested and imprisoned, but a number of his staff and aircraft escaped to England and KLM flew on. The aircraft that had escaped from Holland were operated from Whitchurch Airport, Bristol and a service flew to Lisbon. In October 1942 it was extended to Gibraltar.

It was during the operation of this Lisbon-Bristol service that there occurred one of the war's most famous aviation events, and one that was never fully explained. On 1 June 1943, a DC-3 of KLM, albeit registered in Britain as G-AGBB, took-off from Lisbon for the return flight to Bristol. There were thirteen passengers on board and a crew of four under Captain Tepas. The DC-3 flew its usual course across the Bay of Biscay, heading for southern England. These flights were known to the Germans and until then, there had been no interference from the Luftwaffe. On this occasion, however, the flight was intercepted by eight Junkers Ju88s from an airfield near Bordeaux, and it was shot down into the sea.

The incident made headlines because Leslie Howard, one of the best-known British film stars of the day (he had starred in Gone with the Wind) was on board. Howard had been in Portugal promoting his film The First of the Few, a British propaganda film about the RAF victory in the Battle of Britain. It seems unlikely that the Luftwaffe would have taken their revenge on Howard in such a fashion and a more likely explanation of the incident is that German agents in Lisbon mistook Howard's business manager, Alfred Chenhalls, for the British Prime Minister Winston Churchill. Chenhalls bore a remarkable resemblance to Churchill, and the coincidence was strengthened by the fact that Churchill was at the time attending a conference in Algiers. The KLM service to and from Lisbon was carried out the following day and it continued throughout the war. Five days after the Howard affair, Winston Churchill flew back from Gibraltar along the same route in complete safety.

If the British and European airlines suffered badly by the war, in America the great expansion of the 1930s was not only accelerated, but the demands of wartime led to the production of even better and larger airliners. While the British aircraft industry struggled to produce the bombers and fighters needed in the war with the Germans, the American industry not only supplied large quantities of military aircraft but also found time to develop airliners, three of which would become the major equipment of all world airlines when the war ended.

When America went to war in December 1941, President Roosevelt immediately signed an order which

The potential of the American aircraft industry
is shown in this picture of production of the
Curtiss C-46A Commando in full swing at the
Curtiss-Wright plant at St Louis during 1942.

would have taken over the entire airline industry. However, the airlines persuaded the President that they could serve the national purpose effectively without government direction and the order was reversed. The United States Military Air Transport Service (MATS) was set up to guide the domestic airlines and also operate air transport for the services. The workhorse of MATS was the DC-3 in the early years, or the C-47, as it was called by the USAF. Production of the DC-3 increased to five aircraft a day – an astonishing figure which proved as nothing else did that the United States had become the unchallenged leader in world aviation. To supplement the large number of DC-3s, the USAF ordered the Curtiss C-46, which had been designed to replace the DC-3 on the civil market. The original design provided the C-46 with a pressurized cabin, but this refinement was omitted from the military version. Nevertheless, the cabin was constructed in the distinctive 'double-bubble' shape which was considered the best arrangement for pressurized aircraft at the time. The C-46 was called the Commando by the military authorities, and no less than 3180 were produced during the war. The Commando had a large load capacity and served in every theatre of war. It was provided with two Pratt & Whitney Double Wasp

Top: Large numbers of the Curtiss C-46 were surplus to military requirements in 1946 and were bought up by American civil airlines. Below: The first arrival in Rome of TWA's scheduled service in April 1946 using the Douglas DC-4. Most DC-4s were ex-military aircraft, and formed the immediate post-war strength of airlines like American and KLM.

Opposite page: British Overseas Airways were forced to rely on military conversions as they struggled to rebuild their fleet after the Second World War. A major supplier was the Avro Company of Manchester, with the Lancastrian (top) – a converted bomber seen here in Alitalia colours, and the York, a war-time freighter.

engines, each giving 2000 hp. It could carry up to 62 passengers, which was considerably better than the DC-3. After the war, a number of Commandos were sold as civil airliners and some were still around in the early 1980s.

In 1942, the Douglas Company produced their next airliner, when on St Valentines Day, 14 February, the DC-4 made its first flight. This project had begun originally in the mid-1930s, when the Douglas Corporation set up negotiations with the big five American airlines to provide a four-engined airliner for long-range flights. The first machine produced, called the DC-4E, flew for the first time in June 1938. It was considered to be too large and uneconomic by the airlines, and Douglas set out to redesign a smaller version. This was a much simpler airplane, and the early models did not possess a cabin pressurization system. The triple fins and rud-

ders of the DC-4E were replaced by a single fin and the new aircraft showed excellent potential with a pay-load of 42 passengers.

Initially, orders for 61 aircraft came from American Airlines, Eastern Airlines and United Airlines. At this point, the USAF intervened and all DC-4s were dispatched into military service for the remainder of the war. Immediately the fighting ended, large numbers of DC-4s were sold to the airlines, and converted to civil use. American Airlines opened services with the DC-4 on 7 March 1946 – just eight months after VE day, starting a service between New York and Los Angeles. However, they were not the first to use the DC-4, as American Overseas Airlines (AOA) had started a transatlantic service between New York and London as early as October 1945. There were stops in Newfoundland and Ireland on the way, and the journey took 24 hours. Nevertheless, AOA had broken Pan Am's monopoly of United States overseas routes. It is interesting to note that the service ended at Hurn near Bournemouth, which at that time was an international airport because London Heathrow was not yet open to civilian traffic. At the end of the war, TWA had also been given rights to fly to Europe as well as to the Middle East. The Americans only enjoyed a monopoly of transatlantic services for six months, because KLM also began DC-4 operations to New York in May 1946. Dr Plesman, by this time back as the head of the company, had quickly secured a loan of 14 ex-Air Force machines, and the Dutch airline was once more in business.

With the large numbers of ex-military DC-3s, DC-4s and Curtiss Commandos available for quick conversion to civil use, airlines expanded very quickly in the United States after the war. It

became a habit for Americans to fly any distance which was over 200 miles (322 km) or so, and the railways were never again to have the popularity or the profits that they had before the war. By 1948, over 10 million Americans per year were using the airlines, and 600 American cities could be reached by air. Every major town in the United States had its own airport, and airline services became a part of the booming American economy.

In Europe, the story was very different, and the restoration of air services took another course. Europe was a shattered continent. Most of the national airlines had suffered badly in the war and they lacked organization and equipment. BOAC was faced with the task of linking Britain with the remains of her Empire, and only had converted bombers available in the immediate post-war period. Unfortunately, these machines were hardly satisfactory as airliners. The Handley Page Halifax was converted to carry 12 passengers, and a civilian version of the famous Lancaster was produced. This machine carried even fewer passengers and was called the Lancastrian. The conversion of the Lancaster had originated in Canada, and its nine passengers sat along one side of the cabin facing inward. The Lancaster bomber was also developed into the Avro 685 York transport, which had first flown in 1942. Using the wings and tail plane of the bomber, it possessed a square box-like fuselage and was powered by four of the famous Rolls-Royce Merlin engines. Production of the York reached a total of 257, most of which were used by RAF Transport Command. BOAC had obtained 25 Yorks by 1945, and the type was still in service at the time of the Berlin airlift.

These bomber conversions were no

At the same time, both Qantas and SAA made it known that they were about to order American aircraft in preference to the Tudor. The original order for 79 machines was reduced to 18, and of these, 6 were delivered to British South American Airways, who introduced them in 1948 on the South Atlantic routes. This version was known as the Tudor 4. It was 6 ft (2 m) longer than the earlier version and had 32 seats. The flagship was called *Star Tiger*, and it disappeared in mysterious circumstances in January 1948. When a second Tudor 4 disappeared between Bermuda and Jamaica a year later, the type was withdrawn from service and placed on freight and charter work.

Britain's other four-engined pressurized medium-sized piston airliner, the Handley Page Hermes, had a worse start to its short career than even the Tudor. The prototype crashed on take-off during its maiden flight in December 1945, killing all on board, including the Handley Page chief test pilot. In 1947, BOAC ordered an improved version which was called the Hermes 4. This had four 2100 hp Bristol Hercules radial engines and a tricycle undercarriage. These machines were delivered by 1950, and were the first British aircraft of post-war design to enter service with BOAC. However, they did not match existing American machines and by 1956 had been replaced by the new equipment ordered from the United States. Only then did the Hermes come into its own. The machines were sold to various British private companies, including Air Work Limited and Skyways Limited. These concerns used the Hermes to launch regular services for military transport to Africa and Asia. Flying under contract to the British War Ministry, the Hermes ended up by carrying 14,000 troops and their families

match for the American aircraft, and Britain was so far behind that, in retrospect, it is obvious that it was almost impossible to catch up. The Brabazon Committee had specified the type of machines required as early as 1943, but this allowed only a ridiculously short development time. Whereas the Americans had been able to organize themselves for production and development, the British industry had to start from scratch. Two ambitious projects preoccupied the British civil scene as the war ended.

The first of these was a plan to produce a commercial aircraft capable of non-stop service across the Atlantic. It came from the Avro Company, which had also produced the Lancaster and the York. The Tudor was based on the new Lincoln bomber, and had the wing and engine installation of that machine. In every other respect, the aircraft was

new and was the first British airliner to have a pressurized fuselage. The plan was to carry 24 passengers during the day, and 12 on night flights. Orders were placed by BOAC, Qantas and South African Airways (SAA). An improved version was also planned, which would give a capacity of 60 passengers with a range of 2800 miles (4506 km).

BOAC planned the Tudor to be its main challenger to the Americans, and the prototype flew for the first time on 14 June 1945. From the first, the aircraft was plagued with serious technical problems, and big modifications were made to the tail surfaces. BOAC themselves demanded at least 300 major design changes but, even so, when only 4 aircraft had flown, the British company decided that the machine was unable to meet its requirements and the order was cancelled.

The Avro Tudor II (above) was designed for the African, Far East and Australian services of BOAC, but was cancelled by them before the aircraft came into service. The Tudor was the first British airliner to be designed with a pressurized cabin.

The Handley Page HP81 Hermes 4 went into service with BOAC from February 1950 onwards. Here, a flight crew poses in front of *Hengist*, one of the early machines (below). The engines were Bristol Hercules 763s. The Hermes served the airline for only two years before replacement started with Canadair C-4s. Left: The comfortable ladies powder room on board a Hermes.

The glory that was not to be! The huge Bristol Type 167 Brabazon 1 on engine test outside the Assembly Hall especially built for it (below). The Brabazon 1 flew in 1949 but development problems led to the cancellation of the project in 1952, and the scrapping of the prototype (left). The Brabazon passenger lounges were impressive for size and comfort (right). The manager of the project, the late Frank Chard, is seated centre of the front row.

BRISTOL BRABAZON I

a year, and laid the foundations for later British military transport procedures.

No account of British aviation development after the Second World War would be complete without reference to the gigantic Bristol Type 167 Brabazon 1, which appeared in 1949. Today, the London–New York flight non-stop, with at least 100 passengers on board, is taken for granted. However, in 1943, when the Brabazon Committee made its study of post-war aircraft requirements for Britain, the objective looked very different and it took some six years to achieve. The Brabazon Committee put forward two reasons for the construction of a very large airliner. The first was frankly nationalistic and pointed out the prestige which would be gained by the United Kingdom if she put into service the first commercial aircraft,

capable of flying London–New York non-stop. Secondly, the Bristol Aeroplane company already had more experience than other companies on preliminary designs for a large, long-range strategic bomber. Its range was estimated to be 5000 miles (8047 km) but the proposal had been dropped by the Air Ministry in December 1942. Bristol were, therefore, the logical choice to build the new airliner, and work started in March 1943.

The bomber design was adapted, and the aircraft appeared as a large monoplane with a centrally located wing, eight engines buried inside the wing and a long, circular, pressurized fuselage. The engine installation was interesting. It consisted of eight Bristol Centaurus radial engines, each of 2500 hp, mounted in pairs with each one driving two counter-rotating propellers.

The engines were cooled by means of air intakes in the leading edge of the wing. The object of this engine arrangement was to reduce the drag, although it gave cooling and transmission problems.

So many technical problems had to be overcome that the original completion date of 1947 arrived when the main structure was only just on the point of completion. It was not until 6 January 1949 that the huge aircraft was towed from its hangar for ground tests. These lasted throughout the summer, and the prototype was eventually taken into the air on 4 September 1949 with the Bristol chief test pilot Bill Pegg at the controls. The machine was airborne after a run of only about 1500 ft (457 km), and a ground speed of 87 mph (140 km/h). Following the successful first flight, the Brabazon began a series of test pro-

grammes which were aimed at gathering experience for use on the second prototype, of which construction was well advanced.

Anyone who was lucky enough to experience a flight in the Brabazon found it an aircraft of unbelievable comfort and steady performance in flight. Engineers took pride in balancing coins on the edges of various points of the structure; they would remain there for perhaps a minute before a slight vibration in the airplane overturned them. The cabin was huge, giving a great sense of space, and there was ample room to stretch one's legs. However, such luxury was bought at a price; with American aircraft already operating from the BOAC maintenance base located alongside the Brabazon shed at Filton, any realistic person could see that the Stratocruiser and Constellation were more versatile than the large, slow Brabazon.

Airline interest in the type therefore waned, and the programme was eventually cancelled on 9 July 1953. While it existed, the Brabazon gave a glimpse of the future in the skies over Britain, and its 230-ft (70-m) wing span has yet to be exceeded by modern wide-bodied jets. The 747 has a span of 195 ft 8 ins (60 m), and that is the largest span of the breed.

Post-war Britain did, however, produce a number of successful piston-powered airliners in the medium-range field. The most prominent of these was the Vickers Viking, a 36-seat twin-engined aircraft which was based on the well-tried Wellington bomber. It seemed that the British industry made up for failures in the field of large, long-range commercial aircraft by producing brilliant smaller short-to-medium-range transports. The Viking was one of these, and by the end of 1947 a total of 161

aircraft had been completed at the Vickers plant at Weybridge. The main customer was British European Airways (BEA) and they kept the Vikings in service until 1954, when they were replaced with the turbo-prop Viscounts.

The first Viking's maiden flight was in June 1945, and the production total of 161 aircraft by the end of 1947 rivals anything that the Americans were doing at the same time. It was almost as if the impetus of war production in the British industry had not yet worn out. The Viking used the well-tried Bristol Hercules 634 radial engine and in eight years of service the type flew more than 65 million miles (105 million km) and carried 2,748,000 passengers.

In these immediate post-war years, the Bristol Aeroplane Company produced its type 170 Freighter, an ugly but extremely tough and versatile airplane. It was designed to be as simple as possible, and had a high wing and fixed undercarriage. The power plant was two large Hercules radial engines.

The first prototype flew in December 1945, and over 200 of the type were built before production ceased in 1954. The Freighter had its greatest commercial success in its use as a car ferry across the English Channel, and Silver City Airways began operations in July 1948. In 10 years of service until 1958, the Freighters belonging to that company had travelled 125,000 times to and fro across the Channel, carrying 215,000 cars and 759,000 passengers. Bristol sold the Freighter all over the world, particularly in America and New Zealand, and a military version was supplied to the Pakistan Air Force.

The ultimate piston-engined airliner to come from the British industry was the Airspeed AS57 Ambassador, which operated for almost six and a half years on British European routes from March

1952 to July 1958. It was a high wing machine with tricycle undercarriage, two Bristol Centaurus engines and a wide pressurized cabin which was very comfortable. The fuselage was narrow at either end but extended to a very wide belly and the passengers were seated in two groups on the slope of the cabin. The group in the forward part of the fuselage faced aft and looked directly across to the second group. Twenty one aircraft were delivered to BEA but the Ambassador failed to find any other buyers.

One other European design in these post-war years was the Ilyushin IL-12, the aircraft on which the Russian state airline Aeroflot based its very large network. Altogether some 7000 IL-12s, and its developed version IL-14, were built and they proved themselves to be very successful replacements for the DC-3, of which more than 2000 were built in Russia under licence. The IL-12 owed much of its design to experience with the DC-3. It was a good-looking monoplane, all-metal, and powered with a Russian version of the Pratt & Whitney R1830, which was built under licence as well. The airplane was put into service on Aeroflot routes in August 1947 and a year later was flying on the very extensive network throughout the Soviet Union. The IL-12 was produced in a passenger version and also for freight transport. In addition to being used by Aeroflot, it was supplied to Czechoslovakia, Poland, Ghana and a number of countries world-wide. A larger version, the IL-14, was produced in 1953 and this machine was also built in East Germany and Czechoslovakia. It is fair to say that the IL-12 and IL-14 were to Soviet aviation what the DC-3 had become for Western airlines. This rugged useful machine was seen throughout the world from Vladivostok

Top: A Bristol Type 170 Freighter of Silver City Airways is loaded with motor cars for its cross-channel service which started in 1948. In its first ten years, the service carried 215,000 cars and 759,000 passengers. The Type 170 remained, in terms of numbers built, the most successful civil aircraft to come from the Bristol factory. Above: The Vickers Viking was based on the Wellington bomber, and the wing structure was almost identical, with the characteristic of geodetic design. Right: The Airspeed A557 Ambassador was the last piston-engined aircraft to be used by BEA. Twenty were built between 1947 and 1952.

The Boeing 377–10 Stratocruiser was developed from the B29, one of the best bomber designs to come out of the Second World War. The two decks allowed a bar to be carried on board and ample space for sleeping berths. Although only fifty were built, the Stratocruiser was one of the most significant post-war aircraft and introduced true international mass traffic.

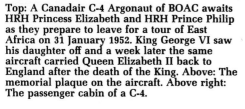

to Buenos Aires, and large numbers remain in service in the 1980s.

All European efforts were dwarfed by the tremendous post-war boom of the American industry. Rightly regarded as the world leaders in aircraft production in 1945, the American industry reacted to the urgent demands of the country's domestic airlines and produced ever-better machines in large quantities. The advantage that the United States enjoys from its huge native airline industry is not always understood in Europe, and certainly attempts by the British government to insist that BOAC always bought British aircraft led to the technical failures and misunderstandings of the immediate post-war years. The big production runs in American factories meant that low unit costs were achieved and world airlines insisted that they be allowed to purchase the better equipment available there. Only by doing so could they remain competitive, particularly on the prestigious North Atlantic services. The final years of development of piston airliners are dominated by the three big American companies Douglas, Boeing and Lockheed. Between 1945 and the mid-1950s, these huge organizations produced a series of airliners in response to demand, often in direct competition with each other. Such was the achievement that three big airliners all competed with each other and all made money.

In 1945, we have already seen that the Douglas company was able to market large quantities of ex-service DC-4s. This machine sold well and was largely equipping most American airlines and several of the prominent foreign ones by the end of 1946. While Douglas considered a development of the machine, there was an interesting offshoot of the design produced in Canada.

Top: A Canadair C-4 Argonaut of BOAC awaits HRH Princess Elizabeth and HRH Prince Philip as they prepare to leave for a tour of East Africa on 31 January 1952. King George VI saw his daughter off and a week later the same aircraft carried Queen Elizabeth II back to England after the death of the King. Above: The memorial plaque on the aircraft. Above right: The passenger cabin of a C-4.

Above: 'Shorten your travel time' says an American poster of the late 1940s.

In 1943, J T Bain of Trans-Canada Air Lines had proposed that the DC-4 be fitted with Rolls-Royce Merlin engines, in order to give it a better performance than the standard version. As soon as the war ended, Bain's idea was put into practice, and both Trans-Canada Air Lines and the Royal Canadian Air Force received deliveries of the machine, which was renamed the Canadair C-4. Trans-Canada used the type on the North Atlantic route from April 1947 onwards, although the machines did not have any pressurization system.

Later models off the production line were pressurized, and Canadian Pacific Air also received four aircraft in 1949.

In mid-1948, the failure of the Avro Tudor to fulfil expectations had left BOAC with considerable problems. The only solution was to order American equipment – a course of action which was against government policy at the time. The Canadian version of the DC-4 offered a way out, and BOAC put a fleet of 22 C-4s in operation. BOAC called them Argonauts, and they were all delivered by November 1949. This was BOAC's first experience of operating American-designed land planes and they have continued to use American equipment in their fleet ever since. The Argonaut proved a particularly successful airplane and BOAC only began to withdraw it in 1958.

The first challenge to the Douglas supremacy came from Boeing. Again it was with an aircraft that was derived from the immense military effort that went on in the United States in the first years of the war. The USAF had asked Boeing to produce a military transport based on components used in the famous B-29 Superfortress. Boeing launched the project using the wing, tail plane, engines and landing gear of the B-29. They redesigned the fuselage, using the double-bubble form which produced a structure strong enough to stand up to the pressurization system. This form of fuselage also gave a much greater load capacity. Fifty five of the military version were ordered after the first flight in November 1944 and the pay-load of 20,000 lbs (9072 kg) with the high average speed of 380 mph (611 km/h) were obviously attractive to the civil airlines. This performance was achieved by cruising at 30,000 ft (9144 m), a feat made possible by the pressurization system. Altogether, 888 of the military aircraft were supplied to the USAF and they were used both as transports and as flying tankers.

The civil version was known as the Boeing Model 377 and it was equipped to carry 100 passengers over long distances. The two deck levels were something relatively new to the airlines and the lower deck was used to provide a bar and additional seating. Alternatively, the Stratocruiser could be used on night services with 55 passengers in bunks. The result was an impressive-looking airplane which gave a sense of power and security to the onlooker. Power was obtained from four Pratt & Whitney Wasps, and the aircraft had a wing span of 141 ft (43 m). The Stratocruiser is particularly associated with Pan Am, who became the largest operators with twenty aircraft. BOAC ordered ten and used them over a period of ten years from December 1949, eventually adding seven more and becoming the second largest Stratocruiser operator. American airlines used eight, North West Airlines had ten, and United Airlines a further seven.

Top: A mobile reservation and ticket office in use during a TWA marketing drive in the early 1950s. Right: TWA led the world in airline promotion in the 1950s. Typical of its publicity schemes was the 'Round the World Survey' of 1952. At this time, the airline seriously threatened Pan Am's position as the major United States overseas operator. Above: Ancient and modern meet as an airfield grass cutter and his horse greet a Lockheed 1-149 Constellation of BOAC. Opposite page: This striking Air France poster portrays a Lockheed Constellation against the profile of Rio's Sugar Loaf Mountain.

AIR FRANCE
AMÉRIQUE DU SUD

Although only 55 were built in total, the Stratocruiser showed itself to be one of the best airliners of the post-war period.

The other major airliner that appeared during the Second World War was the graceful Lockheed Constellation – by any standard of appearance one of the most beautiful airplanes ever produced. In its developed version, the Lockheed Constellation was the final and most efficient expression of piston-engined civil air transport. It was begun way back in 1939 at the request of TWA, which was looking for a long-range machine for its trans-America route. By the time the first flight was made on 9 January 1943, the project had been taken over by the USAF, but only 22 machines had been delivered when the war ended. Using the surplus aircraft remaining from the military order, Lockheed supplied Constellations to TWA and Pan Am, and by early 1946 both airlines had services operating. Pan Am were flying the New York–Bermuda route and TWA operated between Washington and Paris. This was the start of a long series of improved versions of the Constellation, during which time the fuselage was lengthened and its passenger capacity increased from 44 to 81. At the same time, the fuselage was lengthened from 95 ft (29 m) in the original airplane to 113 ft 7 ins (34 m) in the Super Constellation, which appeared in 1954.

The Super Constellation was a completely redesigned aircraft, compared with the Constellation, when that machine was phased out of production with a total of 232 deliveries. Prominent among operators of the Super Constellation were TWA and KLM, but almost all the major companies, including BOAC and Pan Am, operated the Lockheed in the early and mid-1950s. Extended range was obtained by adding wing-tip fuel tanks, and this also enhanced the appearance. The original Constellation had been powered by 2700 hp Curtiss Wright Cyclone engines, but the bigger 3400 hp turbo-compound of the same company was fitted in the Super Constellation.

By the time the Super Constellation was in service, the Douglas company had already produced its DC-6, an updated version of the DC-4. Larger, with more power in the engines, more than 700 DC-6s were sold, and the aircraft was in use right up to the early 1970s.

European orders came in particular from Sabena, and Scandinavian Airlines. An improved version appeared in January 1951 with the DC-6B, which was introduced into service by American Airlines. This proved popular but most airlines considered that the Super Constellation was a better machine, and to meet this challenge, Douglas made a further stretch of the DC-6 fuselage, fitted the same turbo-compound engine as used in the Super Constellation and called the new aircraft the DC-7. This made a break-through that American

Airlines had long wanted; it could fly non-stop between New York and Los Angeles in both directions. This was an improvement on the performance of the Super Constellation, which had to make a refuelling stop at Chicago on the return journey, due to prevailing winds. It was to overcome this problem that Lockheed introduced the extra wing-tip tanks into the L-1049G version of the Super Constellation.

Finally, Douglas produced the ultimate development of its series of piston-engined airliners with the DC-7C of

A sectional artist's impression of a Douglas DC-6B of Pan American World Airlines.

1955. This turned out to be indisputably the best aircraft of the entire series. The Douglas designers produced a new wing which was lengthened by 10 ft (3 m) and rebuilt to include larger flaps and ailerons. This reduced the fuselage vibration and also increased the fuel capacity, thus giving the range required for transatlantic non-stop operations. The DC-7C, named the Seven Seas, was ordered by Pan Am and BOAC. For the British company, the DC-7C proved a godsend, and they ordered it before the prototype had even taken to the air.

This order was placed because BOAC found themselves without a major airplane due to the serious constructional defects that had appeared in their de Havilland Comets. In the course of proving the transatlantic route, a DC-7C of BOAC reached New York from London non-stop on 11 November 1956, in a record time of ten hours forty minutes.

It took a year for Lockheed to match the DC-7C and so recover the ground that TWA had lost to Pan Am. They also turned to wing redesign to improve the performance of the Super Constellation, and this version appeared as the L-1649A Starliner. This had a range of over 6000 miles (9656 km), which was probably the longest of any piston-engined airliner of its size. However, only 43 were built because it appeared in the same year as the first turbo-engined Bristol Britannias were placed in service on the transatlantic route. Then, in December 1957, Pan Am saw the first flight of its first Boeing 707 jet airliner. They put it into service 10 months later and the days of the piston-engined airliner were over.

The DC-7c, known as the *Seven Seas*, was the world's first truly international airliner, being capable of flying the Atlantic non-stop against the strongest head winds. However, its success was short-lived, due to the introduction of the turbine engine.

CHAPTER SEVEN

TRIUMPH OF THE TURBINE

FIVE DAYS BEFORE the invasion of Poland on 1 September 1939, an event of almost equal effect (albeit of a different nature) on world history took place at Merienehe in North Germany. On the airfield of the famous Heinkel factory, the world's first aircraft to fly solely on the power of a jet engine took-off on 27 August. The achievement of Dr Heinkel's design team was reached after a great deal of experiment with jet propulsion at Göttingen University, and one of the researchers, Dr Pabst von Ohain, was engaged to continue the work at the factory. Ohain first ran a small turbo-jet, the HeS 1, in September 1937, and this led to a more advanced engine the following year.

Eventually, this new engine, the HeS 3b, was put into a small high-wing airplane called the Heinkel He 178. It was remarkably similar in design to the first British jet aircraft, the Gloster E28/39, although this did not fly until 1941. The first flight of the He 178 was undertaken by Heinkel's test pilot Erich Warsitz and lasted for thirty minutes. He only achieved a speed of 370 mph (595 km/h), but the success of the flight encouraged Heinkel and the Luftwaffe to develop the jet aircraft. By the end of the Second World War, a number of successful jet fighters, in particular the Messerschmitt 262, were in service with the front line forces of the Reich.

There can be no doubt that the coming of war in 1939 was a significant factor in the development of the jet aircraft as we know it today. Chapter Seven details how the war produced the large piston-engined airplane, but it also spurred aircraft designers into a frantic search for speed and superior manoeuvrability. During the war, all the major powers gained experience of jet propulsion, and development in the United Kingdom, Germany and the

The world's first jetliner (above), the elegant de Havilland DH106 Comet I, first flew on 27 July 1949 and was years ahead of any American competitor until a series of structural failures caused fatal accidents and ended its career. The seating on board a Comet I (right) gave ample leg room for passengers and the four Ghost jet engines were so smooth that cigarettes and coins would balance easily (far right) as the aircraft flew at 500mph (805 km/h).

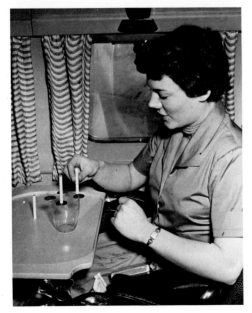

United States ran along remarkably similar lines.

However, the Germans had pioneered the axial flow engine. This meant that the air flowed along the axis of the turbine, starting with a forward compressor, which compressed the air into flame tubes where it was mixed with low-quality kerosene and then exhausted through a turbine into a jet pipe aft. During the 1930s in the United Kingdom, Sir Frank Whittle, a Royal Air Force engineering officer, developed a centrifugal-type turbo-jet. He first ran this very simple engine in April 1937, just ahead of the Heinkel engine in Germany, thus making it the first turbine in the world to be tested successfully. The centrifugal compressor took the air from the intake and compressed it by the use of a spiral compressor acting on centrifugal principles.

After further development, this Whittle engine was flown successfully in the Gloster E28/39 on 15 May 1941. A developed version of it was later fitted to the Gloster Meteor – the only Allied jet fighter to see action in the Second World War. Britain also passed this engine to the United States, where it was fitted to the Bell Airacomet. This engine formed the basis of American and British jet development in the years immediately following the war.

It is a curious paradox that, whereas America developed the piston engine during the war largely to power big transports, both she and the Soviet Union concentrated their design and research efforts after the war into mainly military objectives, which led to the eventual clash between the two super-powers in the Korean war of 1950. The American decision to pursue military development is not hard to understand. Faced with the Soviet threat, she already possessed a large civil airline industry. The American airlines had continued to grow throughout the war and, when it ended, aircraft manufacturers were able to turn their production lines of military transport very quickly over to civil airliners. Therefore, as soon as the war ended in 1945, airlines in the United States were introducing the Douglas DC-4, and the Lockheed Constellation, onto routes nationwide. By the end of the 1940s, the Boeing Stratocruiser was also in service.

While the American airlines were introducing this new equipment, the British aircraft industry was struggling to recover from its wartime efforts. Due to a very limited production strength, Britain had concentrated throughout the war on the production of fighting aircraft. The Royal Air Force had obtained its entire transport fleet from America, following the entry of that country into the war in December 1941. Most of these transports were Douglas DC-3s. When the war ended they had to be returned to their owners, USAF, and British airlines had to use converted bombers such as the Avro Lancastrian. Even so, with all her preoccupations during the war, the United Kingdom had given some consideration to a new generation of airliners, and a committee under the leadership of the aviation pioneer Lord Brabazon was set up to recommend future aircraft requirements to the British government. Aviation historians argue that the results of the committee's work severely handicapped the country's aircraft industry after the war, but one of its recommendations was to have far-reaching consequences.

The Brabazon Type IV was a design of a high-speed, mail-carrying airplane with transatlantic capability. The committee argued that it should be powered by turbo-jets, and this is the first instance on record of the jet engine being considered for use on a civil aircraft. The early jets consumed fuel in large quantities and designers felt their application was restricted to high-performance aircraft. The Brabazon Committee, therefore, were suggesting something very new. Nevertheless, at Hatfield outside London, the de Havilland designers got down to work and finally produced a design for a medium-sized airliner with swept wings, four jet engines buried inside them, and a pressurized cabin which would carry forty passengers. This airplane would eventually be known as the DH106 Comet, and it became the most famous airliner of its day and, eventually, the most tragic. Work began in September 1946 to produce two prototypes, and a production order of 14 followed almost immediately.

The first prototype of the Comet flew on 27 July 1949 with de Havilland's chief test pilot, ex-ace night fighter John Cunningham, at the controls. It was obvious from the first that the Comet was a winner. Its four Ghost jet engines gave it a cruising speed of 490 mph (788 km/h), and allowed 36 passengers to be carried over a range of 2600 miles (4184 km). The aircraft had a clean aerodynamic appearance and soon became a familiar sight on the front pages of the world's newspapers. It was obvious to all that with the Comet, Britain had produced an airplane years ahead of America's designs, and it placed her in a favourable position to overtake the American lead in commercial air transport.

The development programme of the aircraft raced ahead and several world distance records were broken during the route-proving flights. The first Certificate of Airworthiness for a commercial jet airliner was awarded to the Comet on 22 January 1952 and passenger services started from London to South Africa on 2 May.

By this time, the advantages of the axial flow engine over the centrifugal type had been well established, and Rolls-Royce Avon engines were fitted from the sixth aircraft onwards. This allowed the de Havilland Company to announce a new, larger, Comet 3 which would carry 78 passengers over a range which increased by sixty percent. By this time, many world airlines were showing interest in the aircraft and orders came in from Canada and Brazil. Another early customer was Air France, who were soon joined by Japan Airlines. The impossible was achieved in October 1953 when Pan Am ordered three Comet 3s, with an option on a further seven. By the end of 1953, orders for over 100 Comets were being negotiated and the aircraft looked set to become one of the most successful airliners of all time.

At the beginning of 1954, it was obvious that Britain had a commanding lead of some five years over the rest of the world, particularly the United

THE COMET
Britain leads

DE HAVILLAND ENTERPRISE

The Comet became a prestige symbol for British technology, as a de Havilland advertisement from 1950 shows.

States, in the production of jet airliners. The Comet 3 was obviously capable of transatlantic flight and production at three factories (Chester and Belfast had been added to Hatfield) was in full swing. There were no other aircraft likely to be available in the immediate future from other countries, and the only problems to date had been the crash of a Canadian Pacific machine in Pakistan and the loss of a British Comet in Calcutta. The accident reports on both aircraft were considered to give sufficient explanation for the disasters and the Comet flew on to a storm of worldwide applause.

Then, on 10 January 1954, a Comet 1 of BOAC crashed into the Mediterranean off the Italian coast near Elba. No immediate reason for the accident was apparent (the machine broke up in mid-air and no one survived), and all the airliners remained in service after a check-up. Almost three months later, on 8 April 1954, another Comet broke up in mid-air and crashed into the same Mediterranean Sea, about 200 miles (322 km) further south, near the volcanic island of Stromboli. The Comet's Certificate of Airworthiness was immediately withdrawn and all Comets were grounded.

The tragedies at Elba and Stromboli shattered the British aircraft industry, and titanic efforts went into the attempt to explain the accidents. The Royal Navy put its most experienced diving teams into operation off the Italian coast and these succeeded in raising a sufficient quantity of wreckage. This was then sent to the Royal Aircraft Establishment at Farnborough, where a reconstruction of the airframe showed that the trouble was caused by weaknesses in the design of the cabin window structure on each side of the fuselage.

The aircraft was the result of a long
development programme which started in 1944
and an early version of the wing is shown in a
wind tunnel model (below). The aircraft cabin
and nose profile was tested in the air by
mounting it on a *Horsa* glider, towed aloft by a
HP Halifax III (right). After the accidents to
Comet I in 1954, a long redevelopment
programme, concentrated on structural
improvement, produced the Comet IV (below),
which was an excellent aircraft but
overshadowed by the Boeing 707.

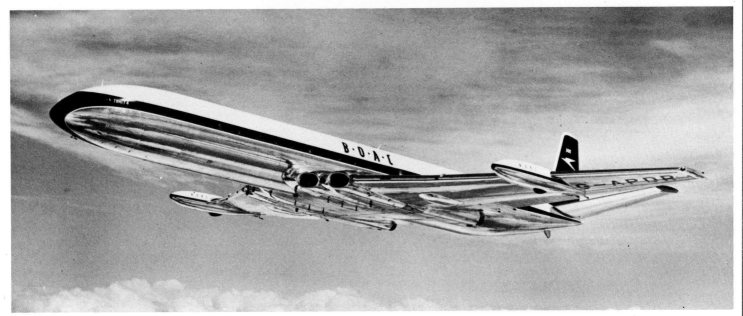

The misfortunes of the Comet had given American designers the time to develop a turbo-jet airliner. The 707 (top) was the first of a long line of successful Boeing jets. The DC-8 entered service a year after the 707. Both aircraft were almost identical in appearance. Right: A DC-8 in the exotic livery designed by Alexander Calder (above) who was commissioned by Braniff International in 1973 to produce a series of hand-painted designs for their South American routes. Opposite page: A poster by French artist Jean Colin for Union Maritime Transports (now part of Union de Transports Aeriens), a privately-owned French airline serving Africa.

UAT SERT L'AFRIQUE PAR JET DC-8

Prior to the Comet accidents, aircraft structure had not been considered by designers to need extreme physical testing during development. The Comet accidents changed all this and now every major aircraft project is required to have at least one test specimen, representative of the flying aircraft, under test and simulating flying hours well in excess of those flown by machines in service. The results of the Comet investigation meant that radical improvements had to be made to the aircraft, and the Comet 4 did not appear until April 1958. The type went into service with BOAC later that year, but by then, the British five-year lead had been overtaken and the great Boeing domination of world airlines was about to begin. With their Model 377 Strato-cruiser successfully in service, Boeing began to produce design studies for a jet-powered replacement in the spring of 1950. By this time they had gained considerable experience with their medium-range jet bomber, the B-47. In this machine, Boeing had used turbo-jet engines mounted in pods below the wings.

The success of the B-47 led the Boeing design team to think that the basic layout could be applied to a civil transport, and in 1952 the board of the company resolved to proceed with the machine (the so-called Dash 80), as a private venture. This must rank as one of the most significant commercial decisions of all time. The Pratt & Whitney JT3 engine was chosen for the machine and it flew for the first time on 15 July 1954. By the time of the first flight, the company had renamed it the Model 707, and it was eventually to become one of the great classic airliners of all time.

A very handsome aircraft in appearance, the 707 was able to carry 130

The Sud-Aviation SE210 Caravelle has proved to be the most successful European jetliner to date, with 280 copies sold. The nose section of the aircraft was a direct copy of the de Havilland Comet design. In 1962, an improved version using the Pratt & Whitney JT8 engine (below) appeared with a range improvement of fifty percent.

passengers and a crew of 8 at a cruising speed of just over 600 mph (966 km/h) at 25,000 ft (7620 m). Fully loaded, it had a range of 4700 miles (7564 km) and was obviously an aircraft of great potential. By the time the prototype appeared, the USAF was expressing interest in the 707 and Boeing accepted this in order to get military support for the aircraft funding.

Commercially, in the first year or so, orders for the 707 did not materialize in any quantity. Most of the big airlines had recently re-equipped with numbers of Super Constellations and DC-7s but in October 1955, Pan Am placed an order for 23 of the new Boeing jets. These machines were ready by 1958 and Pan Am immediately placed them on its services from New York to London and Paris, the first take-off being made on 26 October.

Ironically, BOAC had introduced the first Comet 4 only three weeks previously, and thus can claim to have flown the first jet scheduled services across the Atlantic. By the time that the 707 made its first passenger-carrying flight, orders were flooding in and 180 machines of various specifications were then on order. Boeing were able to offer the machine in a variety of different marques, including STOL and short fuselage versions, while others were larger and heavier, using an uprated version of the Pratt & Whitney JT3.

Two interesting developments of the 707 followed in the years ahead. The -420 Intercontinental series, sponsored by BOAC, was powered by four Rolls-Royce Conway 508 engines, each delivering 17,500 lbs (7938 kg) thrust. The combination of the Boeing airframe and the Rolls-Royce power plant was particularly successful. The second development was the introduction of a modified design for short- and medium-

range operations. This allowed the passenger capacity to be increased, and a new type number, the Model 720, was allocated for this.

By January 1980, 25 years after the prototype flew, 941 Boeing 707s had been ordered and a further 154 Boeing 720s had also been supplied. A total of 594 aircraft of the two types were in service around the world. The 707 deserves its place in the history of aviation as the aircraft which more than any other was the first reliable and profitable jet liner, making a great contribution to the revolution in air transport that occurred in the 1960s. It is obvious that the Boeing 707 will be around the skies of the world for a number of years to come. In the course of its incredible career, it has set up a number of records. Probably the most sensational is that set on 3 February 1960 by a Pan Am Intercontinental 707-320. Using a following jet stream at high altitude, this aircraft flew the 1885 miles (3037 km) between Tokyo and Hong Kong at a ground speed of 760 mph (1223 km/h).

When Pan Am first ordered the Boeing 707 in 1955, it is only fair to mention that at the same time the airline ordered six of the rival Douglas DC-8. Douglas had not given great priority to the design of a jet transport until the work of the Boeing airplane was well advanced. This was due to the lack of available capital needed to support a private venture and the Douglas company did not announce the DC-8, as they named their first jet liner, until almost a year after the prototype Boeing 707 had first flown.

The two airplanes were very similar in appearance, and almost identical in size and performance. The DC-8 cruised at 588 mph (946 km/h), at 30,000 ft (9144 m), and could lift 116 passengers

over 4280 miles (6888 km) with a crew of five. Like the 707, the DC-8 was offered in a variety of different layouts and capabilities. However, the Douglas design team concentrated on American internal air routes and offered high-density passenger capacity, therefore laying the foundations of economy-class air travel. The DC-8 was the first big jet to allow six-abreast seating, compared with the five-abreast of the 707.

Following the order for 25 DC-8s from Pan Am, three other American airlines also placed orders, and by the time of the first flight of the prototype on 30 May 1958, a total of 130 aircraft were on order. This figure alone shows the faith that the aircraft operators of that time had in the Douglas aircraft company and its ability to produce fine airliners. The DC-8 went into service almost a year after the Boeing 707, when on 18 September 1959 Pan Am began services with the type.

Although it never quite achieved the total orders placed for the Boeing jet, the DC-8 turned out in some ways to be a more versatile machine than its rival, particularly at low speeds. By 1980 556 Douglas DC-8s had been built in a number of different versions, and 424 were still in service. The major users were Alitalia, Iberia, KLM, Pan Am, SAS, United, Air Canada, Japan Air Lines and Swissair. Meanwhile in Europe, Britain had eventually produced the Comet 4 and put it in service on the North Atlantic, but it had been replaced by the Boeing 707 as soon as that type came available.

So, three aircraft – the de Havilland Comet, the Boeing 707 and the Douglas DC-8 – pioneered the jet air routes and opened up the possibility for mass, safe, cheap travel throughout the world. In terms of airport development alone, the introduction of the big jets with their increased passenger capacity led many major airports to improve their facilities and offer better turn-round times. The safety record of the jet airliner also increased public confidence, and the pioneer years of the 1950s, which lasted from 1952 until 1960, laid the foundations of the mass aircraft industry that exists today.

One other European pioneer jet liner must be mentioned. This was the Sud-Aviation SE210 Caravelle, and it was the first commercial jet to be built in France and also the first to have engines mounted at the rear. In time, the Caravelle turned out to be the most successful of all European civil aircraft and it was operated by most major airlines in Europe with the exception of BEA. The first prototype flew on 27 May 1955. Production was undertaken at the Sud-Aviation factories at Toulouse and the aircraft went into service with Air France on the Paris-Rome-Istanbul route on 12 May 1959. A long period of development and commercial success followed. The early aircraft used two Rolls-Royce Avon turbo-jets and could carry between 64 and 99 passengers over a range that varied up to 1000 miles (1609 km). This capability made it an excellent airplane on European routes, and it was not until 1962 that a stretched version appeared, using Pratt & Whitney JT8 engines. This improved

the range by up to fifty percent. When production stopped in 1972, 280 Caravelles had been supplied to the airlines.

If the world had watched the struggle between Britain and America to place the first jet liner in service with a blaze of publicity, the Russian aircraft industry produced its first jet liner almost unnoticed. Certainly the de Havilland Comet was the first airplane of its type to fly, but the Russians undoubtedly take second place with their Tupolev 104 which made its first flight on 17 June 1955. As usual in the Soviet Union, the whole Tu-104 programme was carried out in complete secrecy and so the prototype caused a stir when it arrived at London Airport in March 1956. The Tu-104 was a twin-engined, swept-wing, medium-range aircraft, powered by two Mikulin AM-3 turbo-jets. It had a capacity for seventy passengers and a crew of five, and went into service with Aeroflot on 15 September 1956, flying on the Moscow-Omsk-Irkutsk route. At the time, it was the only commercial jet flying a regular service anywhere in the world, as the Comet had been withdrawn two years earlier following the accidents over the Mediterranean. Little is known even today about the development stages of the Tu-104 but, as in the United States, the airplane owed much to earlier designs for jet-propelled bombers.

Many of the early Russian jets including the Tu-104, were provided with an observation panel in the nose of the aircraft. The exact production figures for the Tu-104 are not known but it is estimated that over 200 were built and some supplied to Soviet satellite airlines.

The gas turbine developed in other ways, however, than simply the pure jet with which we have been concerned until now. In the early days of gas turbines, many aircraft designers argued that the high fuel consumption would make the cost of commercial operation prohibitive, and possibly fifty percent of all development effort went into research to produce propellor turbine engines, or turbo-props, as they became known. The use of propellers gave a comparatively more economic performance than turbo-jets and the resulting engines proved to be smooth and very quiet in operation.

Once again, it was the United Kingdom that took the lead. The proposal to build a civil transport powered by turbo-props came originally from Lord Brabazon's committee, which issued a requirement in 1945. The order went to Vickers and the project was taken over by their new chief designer George Edwards in September 1945. Edwards immediately decided that the new machine would be powered by the

Rolls-Royce Dart – a choice which made the Dart the first turbo-prop engine to go into service. Thirty years later the Dart was still in use, notably on the Hawker Siddeley 748 medium-range feeder liner.

Then came a setback to Vicker's plans. The project was nearly abandoned when BEA decided to order the piston-engined Airspeed Ambassador, which appeared to have better economic prospects than the proposed turbojet. Nevertheless, Vickers proceeded with one prototype on their own initiative and this first flew on 16 July 1948 with the legendary Mutt Summers, Vicker's chief test pilot, in the cockpit. The new airplane was named the VC2 and called the Viscount. An earlier proposal to call it Viceroy was dropped when the United Kingdom gave independence to India in August 1947. Nevertheless, it took Vickers nearly two years to convince a reluctant BEA that the Viscount was the best small airliner on offer anywhere in the world at the time. Eventually the prototype carried out experimental flights between London and Paris, and London and Edinburgh. Everyone involved in these trial trips was pleased with the comfort and smoothness of the aircraft. Therefore, in August 1950, twenty Viscounts were put on order and the first aircraft was delivered in early January 1953. It went

Vickers started the design of the Viscount (bottom, in Alitalia colours) in 1945, but had difficulty in persuading BEA to accept it, the airline preferring the piston-engined Ambassador. When the Viscount eventually entered service in April 1953 some 445 were sold, including 147 in North America. The Viscount shared its success (and also the Rolls-Royce Dart engines) with the Fokker F27 Friendship (above), introduced to succeed the Viscount on short-haul routes. The Friendship first flew in January 1957 and production continued into the late 1970s. It was also produced by Fairchild Hiller under licence in the United States. Another successful short-haul airliner appeared bearing Rolls-Royce Dart engines. The Hawker Siddeley 748 (right) is in the colours of the British independently operated Dan-Air. The 748 has remained in production for over two decades and has been sold to over 500 airlines.

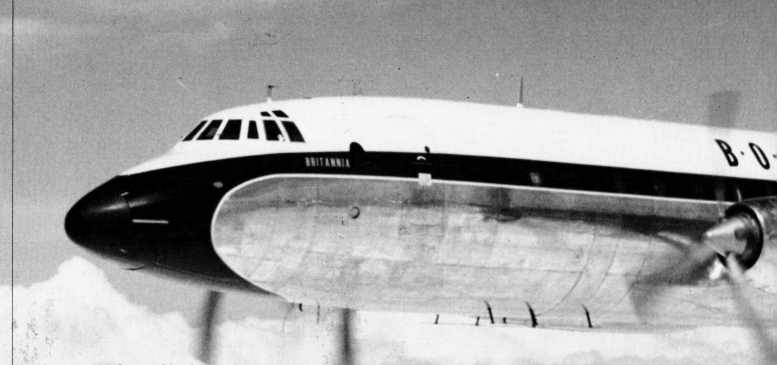

into service as the world's first turbo-prop airliner in April of that year and has continued to fly on world air routes, particularly in Europe, ever since. Something like 440 Viscounts were sold, including 147 to various American airlines – an impressive performance by the Vicker's sales team. In January 1980, about 120 Viscounts were still flying and the type appears to be set to rival the DC-3 for a record length of airline service.

Vickers followed the Viscount with a larger turbo-prop airliner, and the first prototype of this machine, called the Vanguard, flew on 20 January 1959. It was basically an enlarged Viscount, and could carry 139 passengers. It used four Rolls-Royce Tyne turbo-prop engines but did not make anything like the same impact as its predecessor. Only 43 were built, because by the time the Vanguard appeared, most airlines preferred the Lockheed Electra.

The Electra had been produced by Lockheed at the request of American Airlines, and orders were also received from the big carrier Eastern Airlines. The airplane first flew on 6 December 1957, by which time the astonishing total of 144 orders had been placed. The Electra went into service only 14 months later, on 12 January 1959. The first company to fly them was Eastern, with American Airlines following only

11 days later. Subsequent accidents revealed weaknesses in the wing structure, and a long technical inquiry, followed by far-reaching modifications in the wing, meant that a loss of time and money badly affected the Electra's career. The whole affair cost Lockheed over $30 million and raised doubts with airline operators about the viability of turbo-driven airliners.

These years of the 1950s saw the design of two small turbo-liners which have remained in service ever since. The Avro 748 was the last project to bear the name of that company before it was absorbed by Hawker Siddeley in 1963. The specification was for a small, twin-prop airliner which could carry 40-50 passengers over a range of 500 miles (805 km). There was nothing fancy about the Avro 748. It was a rugged airplane which could operate in almost any conditions and was a proven success. It was still in production in 1980, by which time a total of about 400 had been sold in different versions. Fourteen countries had bought military types while the remainder had been sold to fifty airlines in thirty six countries. Even today, Avro 748 (now known as the British Aerospace 748) is probably the most widely distributed airliner in the world.

In 1955 the Fokker Company re-entered the civil aviation market with a

beautiful-looking airplane, the F-27 Friendship, which was directly aimed at the same short-haul market as the Vickers Viscount. It was also powered by a pair of Rolls-Royce Dart turbo-props, could carry 28 passengers and made its first flight in November 1955. Today, it remains one of the most popular twin-engined airliners and has had great success with smaller companies both in Europe and the United States, where over 200 have been built under licence by the Fairchild Company. The Friendship has been bought by operators in 56 different companies and used by more than 60 airlines. The Friendship was a high-winged monoplane with a pressurized fuselage and had room for between 40-52 passengers, depending on the version ordered. In many ways it was similar to the Handley Page Herald, which appeared at almost the same time, but did not enjoy the success of the Friendship.

The Soviet Union built a number of turbo-prop aircraft in the 1950s. The most important was the Ilyushin 18, which went into service with Aeroflot in April 1959. The airplane was very similar to the Lockheed Electra in shape and performance and it is likely that over 400 were built. In 1967 Aeroflot claimed they were moving 10 million people a year using the type. The IL-18 also appeared in airlines operated by

The Bristol Britannia 301 makes an imposing sight at full power on a test flight in 1957. The *Whispering Giant* enjoyed an enviable reputation for safety and comfort, but suffered from power plant de-icing problems which led to late deliveries to customers.

Czechoslovakia, East Germany, Hungary and Poland, together with a number of African countries. Russia also produced the very large turbo-prop airliner, Tu-114, which was a civil version of the Tu-20 long-range bomber. Altogether, thirty or so of this huge machine appear to have been built. It had capacity for 170 passengers over a range of 3800 miles (6115 km), although this could be extended with smaller loads to 6215 miles (10,002 km).

Without doubt, the most important turbo-liner ever built from the standpoint of performance and safety was the Bristol Type 175 Britannia, which became the first airliner to operate a non-stop Atlantic service. This dream of the pioneers became a reality at last when BOAC opened a service with Britannias on 19 December 1957. The big, elegant four-engined turbo-prop was the first airplane in the world to make this regular flight. It was developed as the result of the specification issued by the British government in December 1946. This was for a medium-range aircraft which would carry 32 passengers. The design submitted by Bristol was one of five and proved successful, being accepted by the government in April 1947. Originally, the machine was to be powered by Centaurus radial engines but, following a requirement from BOAC for increased

passenger capacity, the Bristol Proteus turbo-jet was adopted instead. The first prototype Britannia made its maiden flight from Filton on 16 August 1952, piloted by Bristol's chief test pilot Bill Pegg. A second prototype followed a year later and a production order of 15 Britannia 102 aircraft was placed by BOAC.

However, development of the Britannia was proving difficult, due to the layout of the Proteus engine. In order to obtain a compact power unit, the air-flow through the engine was doubled back on itself, but icing problems occurred at the turning point of the jet stream. This led to a long development programme before the ice could be successfully removed. It meant that the Britannia 100 series did not go into service on BOAC routes to South Africa until February 1957. However, great interest was shown in the Britannia from airlines from all over the world. Orders were received from American, Canadian, Israeli and Cuban operators for the Britannia 300, in which the fuselage was lengthened by about 10 ft (3 m). Eighteen were ordered by BOAC, and it was this machine which opened the New York service in December 1957. Nicknamed the *Whispering Giant* because of its quiet flight, the Britannia proved itself popular with passengers and extremely airworthy and safe. If

the engine problems had not occurred (an event about which American newspapers made great play), the Britannia could have been a world-beater. There was no real competitor around at the time of its first flight and its size, payload, range and speed made it an extremely economic airplane to operate.

By the time that the Britannia was in transatlantic service, however, the Boeing 707 was almost ready to be introduced. The turbo-prop was cheap and reliable but it did not have the speed of the pure jets. The President of the United Airlines, W A Patterson, put the matter clearly when he said 'We think that if you buy a turbo-prop plane today your competitor can buy a jet and whip you by 200 mph'. Airlines sell speed as their principle commodity and it was this factor alone that ensured the pure jet would be successful over the turbo-jet. Nevertheless, a number of turbo-jets still operate world-wide today and the type played its part in the development of jet transport. The Viscount and the Britannia, together with the ill-fated Comet, were Britain's contribution to the great technical development that took place in the 1950s. If the Boeing 707 eventually emerged supreme, it was largely because of the experience gained by the earlier pioneers, and the three British aircraft were in the front line of the battle.

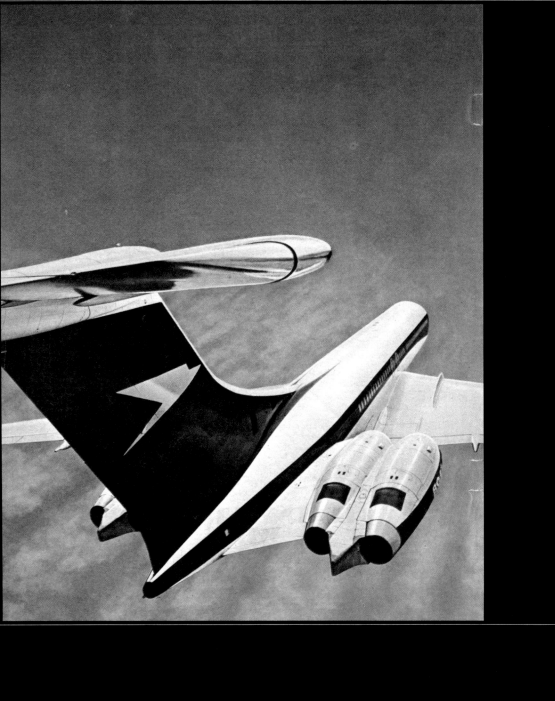

CHAPTER EIGHT

WALKING FREIGHT

TODAY, AS CIVIL AVIATION enters the decade of the 1980s, it has become big business in every way. In 1980, the world's airline operators, from big international carriers to small local services, will have a turnover of more than £150,000 million. The 110 airlines belonging to the international organization International Air Transport Association (IATA) employ nearly 900,000 employees of all types. Many thousands more work for the various companies that are based in airports around the world. In 1979, the airlines belonging to countries which had membership of the International Civil Aviation Organization (ICAO) carried 745 million passengers and 12½ million tons of freight. This performance accounted for 65 percent of the total aircraft capacity available in those countries.

The load factor – the percentage of total capacity that is actually used – is vital to the profits of an airline. Throughout the 1960s and early 1970s, the airlines were content with a 55 percent average load factor, and the improvement in the late 1970s has been largely due to the fare reductions which have resulted from aggressive financial policies by United States airlines and the activities of entrepreneurs, such as the owner of the British Skytrain, Sir Freddie Laker. These low fares have become a feature of the world travel market, and British Airways predicted, as long ago as 1978, that by the middle of the 1980s, eighty percent of its traffic will be composed of low-fare holiday travellers.

The low fare revolution came along just as the airlines were facing record increases in fuel costs. The quantities of fuel used by jet engines are enormous, although when related to the size of the business, a modern jet airliner can be operated at about the same cost per passenger mile as an average family car. A Boeing 747 uses about 3100 gallons (14,093 l) an hour when cruising. The average transocean jet is in use for 12 hours every day but, because it has a high speed and a large passenger capacity, it can use as little as 7.7 gallons (35 l) per flying hour per seat. This allows it to achieve 36.5 passenger miles (59 km) per gallon (litre) – a performance that many motorists would envy. This figure allows for the empty seats that occur on all scheduled flights (those operating on a regular timetable). A charter flight (a special flight pre-arranged and fully booked), can get as high as 45 passenger miles (72 km) per gallon (litre). These figures are important in the context of the steep rises in fuel costs. In January 1979, jet fuel could be purchased at an average cost of 45 cents per US gallon. A year later, the price had doubled to $1 per gallon and there was little sign of stabilization. Add the price of wages and operating charges (it can cost well over £3000 to land a 747 once at London Heathrow) to the fuel costs, and the problems facing airline operators in the 1980s become immense.

The capital investment required to support the flying effort is gigantic. A small airliner such as the Fokker F-28, carrying only eighty passengers, can cost up to £6 million, while a Boeing 747 costs over £30 million. Even when the aircraft have been purchased, there are further costs because they require constant maintenance and modification. They normally have a service life of about fifteen years, although some machines last for twenty or more. At present, more than fifty percent of the world's total of jet airliners are more than ten years old.

All the costs mentioned above are eventually carried by the passenger, and the pricing of air travel tickets is a delicate and complicated business, usually decided by international agreement and backed by government policy. The more freedom a passenger requires, the more costly his ticket is likely to be. The first class and economy fares offered by most airlines who operate scheduled services means that the passenger can travel on the date of his choice, provided that he makes a firm reservation. He can still change to another airline, break his journey along the route, or even divert to other destinations, providing he travels the distance he has paid for from his starting point. He can even get his money back if he fails to turn up. By booking a long way ahead, a passenger can make substantial cuts in the fare he has to pay, and the cheapest way of all is to fly with a charter airline, although the passenger is often committed to fixed travel dates many months before the flight departs.

This variety of travel available to commuters in the last quarter of the twentieth century relies on the jet airliner. In all, there are only 15 or so different types of jetliner in service, discounting the aircraft flying in the Soviet Union. Of these, four are of the big wide-bodied jumbo-type, which have made such an impact since their introduction in 1968.

The birth of the jumbo jet can be traced back almost to 1960. In that year, the success of the Boeing 707 and Douglas DC-8 had clearly been established. The long-range jet aircraft had proved itself, and the world's airlines were experiencing a boom in mass travel by air. Paradoxically, this would lead to a slump in airline profits during the early 1960s, because the traffic grew more slowly than the available capacity. Boeing lost money steadily during the early years of the 707 programme and

The first Boeing 747 is rolled out at Everett on 30 September 1968 to inaugurate the age of the wide-bodied jet. By that date Boeing had received orders for 158 copies from 26 airlines, all of whose insignia can be seen displayed on the aircraft.

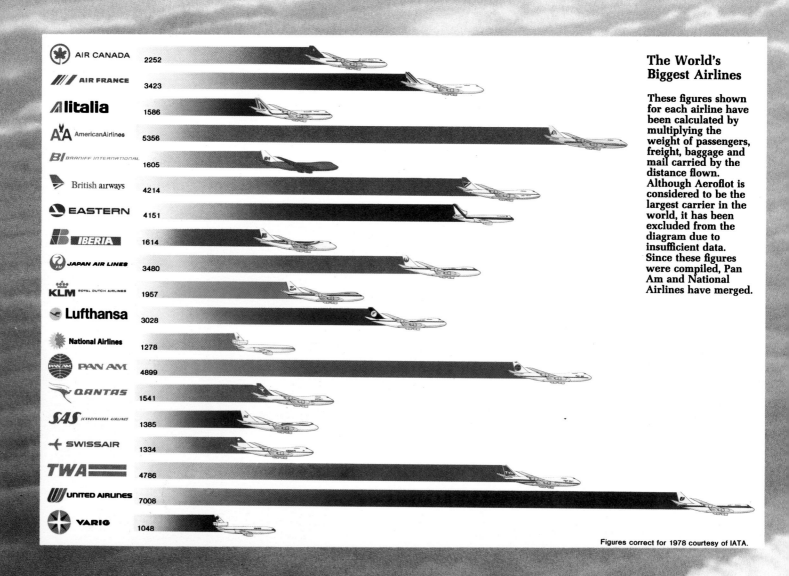

Airline	Figure
AIR CANADA	2252
AIR FRANCE	3423
Alitalia	1586
American Airlines	5356
BI Braniff International	1605
British airways	4214
EASTERN	4151
IBERIA	1614
JAPAN AIR LINES	3480
KLM Royal Dutch Airlines	1957
Lufthansa	3028
National Airlines	1278
PAN AM	4899
QANTAS	1541
SAS Scandinavian Airlines	1385
SWISSAIR	1334
TWA	4786
UNITED AIRLINES	7008
VARIG	1048

The World's Biggest Airlines

These figures shown for each airline have been calculated by multiplying the weight of passengers, freight, baggage and mail carried by the distance flown. Although Aeroflot is considered to be the largest carrier in the world, it has been excluded from the diagram due to insufficient data. Since these figures were compiled, Pan Am and National Airlines have merged.

Figures correct for 1978 courtesy of IATA.

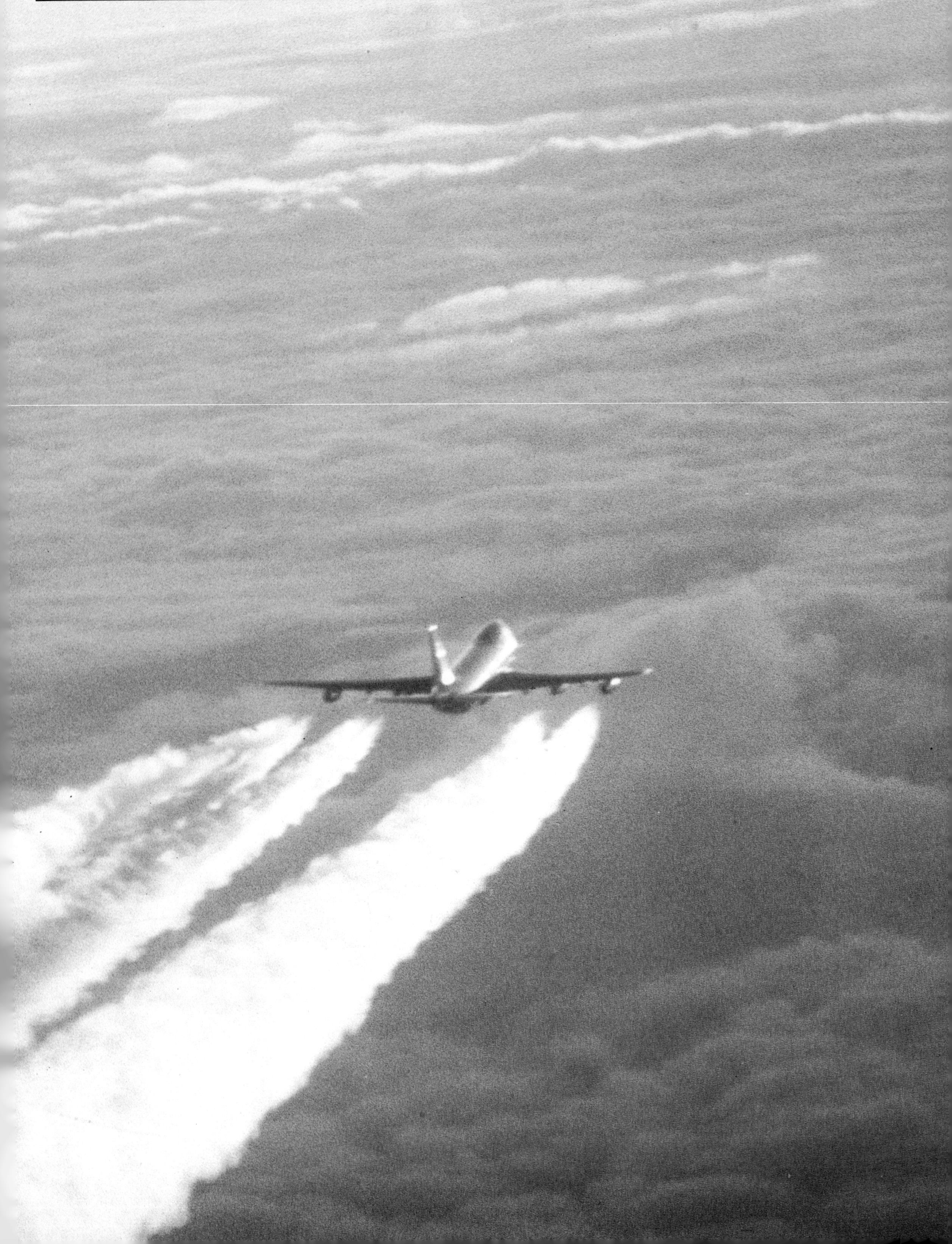

did not break even until 1964, while it is doubtful that Douglas ever made a great profit from the DC-8. However, 1960 saw the introduction of new engines, particularly the bypass types such as the Rolls-Royce Conway and the rival Pratt & Whitney JT3D. These engines gave the DC-8 and 707 much better performances and enabled Europe to be linked non-stop over the North Pole to the American West Coast. This route had been pioneered with piston-engined aircraft – in particular the Douglas DC-7C – but it required a stop at Anchorage in Alaska. This new long-range capacity of the improved 707 using the JT3D meant the virtual extinction of the piston-engined airliner from the big international routes.

These years established Boeing as the world's dominant airliner constructor. Douglas were their only real competitor, and by 1964 they had sold several hundred four-engined jet airliners. Nevertheless, the British aircraft industry made a valiant attempt to break the American monopoly, with the Vickers VC10.

The VC10 was not Vickers' first big jet airliner. As long ago as 1953 they had built the V1000, whose civil version was to be the BC7. The V1000 was developed for the RAF, using many components of the Valiant bomber. However, the British government cancelled the V1000 in early 1956, and Britain lost her final chance to get into the big jet market. Despite this, and after some prodding, BOAC placed an order for an all-British pure jet aircraft in 1957. An agreement to buy 35 VC10s was signed on 14 January 1958, and the Weybridge design team under Sir George Edwards produced a beautiful aircraft. It had an elegant low wing with four Rolls-Royce Conway engines mounted in pairs on the rear fuselage.

The first VC10 flew on 29 June 1962 and a Certificate of Airworthiness was issued on 23 April 1964. It went into service with BOAC six days later.

The VC10 had accommodation for up to 163 passengers in its later version and cruised at 568 mph (914 km/h), giving a range of 4630 miles (7451 km) when fully loaded at its maximum of 335,000 lbs (151,953 kg). BOAC had specified that the aircraft must be capable of operating across the Atlantic and also on Commonwealth routes. This meant that it had to be capable of operating at airports in the Commonwealth countries where runway lengths were shorter than those available in Europe and America. Hence Vickers had to provide a large high-lift wing to get short runway performance. This meant that the wing of the VC10 was complicated and expensive, and inevitably the aircraft had a lower economic performance than its American rivals. Incredibly, BOAC also criticized the design in certain public statements, and this criticism and the powerful competition from America led to only 54 VC10s of all types being built. Nevertheless, it remains one of the most attractive airliner designs to have appeared during the jet age.

By the time the VC10 project was well advanced, Vickers had joined with the Bristol Aeroplane and English Electric companies to form the British Aircraft Corporation (BAC), and the new company came into being in 1960. BAC also acquired part of the Hunting Group's aircraft interests, including a short range turbo-jet successor to the Vickers Viscount. This machine would have twice the speed of the Viscount but be able to operate from short runways and require little maintenance.

The engine chosen for the new machine was the Rolls-Royce Spey – a medium-sized turbo-fan. The introduction of the turbo-fan has revolutionized air transport and all modern airliners use this type of engine. It has the best features of the turbo-jet and turbo-prop. The turbine drives a large fan at the intake entrance and surplus air, which does not go through the main engine, bypasses it on the outside and is then discharged through the jet pipe. This technique dramatically reduces fuel consumption and, almost as important, noise, but does mean loss of performance.

Airlines showed great interest in the new BAC machine, which was originally called the BAC107, but later became the well-known BAC One Eleven. By the time the first prototype flew on 20 August 1963, BAC had obtained orders from a number of American operators, including 15 from American Airlines. In October 1963 the first prototype crashed, but the company handled the ensuing inquiry so well that the order book was maintained and eventually over 200 of the various series of BAC One Elevens was sold. Limited production of the type has continued into the early 1980s, with export orders to Romania, and the One Eleven remains a useful and competitive short-range airliner.

The undoubted reason for the success of the One Eleven was the decision to fit the Spey turbo-fan. The same engine was used on the other prominent British airliner of the 1960s, the Hawker Siddeley Trident. Ironically, in the light of later events, the Trident was the world's first three-jet airliner. It was built for BEA in response to a requirement for a medium-range airliner for use in European services. Twenty four aircraft were ordered in August 1959 and the first Trident flew in January 1962. The Trident filled a very important place in

The Hawker Siddeley Trident was produced in
three variations and formed the backbone of
the BEA fleet on European routes from 1964
onwards. The other significant customer was
the Peoples Republic of China. The offset nose
landing gear was so arranged to save space.

In-flight entertainment is not the exclusive preserve of the 1970s! Passengers on board a Ford Trimotor of American Airways (right) enjoy a radio broadcast in-flight from New York to Chicago some time in 1933. In-flight movies (below) aboard a Boeing 747 of the Israeli airline El Al.

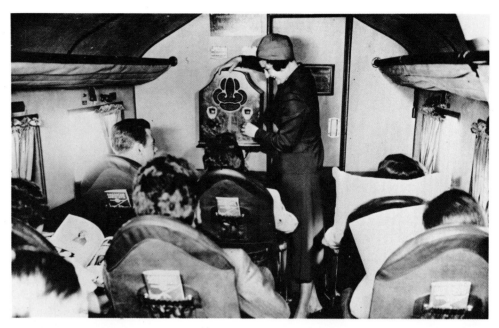

The Boeing 727 (top) is the world's best selling jetliner. It bears a striking resemblance to the Hawker Siddeley Trident which preceded it into the air. By January 1980, 1720 Boeing 727s had been ordered. A BAC One Eleven (above) of Tarom, the Rumanian state airline. The type had a useful route length which proved most economic and has maintained a high second hand sales value for almost two decades.

the airliner market. Its later version, the Trident 3, carried 152 passengers and cruised at 600 mph (966 km/h) over a range of 2500 miles (4023 km). In all, 117 Tridents were built, 35 aircraft going to the airlines of the Peoples' Republic of China.

So it was that the United Kingdom in the early 1960s had put two significant airliners into the skies ahead of the Americans. The BAC One Eleven was the world's first true bus-stop airliner, and the Trident the first medium-range three-jet machine, giving high passenger capacity over medium-range routes. However, the powerful position of Boeing and Douglas, with their reputation as the main builders of the airliners of the West, proved impossible to beat, and most of the world's airlines preferred to place orders with any possible scheme that the two American giants would present.

These proposals were not long in coming, and when they did, they bore a remarkable resemblance to the British machines.

The aircraft that came from the American industry turned out to be the Boeing 727, the Boeing 737 and the Douglas DC-9. Just as it had in the race to build piston-engined airliners after the war, so once again the American industry proved itself capable of out-building and out-selling all its rivals. All three aircraft types were to sell in their hundreds, and the Boeing 727 holds the record of being the world's best-selling jet airliner to date. By January 1980, 1720 Boeing 727s had been ordered.

The Boeing 727 bore a striking resemblance to the Trident 1. Although the British aircraft flew over a year before its American rival, a change of specification required by BEA allowed the

American airliner to catch up, and it actually entered service ahead of the Trident. A big, unattractive three-engined machine, the 727 uses Pratt & Whitney JT8D-11 turbo-fans and gives a very versatile performance. The type first flew on 9 February 1963, by which time orders for over 100 machines had been placed, particularly from Eastern Airlines and United Airlines. It went into service on 1 February 1964 and has been used throughout the world ever since. By 1967, 500 had been sold and today it is operated by over 80 airlines.

The delay to the BAC One Eleven programme which followed the crash of the first prototype in October 1963 allowed its first American competitor to reduce BAC's lead before the One Eleven entered service in October 1964. The One Eleven accident was caused by so-called deep-stall – a condition of flight which is unique to T-tail aircraft. In some conditions, the wing will stall and the turbulence set up can be so great that a T-tail will not allow the aircraft to recover. All T-tail jets are now fitted with a warning system which makes the control wheel shake if the stall condition is approached.

The new American airplane, not surprisingly, came from the Douglas company. In 1962, Douglas had shown the airline companies a design for a similar aircraft to the One Eleven, but based on the JT8D. This design became the DC-9, which made its first flight in February 1965.

Originally, the DC-9 was a smaller version of the DC-8, but Douglas saw the advantages of placing the engines aft, as in the Caravelle and the One Eleven. The resulting aircraft owed much to the experience gained by the European companies, but the DC-9 has proved capable of such development that the latest versions have become almost unrecognizable compared to the original machine which flew in 1965. The Series 10 DC-9 was capable of carrying between eighty and ninety passengers. With the appearance of the Boeing 727, Douglas recognized that larger capacities would be required and the machine has been so refined that the latest member of the series, the DC-9 Super 80, can carry 179 passengers.

The arrival of the DC-9 on the market led to immediate orders from a number of airlines, and Douglas were faced with production requirements beyond the capability of their plant. Nevertheless, they marketed the DC-9 aggressively and sales soon overtook those of the BAC One Eleven. BAC flew a stretched version of their machine, the One Eleven 500 – a 117-seat version for BEA – and this order allowed the One Eleven to be sold in small numbers throughout the 1970s. It became the best-selling European jet after the Caravelle. But its total of 220-plus sales was small indeed when compared with the DC-9. Production of the DC-9, however, proved a difficult task for Douglas. They took on a variety of design changes required by various airlines, and programme delays ensued. With some companies threatening to sue for late delivery in 1966, Douglas almost went out of business and were bought up by the McDonnell Corporation. Today, the

The popular Boeing 737 had an uncertain start to its career and owes much of its success to support from the German airline Lufthansa. Today it is a firm favourite with passengers world-wide.

McDonnell Douglas Aircraft Company represents one of the world's largest aircraft businesses. After the takeover, the DC-9 programme continued unabated and, in January 1980, 1034 had been sold. The most popular version was the Series 30, first ordered by Eastern Airlines, and in Europe by KLM, Alitalia and Swissair. This places the DC-9 second to the Boeing 727 in the Western world, but reports from Russia show sales of the Antonov An-24 to be at a total of over 1100.

The emergence of the DC-9 gave Boeing an immediate problem. They needed a short-range jet to compete directly, otherwise they could see that the greater capacity of the Series 30 DC-9 could make serious competition for their 727.

They therefore quickly got underway with a design for a twin jet, which eventually emerged as the popular Boeing 737. It was based on the same fuselage design as the 707 and 727, and Boeing relied on the well-tried wing-slung engine fixture with their traditional pylon design. The engine would be the ubiquitous Pratt & Whitney JT8D. The aircraft badly needed a production order and this came from the German Lufthansa, who urgently needed a commutor jet on their internal services. When Boeing finally decided to proceed with the 737 it was on the basis of the German order only, and the future looked far from rosy when Eastern Airlines ordered the DC-9. Boeing therefore offered a stretched version of the machine, the 727-200, which could seat up to 130 passengers. An order for 30 came from United Airlines, who eventually took a total of 58. They were the only large United States operator to buy the 737-200, because of a ruling by the United States pilots' union that three-man crews were mandatory, although

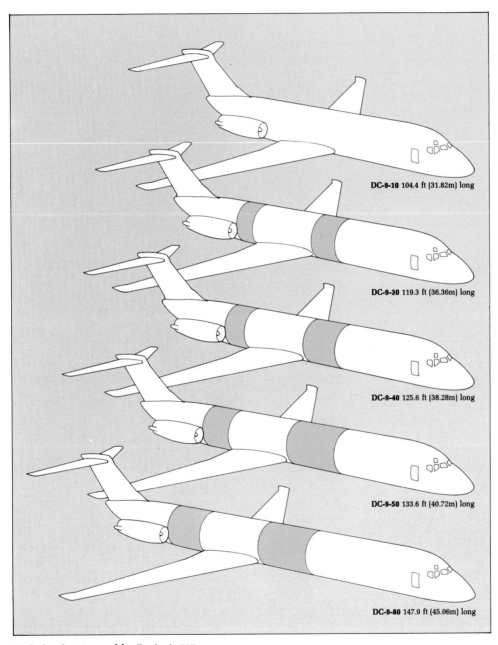

DC-9-10 104.4 ft (31.82m) long

DC-9-30 119.3 ft (36.36m) long

DC-9-40 125.6 ft (38.28m) long

DC-9-50 133.6 ft (40.72m) long

DC-9-80 147.9 ft (45.06m) long

With the threat posed by Boeing's 727, McDonnell Douglas began to extend the fuselage of the DC-9, so that in 15 years it had been lengthened by 43.5 ft (13.26m) and carried an extra 80 passengers, making it one of the most 'stretched' aircraft flying.

the DC-9 escaped this problem because it was in service before the rule was introduced.

After the introduction of an advanced 737-200 in 1972, the 737 began to sell well and, as it could be converted to a freighter, it was especially attractive to African and Asian operators. A total of 742 had been sold by the end of 1979.

The McDonnell Douglas DC-9 and the two Boeing machines have been marketed and sold in such large numbers throughout the 1970s, and have proved so profitable to their owners even during the world oil crisis, that airlines appear reluctant to enter the inevitably costly process of replacement. Orders are still being obtained for all three types, and they have good sales prospects for well into the 1980s.

Apart from the BAC One Eleven, from the early 1960s the United States aircraft industry has dominated the medium- and short-range jet market. Fokker-VFW have had a certain success with their F-28 Fellowship, having sold about 150 aircraft, although none of these had gone to the United States by the end of 1979. The arrival of hundreds of jetliners in the mid-1960s heralded a period of prosperity for the airlines, and they became a mass production industry, in every sense of the term. The carefree days of the 1930s were long forgotten. Any pretence of luxury that remained was found in the small first class compartments that some airlines still maintained in exchange for a sharp increase in fares. However, even the free drinks of the first class accommodation did not in any way make up for the superb food and careful attention that passengers received before the war. Airfields became mass commuter processing areas where passengers were booked in and then led (literally, at some places), along a conveyor belt to

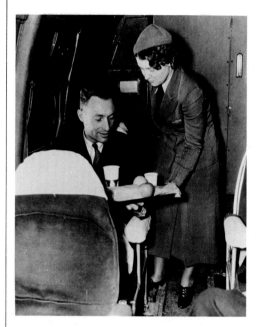

The PRESIDENT SPECIAL

BOISSONS

APERITIFS

Sherry   Dubonnet   Campari   Dry Vermouth

COCKTAILS

Bloody Mary   Manhattan   Martini

Vodka Martini   Screwdriver   Whiskey Sour

WHISKIES

Scotch   Bourbon   Canadian

Gin and Tonic   Tom Collins   Vodka Collins   Gin   Vodka

Beer and Soft Drinks

NOTRE SÉLECTION DES GRANDS VINS

OUR SELECTION OF VINTAGE WINES

Bourgogne Rouge Tête de Cuvée   Bordeaux Blanc Grand Crû classé
RED BURGUNDY   WHITE BORDEAUX

Champagne Brut Millésimé—Cuvée spéciale pour Pan American
CHAMPAGNE SPECIALLY SELECTED FOR PAN AMERICAN

LIQUEURS

Cointreau   Drambuie   Bénédictine

Crème de Menthe   VSOP Cognac   Bénédictine and Brandy

Refreshments available throughout your flight

DÎNER

HORS D'OEUVRE

Le Caviar Malossol de la Caspienne   Le Jambon de Westphalie et Melon
CAVIAR MALOSSOL FROM THE CASPIAN SEA   WESTPHALIAN HAM AND MELON
Vodka ou Champagne   *Bordeaux Blanc*

POISSON

Le Coquille St. Jacques Duchesse
LONG ISLAND BAY SCALLOPS DUCHESSE
Bordeaux Blanc

ENTRÉES

Le Filet de Boeuf rôti
ROAST FILLET OF BEEF
Bourgogne Rouge

Le Ris de Veau Financière   Le Côte d'Agneau grillée
SWEETBREADS FINANCIÈRE   GRILLED LAMB CHOP
Bourgogne Rouge   *Bourgogne Rouge*

Le Médaillon de Veau à l'Estragon   L'Aiguillette de Boeuf Tastevin
VEAL STEAK WITH TARRAGON SAUCE   SAUTÉED BEEF TASTEVIN
Bourgogne Rouge   *Bourgogne Rouge*

Le Pigeonneau farci – Sauce Porto
STUFFED SQUAB WITH PORT WINE SAUCE
Bourgogne Rouge

Les Légumes du Jardin   Le Riz Pilaff   Les Pommes persillées
GARDEN VEGETABLES   PILAFF RICE   PARSLIED POTATOES

FROMAGES

La Sélection de Fromages de Pays
SELECTION OF CHEESE
Bourgogne Rouge

DESSERT

Les Cerises Jubilé – La Glace Vanille   Friandises
CHERRIES JUBILEE–VANILLA ICE CREAM   COOKIES
Champagne

Un Choix de Fruits des Îles et des Continents
FRUIT BASKET

Café Américain   Café Sanka   The Orange Pekoe
AMERICAN COFFEE   SANKA COFFEE   ORANGE PEKOE TEA
Liqueurs

PAN AMERICAN CUISINE BY MAXIM'S DE PARIS

"La bonne Cuisine est la base du véritable bonheur." Escoffier
"GOOD FOOD IS THE BASIS FOR TRUE HAPPINESS"

In-flight catering was initially just a sandwich or cold snack (above left), but as the size of aircraft increased, more and more elaborate meals became available. The pre-war flying boats offered meals totally prepared and cooked in-flight (above). The Pan Am menu (left) was prepared by Maxim's of Paris and shows the sort of food offered to members of the exclusive Clipper Club. Top: Loading catering supplies aboard a DC-3 of Qantas by hand.

the aircraft. The techniques of mass transport ensured that, to a large extent, passengers became 'walking freight', as one writer pointedly described them.

Nowhere was the change more apparent than in the supply of food on-board aircraft. Mass travel demands mass catering. A large airline, such as British Airways, serves over 20 million meals in the air every year. These days the food is prepared in vast specialized catering centres. The work is performed by specialist companies who have lucrative contracts to supply food to flights about 45 minutes before take-off. The food is entirely pre-cooked and is then reheated in the aircraft galley. These are fitted with food units which are replaceable and supplied fully packed, while the empties are removed in the same manner as milk bottles. Inevitably, this mass processing of food means that variety is sometimes difficult to achieve. The airlines try to provide a meal that is as attractive to as many people as possible, and chicken and steak predominate. Nevertheless, some companies do attempt to give a special character to certain meals. As an example, Pan Am always serves turkey and cranberry sauce on Thanksgiving Day.

Aircraft catering is now big business. In an average week, British Airways handles over half a million items of cutlery, 168,000 glasses and 40,000 cups and saucers, and they send 100 tons of linen and blankets to the laundry. It is all a far cry from Imperial Airways, when the potatoes were peeled on-board!

The passenger often does not realize that the meal he gets included with his economy class ticket is very carefully controlled by IATA, and that no member airline is allowed to provide a better meal than the standard specified. The passenger is allowed a glass of fruit

Today, airline catering is a big business with millions of meals being suplied annually (above). First class passengers have always received better facilities, as can be seen from this first class lounge on a Boeing 747 of United Airlines.

juice or one cup of soup, but not both. Some airlines interpret the IATA rules more liberally than others, and the regulations do not apply to first class passengers in any case. In 1970, Pan Am was serving caviare and a choice of six main courses to its pampered first class passengers.

Statistics of air travel in the Soviet Union are difficult to obtain but Aeroflot, the state airline, is by far the largest carrier in the world, and currently operates an enormous network of services for passengers and freight throughout the country. In 1976, the airline carried over 100 million passengers for the first time, and the 1976-1980 Five Year Plan calls for an increase of thirty percent. Aeroflot controls its vast fleet (all Russian-built) through thirty directorates, which are really complete airlines in themselves.

During the 1960s and 1970s, the Rus-

sian aircraft industry, although preoccupied with military expansion, has supplied Aeroflot with a continuous flow of aircraft which have closely paralleled design practice in the West. The Tu-104 and the Il-18 have continued in service through both decades and the Tupolev bureau have followed the 104 with the Tu-124, a twin-engine, 65-seat, scaled-down version of the 104. This was the first short-range jet with bypass engines (two Soloviev D-20 turbo-fans) and Tupolev followed it with a far better airplane, the Tu-134 of 1964, of which over 520 were built. Despite this progress, the Soviet Union was late to provide Aeroflot with any machine that approached the Boeing 727, and it was not until 1968 that the trimotor Tu-154 made its first flight.

The other Soviet equipment supplied in the 1960s and 1970s came from the design bureaux of Alexander Yakolev

and Serge Ilyushin. The most important products of these two distinguished designers is the Ilyushin Il-62 – a long-range airliner with its four engines aft and bearing a close resemblance to the British VC10. It went into service in 1967 between Moscow and Novosibirsk, and then on international services to Montreal and New York. It has remained the main Russian prestige international airliner for over a decade.

The Yakolev bureau has, meanwhile, concentrated on its Yak-40 and 42 series of three-engined, small-capacity, short-range jets which are useful in the Soviet Union because of their ability to operate from grass fields and so reach remote areas with air services. These versatile little aircraft have enjoyed great success and have even won small export orders in the West.

It is in the United States, however, that developments occurred, which to

The Il-62 is the most impressive of modern Soviet jets and bears a strong resemblance to the Vickers VC10. Operating costs are reported to be high by Western standards.

The Soviet aircraft industry has kept Russia and her allies well supplied with a series of jet airliners for a variety of roles. The Tupolev Tu-134 (top) dates from 1964 and over 520 were built. It has been supplied to a number of Warsaw Pact powers and this example serves LOT, the Polish state airline. Above: A Yakolev Yak-40 of CSA (Czechoslovakia Airlines). The Yak-40 has a versatile performance and can operate from grass runways in remote areas. It has been sold in the West, a unique achievement for a Russian aircraft.

many must represent the apotheosis of the airliner. On 13 April 1966, Boeing revealed the design of its Type 747 to the world and at the same time announced orders from Pan Am for 25 machines. So dawned, with remarkable speed, the age of the jumbo jet. The years from 1960 onwards had been taken up with the vast efforts to produce the supersonic airliner, and it was only in 1964-5 that manufacturers realized that this was not the way in which the airliner industry was going to develop. The production of the big powerful turbo-fans, whose economy had been demonstrated so clearly in the later generation of jets, gave scope for machines with no increase in speeds but with wide-bodied fuselages and hence immense passenger capability measured on existing standards. These ideas paralleled military requirements for larger logistical transports, and the

middle of the decade saw work start at Burbank on the huge Lockheed C-5A Galaxy. Boeing had also tendered for this contract, and losing it to Lockheed allowed them to divert their ideas into the 747. For the engines, Boeing renewed their well-proven partnership with Pratt & Whitney, and chose their JT9D power plants. Even before the aircraft flew, it had received orders for 158 copies from 26 different airlines, but engine troubles delayed the programme. The first machine was two months late, taking to the air on 9 February 1969.

The 747 is in all ways a remarkable machine. It has a versatile structure and is capable of being produced in several versions – mass density and short-range, wholly freighter or part-passenger, or part-freighter. It can be adapted for various power plants, and the latest machines for British Airways are fitted

with the Rolls-Royce RB211 engine. But its great importance lies in its size of cabins and the 350-500 passengers that it can carry in its various versions.

Where Boeing led the way, they were soon followed by their old rivals, Lockheed and McDonnell Douglas. Lockheed began work in January 1966 on the L-1011, which has now become the famous TriStar, making its first flight on 16 November 1972. The TriStar was the result of American Airlines' request for a medium-range wide-bodied jet, and both aircraft and engine builders suffered financial troubles in its creation. Rolls-Royce had to be rescued by the British government when the RB211 proved beyond their capacity to finance, and Lockheed tottered on the edge of insolvency until the big airliner proved itself to be a winner.

The third wide-bodied jet was the Douglas DC-10, which originally was designed as a four-engined aircraft with the incredible load of 650 passengers. But by the first flight in August 1970, it had conformed to airline requirements and appeared as a trimotor, using General Electric CF6 engines. Despite a series of troubles and several fatal crashes in airline service, the DC-10 continues to sell well and 360 had been ordered by January 1980. This is compared with 507 for the Boeing 747, and 216 for the Lockheed TriStar.

The financial resources required to launch a wide-bodied jet are immense, and Boeing in particular shared the load with a number of sub-contractors world-wide, who also shared the commercial risks. Parts of the 747 are built in locations as far apart as Japan and Northern Ireland. This partnership principle has produced the only European wide-body – the Airbus Industrie A300B Airbus, produced by a consortium of French, British, Spanish, Dutch and German companies. Conceived as a short-range, high-capacity transport, the A300B also uses the General Electric CF6 and can seat up to 345 passengers. After an indifferent start, the type made its break-through into the American market in 1978 when it was ordered by Eastern Airways, and 189 machines were on order by the end of 1979.

The only other developer of a wide-bodied airliner is Ilyushin, who flew their Il-86 in December 1976. The Russians planned to have many of the type in service by the time of the 1980 Olympic Games in Moscow.

There is obviously a long future ahead for the wide-bodied airliner. It has capacity and economy, the two vital qualities that any airline requires, and it will be the mainstay of world airlines while they look forward to the twenty-first century.

The McDonnell Douglas DC-10 was the third of the American wide-bodied jets to appear, and despite well publicized troubles, continues to sell well to world airlines. Far left: The spacious interior of a DC-10. Right: A Lockheed L1011 TriStar of British Airways. Both airframe and engine suppliers had financial difficulty in launching the L1011, but by 1980 it was firmly established, being popular with aircrews and passengers alike. The Airbus Industrie A300B (above), the European Airbus, was produced by a consortium of five countries and was assembled at Toulouse in France.

CHAPTER NINE

THE
HUMAN
ELEMENT

THE FOUNDER OF THE GREAT Dutch airline KLM, Dr Albert Plesman, once said in a public speech that 'The ocean of the air unites all peoples'. Plesman in the 1920s saw more clearly than most of his contemporaries the great potential of the airliner, and his quotation is apt. The air is an ocean; it has its storms, eddies and currents, in the same endless confusion as the ocean below. Ice, snow, thunder and tempest all thrust danger in the path of the airman yet, if that same airman has mastered the skills and sciences of aeronautics, then he can sustain himself with complete safety in the ocean of the air.

Air transport has proved to be the safest method of transport in the history of man's travel on this planet. Only in this century has overland travel become safe from bandits and robbers and, not infrequently, from authority too. Only 150 years ago, one out of every five ships that crossed the Atlantic could be expected to disappear, and insurers set their rates accordingly. Aviation, on the other hand, has not suffered these losses, although there have been accidents, as there always are in any form of travel. But, from the very early days, the airline industry has made flight safety its very special preoccupation – something unique in the history of twentieth-century big business.

The reasons for this are not hard to define. No travel system can prosper and return profit unless it has the confidence of its passengers, and also of the crews that lead and sustain it throughout its journey. Nowhere can confidence disappear more quickly than in the ticket sales of an airline that suffers a number of major accidents. While flying is an exciting and pleasing experience, the results of an accident are spectacular, and usually result in the complete destruction of the airframe

and the death of all on board. The latter circumstance is usually achieved either by complete physical disintegration or incineration. The consequent emphasis on flight safety is therefore understandable, and it is a matter of record that the aircraft industries in both Europe and the United States have achieved safety standards that have largely eliminated technical failure, so that most aircraft accidents are usually attributed to human error.

With the arrival of the wide-bodied jet in the late 1960s, the airlines found themselves at last carrying in one machine the quantities of passengers that the shipping companies had dealt with for centuries. Whereas beforehand, the total loss of an airliner would result in perhaps something over 100 casualties, a fatal crash would now result in the loss of three times that number. It was perhaps inevitable that incidents involving the big jets would occur, and that when they did so, world-wide attention would be focused on the unfortunate machine and its operators. The big jets numbered over 1000 machines in 1980, and had carried out more than 1 million passenger flights. The simple statistic of only four accidents in twelve years of concentrated operations emphasizes the superb safety record of these wonderful machines.

Nevertheless, when incidents have occurred the results have been both tragic and frightening. On Friday 29 December 1972, Eastern Airways flight 401, operated by a Lockheed L-1011 TriStar, left New York's Kennedy Airport on a routine late-evening flight to Miami. Although it was the Christmas holiday season, only 163 of the 300 seats were filled, and in all there were 176 people on board. The flight proceeded normally, and the TriStar had been

cleared by Miami Approach Control for a landing, when the flight crew noticed that the landing gear indication lights were showing that the nose leg was not locked down. This snag is a nightmare for the pilot, as usually it is a failure of the lamp filament, rather than the undercarriage leg. However, the pilot has to decide whether to attempt a landing or not, and the responsibility is his alone. In earlier days, this kind of undercarriage problem was fairly commonplace, and some modern aircraft have the facility for the crew to see the landing gear through observation panels in the wheel wells. It was while the flight engineer of the Eastern TriStar was doing this, and the two pilots were so preoccupied that they failed to notice a gradual loss of height, that flight 401 plunged into the Florida Everglades, 20 miles (32 km) west of Miami, and broke up. Incredibly, there were 77 survivors. The muddy waters of the Everglades prevented a major fire, beyond the initial explosion as the fuel already in the engines ignited.

The TriStar was, and still is, a firm favourite with air crew and passengers, both for its docile handling qualities and for the quiet comfort and spaciousness of its passenger cabins. The giant planes were the pride of Eastern Airways, which had fifty of them on order at a price of $20 million each. Eastern called the TriStar 'the quietest, cleanest plane in the skies', and they were correct. It was promoted as the 'whisper liner' and got this designation from the quiet performance of its three Rolls-Royce RB211 turbo-fans. It was imperative that the cause of the accident to flight 401 be determined immediately, and an investigation was underway within hours. Among those first at the site was Apollo astronaut Frank Borman, by then a vice-president of East-

Accident investigation is a meticulous and painstaking affair which requires great skill and experience. The picture shows the wreckage of a Bristol Britannia being carefully analysed to determine the reason for an accident to a Series 300 prototype in 1958.

Flight safety is the paramount concern of everyone in aviation and strict legal and manufacturers' regulations govern the servicing of aircraft. Top left: The port engine of an Alitalia DC-9 is removed for inspection and service. Top right: Engine testing in progress on a McDonnell Douglas DC-10 of Swissair. Bottom left: Aircraft passenger seats under service. The strength and anchorage of seats is critical in emergencies. Bottom centre: The complex services which the passenger never sees show up well when wall panels and floor boards are removed. Bottom right: Fitting new wing skins to a Lufthansa Boeing. Normally this type of work would be carried out by a manufacturers' working party.

ern. The investigation was complicated but the final report of the United States National Transportation Safety Board said that the crash was not the result of a single error, but that the crew failed to monitor the flight instruments during the final minutes of the flight, and that the problem with the landing gear warning light had drawn attention away from the unexpected descent until it was too late. The Board also made recommendations for improvements on the flight deck, but the TriStar, a much-loved and respected airplane, was cleared.

Just over a year later in early 1974, a McDonnell Douglas DC-10 of Turk Hava Yollari, the Turkish State Airline, went out of control soon after take-off from Orly Airport in Paris and crashed, killing all 345 people on board. During the development of the DC-10 there had been problems with the locking mechanism of the aft cargo doors. In certain circumstances it was possible for the door to come open in-flight, causing the fuselage to decompress. Decompression can cause structural failure and, in this case, control runs were cut. An accident from the same cause had been narrowly avoided by a DC-10 of American Airlines on 12 June 1972 and the Turkish machine, which crashed on 3 March 1974, had not been modified. No more problems were experienced with the DC-10 until May 1979, when American Airlines lost one of their fleet of thirty DC-10s, which crashed on take-off at Chicago O'Hare Airport. Immediately, the American authorities grounded all DC-10s for structural checks which concentrated on the underwing engine pylons, but the investigation seems to have cleared pylon failure as a possible cause.

The Paris crash was the worst air disaster in history and remained so until the afternoon of Sunday, 27 March 1977. On that day there was an incident at Las Palmas Airport in the Canary Islands. The local nationalist movement planted a bomb in the terminal buildings and, as a result, all traffic into Las Palmas was diverted to neighbouring Tenerife. Los Rodeos field on Tenerife is known to pilots as a difficult airport, and it has only one runway, 2 miles (3 km) long. The air traffic control system was heavily loaded due to the diversions and visibility was poor. It was in these circumstances that a KLM Boeing 747 called *Der Rijn*, with 229 passengers and 15 crew, crashed into a Pan Am 747 which, incredibly, was taxiing across the runway as the Dutch machine attempted to take-off. There were 364 passengers and 14 crew on the Pan Am airplane and, in all, 563 people died and 49 were injured. The Tenerife disaster holds the grisly record of being the world's worst air crash to date, yet it did not take place in the air and there was no malfunction of either of the aircraft involved. The incident demonstrated that despite the great advances made in flight safety, the human factor can always have the last word. In the aircraft business, technicians call it Sod's Law – if something can go wrong it will do so.

The record of man's patient attempts towards perfect flight is a long one, and progress at times has been painfully slow. Today, flight safety procedures have become almost infallible and it is only when man takes over that problems occur. That does not mean that today's aircraft captains are not as skilful as the pioneer pilots in the 1920s and 1930s, but only that the process of flying is now taken much closer to the limit of human experience and capability, time factors in which action can be determined and initiated are much shorter, and the consequences of an accident can be of almost catastrophic proportions.

Crew training is therefore the first and most important aspect of flight safety. An airline pilot has usually undergone at least three years' training before he is accepted by a company as a junior pilot. Something approaching half of all applicants for training fail on eyesight reasons alone. A pilot is required to undergo a strict annual medical examination to remain qualified for a commercial pilot's licence, and this period is reduced to six months for senior pilots, and for all pilots over the age of forty. No pilot becomes a Captain until he has extensive experience as a First Officer or Co-Pilot. In the United States, in particular, this may not happen for years, as American Captains have to clock up thousands of flying hours in order to wear the coveted gold oak leaves on the peak of their uniform caps. In the United Kingdom, the rules are not extensively based on experience and more notice is taken of qualifications and flying ability. Nevertheless, in most countries it is unusual to find a Captain of a Boeing 747 who is not aged about fifty, with perhaps thirty years of flying experience and earning the equivalent of £40,000 per year. These salaries are a measure of the responsibility of the rank, because the authority of the Captain is absolute from the moment the engines start up, and it is on him alone that all decisions fall, and on him that the safety of his passengers and crew depend. All airliners carry two pilots by law and usually (but less frequently today), the larger machines carry a flight engineer. Basically, he has two responsibilities. His is the ultimate authority for clearing the aircraft as fit for flight, and he will make his own inspection to see that all

Top left: Life raft drill in progress for Lufthansa cabin staff. All crew members are fully trained in the use of all emergency equipment. Above left: Trying out a life raft carried by Qantas DH86s in the 1930s. Above: All large modern aircraft carry inflatable escape chutes which operate automatically in an emergency. Aircrews carry out regular drills to practice rapid evacuation of the aircraft.

maintainance and preparation for flight including refuelling has been carried out to the standards required by the aircraft operational manuals. Once airborne, he monitors the flight, keeping a note of the speed, altitude and distance covered, and keeing a close eye on fuel consumption. He will watch over a complicated set of instrument panels which will continuously present information about the aircraft's state, and also be able to give a warning in case of any conceivable emergency.

Before take-off, the cabin crew will have instructed all passengers in the use of safety equipment carried on board. The most likely time for accidents is on take-off and landing, and therefore smoking is not permitted at these times. All passenger seats are required by law to be fitted with safety belts, and all persons onboard, including all crew members, must be seated at take-off and landing with safety belts fastened. Passengers are also required to remain in their seats when the aircraft is passing through any areas of turbulence. The other piece of personal safety equipment for passengers is a life-jacket, which is usually located under the seat. Instructions on how to use the life-jackets are given verbally, with a demonstration at the start of each flight and the position of the emergency exits pointed out. Printed instructions are also placed in all passenger positions, and it is possible to evacuate a pancaked aircraft in a very short time, provided that fire has not occurred. This is done by pneumatic escape chutes, which inflate automatically when the cabin staff open the doors and emergency exits. Passengers are dispatched down the chutes at the rate of one every one and half seconds.

Should the aircraft suffer a loss of cabin pressure for any reason, all on board can be supplied with a personal oxygen supply. This is delivered through masks which fall automatically from the cabin ceiling or the light luggage racks, the usual critical actuation pressure being the equivalent of 14,000 ft (4267 m) above sea level.

If the airplane is unfortunate enough to ditch in the sea, life-rafts which have sufficient capacity for all on board, are carried. These are inflatable and usually cater for 20-26 passengers. A full inventory of survival equipment is stowed in the life-raft, and food and water is available. The aircraft also carries a wide range of fire-fighting appliances and medical supplies. All aircrew are trained continuously in emergency techniques, which have proved themselves in incident after incident.

Much of the safety equipment carried on modern airliners is the result of aviation law, which now regulates most things in civil aeronautics from the licencing of pilots to the distance between the passenger seats. Much of air safety law springs from the Chicago Convention of 1944, when 52 nations met and agreed to set up ICAO. This has now become a United Nations agency, and recommends, amongst other things, safety standards to member nations. These are invariably carried out by national governments and usually each has its own flight safety authority. In the United Kingdom, it is the Civil Aviation Authority (CAA), while in the United States it is the Federal Aviation Authority (FAA). It is these bodies that issue Certificates of Airworthiness, without which no airliner is permitted to carry fare-paying passengers. An aircraft type will only be certified after it has undergone many hours of ground and air tests of all its systems, and the board's own pilots make the final checkouts. Once the aircraft type has been awarded a Certificate of Airworthiness, each succeeding model must also conform to the specification, modifications must obtain full approval and the properly approved maintainance procedures followed.

The navigation of the airplane along one of the authorized air routes of today is a complicated business, calling for smooth organization and very sophisticated equipment and techniques. However, it is a process designed for safety, and it says much for air travel that insurance rates are roughly the same as for surface travel, and have been so since 1933. This is in spite of the heavy liabilities that can face underwriters in case of an accident. IATA itself sets compensation rates for passengers, largely based on agreements springing from the Warsaw Convention of 1929. Although the rates are higher in the United States, loss of baggage compensation is currently set (late 1979) at £5 per pound for checked-in luggage, while injury will cost the airline £5,000 and death £10,000. In the United States, the airlines and aircraft manufacturers do not enjoy protection from international insurance conventions, and therefore the above-named payments are not automatic, as they are elsewhere. It is, however, possible to sue the manufacturer or the airline or both, and this occurred after the DC-10 crash at Paris in 1974. The relatives and dependents of the victims opened an action in California and the defendants, who did not admit liability, nevertheless decided not to contest the suit. Four years later, with many pleas still to be heard, $26 million had been paid in compensation.

The average airline passenger sees little of the air traffic control organization that is responsible for his well-being while he is with the airline. He may glance at the control tower, which often is the only building to rise above the skyline of an airport, but probably gives it little thought. However, this is the nerve centre that will control the first part of the journey. Here, the Captain will file his flight plan which the company computor will have prepared from all the available data. This plan takes into account the pay-load of the aircraft, the distance, fuel required and the latest state of the weather at the flight altitude. This latter information will probably have been obtained from the European Space Agency weather satellites. The meteorological unit stationed at the base will inform the Captain of the surface weather conditions at the airport. The aircraft will be allocated a course along the appropriate airway. These airways are the air-lanes of the world. They are all numbered like motorways on the ground, and are closely monitored by ground stations. Radio beacons are located at various intervals as navigational aids and at airway junctions. The aircraft flies along the airway at a given height and is passed from one control zone to another, until it is eventually taken under the controller of its destination airport, who will supply details for landing, such as runway and weather conditions, and advise on the need for automatic or assisted landing systems. Ground control in the vicinity of a busy airport requires great skill and concentration, and modern radar caters for literally dozens of aircraft arriving and departing at the same time.

These aircraft in the vicinity of the airfield are usually dealt with by the approach controllers, who sit in the radar rooms, operating their sets in almost complete darkness, and pinpointing aircraft position and height on

The flight deck is the nerve centre of the aircraft and the instruments guide the Captain on aircraft state. Great progress has been made in less than a decade from the Fokker FVII (left) to the Douglas DC-2 (above). These should be compared with the Douglas DC-9, a contemporary jetliner (right).

the illuminated screens. At the same time, they are in touch with the Captain of the machine, who is up to 40 miles (64 km) away. Aircraft in the process of taxying on the ground, taking-off or landing, are controlled from the visual control room located on the top of the tower.

The Captain, his flight crew in the sky and the controller on the ground are the leaders in a vast army of technicians that control and service the aircraft, navigational and radar equipment which provide the high standard of safety that exists on the airlines of today. It is all an age away from the primitive radio sets and visual aids of the 1920s and 1930s, like the windsock and weather boards. Nevertheless, accidents sometimes do occur, but even they are catered for in this magic world of technology. To the general public, the flight data recorder is better known as the 'black box', as this bit of equipment was dubbed when it was first used in 1965. The apparatus consists of tape recording equipment mounted in a shock-proof container (normally brightly-coloured and not black at all), designed to withstand the impact of the worst possible crash. It records such data as airspeed, altitude and aircraft attitude, and later versions also record the conversations of the flight crew. The tapes are renewed every half hour, so that there is a record of every aspect of the aircraft's performance, right up to the point of impact. Flight recorders have proved themselves invaluable in the short time that they have been in use. As an example, the recorder was recovered intact when a DC-10 of Air New Zealand crashed into Mount Erebus, an Antarctic volcano, on 28 November 1979. Ground conditions were very difficult, yet the recovery of the black box allowed the New Zealand

Chief Inspector of Accidents to state that the aircraft was airworthy right up to the moment of impact.

Despite the ever-constant research aimed at removing all unplanned incidents from modern air travel, every departing passenger is reminded that the day of the pirate is not yet over, when he passes through security checks which are now standard protection against the scourge of hijacking. Crime in the sky is not new, and many airports have been plagued with theft of cargo, especially valuables. The first hijack has been attributed to a Fokker F-7 in Peru as long ago as 1930. In the mid-1960s, the crime reached troublesome proportions, largely in the United States where it became a reliable method of escaping to Communist Cuba. Air crews have standing instructions that passenger safety must always come first, and

therefore the instructions of the hijackers are invariably complied with when the aircraft is in the air, and nothing is done to provoke fatalities on either side. The hijackings to Cuba were almost routine, even when on 2 August 1970, a certain Rudolfo Rios made history by becoming the first man to hijack a 747. When the big Boeing arrived at Havana, no less a person than Prime Minister Fidel Castro himself hurried to Jose Marti Airport to inspect and admire the new monster.

However, when the Popular Front for the Liberation of Palestine (PLP) made hijacking a major part of its terrorist campaign, world opinion had had enough, and stringent security precautions became standard throughout the air transport industry. Despite this, there have been over 400 attempts since 1969, over fifty percent of which, unfor-

tunately, were successful.

The PLP made its most notorious operation on 6 September 1970, when the first aircraft of the day – a Pan Am Boeing 747 – was seized on a flight from Amsterdam to London, and eventually taken to Cairo, where it was blown up, after the passengers and crew had been released. Other groups took over a Swissair DC-8 over Paris, a TWA Boeing 707 over Frankfurt and a BOAC VC10 from Bombay. All three aircraft were taken to Dawson Field near Amman in Jordan, while various political demands were made. The only failure was the attempted hijacking of an Israeli Airlines (El Al) 707 by the well-known Palestinian activist Leila Khaled. Her companion was shot dead by a steward, because the Israelis have a different approach to terrorism, and Miss Khaled was handed over to the

Incidents such as the hijacking and destruction of three airliners by the PLP at Dawson Field, Jordan on 12 September 1970 have led to security checks of passengers and baggage becoming familiar scenes at all airports (bottom).

British government when the plane landed at London. She was later released.

All five planes were flag carriers from major airlines. Four of them were destroyed (those at Dawson were blown up on 12 September) at a cost of $52 million. A total of 430 passengers had been held hostage in very difficult conditions and 769 men, women and children had found their lives put at risk for reasons with which they had nothing to do, and over which they had no control.

Such incidents could not be allowed to plague the world's airlines, which is why all passengers now pass through metal-detecting devices before they board their aircraft, while their luggage is subjected to examination by X-ray. It is all part of the never-ending battle to make the sky a safer place.

CHAPTER TEN

FASTER
OR
BIGGER?

THE HISTORY OF AVIATION belongs to the twentieth century, and many people who remembered the first tentative flights of the Wright Brothers were still alive when supersonic flight was achieved for the first time in the middle of the century. In their old age, the same people saw the birth of the wide-bodied jet, with its capacity to transport several hundred passengers in safety and comfort along international air routes. So rapid has been the development of aeronautical science that no one can say with safety that an end has been reached or that there is any limit to the ability of man to develop flight at the same pace in the next century.

However, it is possible to forecast in broad terms the likely development of the airliner for at least the first two decades of the next century. Costly as it will be to develop, the next generation of the supersonic transport has a great measure of support among aeronautical opinion, and design studies are going on in America and Europe over the possibilities of a successor to Concorde. In the field of medium- and wide-bodied jet liners, the so-called 'War of the Paper Airplanes' of 1978 largely determined the shape of the airliner on conventional subsonic routes from the mid-1980s onwards. The problems of noise, the short supply of fossilized fuels and the environmental impact of airports continue to have a large place in the arguments facing governments, aircraft constructors, airlines and designers as the year 2000 approaches. Apart from these mainstream developments, there are those who argue that the future of the mass movement of cargo and freight lies in the sky, and the case for the large freight-carrying airship is frequently put forward, sometimes with more enthusiasm than scientific practicality.

The history of supersonic flight dates only from the years that followed the Second World War. The first controlled-level flight through the sound barrier by a piloted aircraft was made in October 1947 by the Bell X-1, a small rocket-powered airplane which was carried into the air by a Boeing B-50 bomber and which had a supply of fuel sufficient for 2½ minutes of powered flight. Even at that time aircraft companies were toying with the idea of supersonic flight, and Boeing carried out a feasibility study for an SST in 1952. The conclusion reached was that no real development was likely for thirty years.

The problems surrounding supersonic flight are considerable. The speed of sound varies with both altitude and temperature, so for practical purposes the speed of an airplane flying close to the speed of sound is expressed as a factor of whatever the speed of sound happens to be in those particular conditions. This factor is known as the Mach number, and at 36,000 ft (10,973 m) it is about 660 mph (1062 km/h). The main problem of supersonic flight is the change in the speed and pressure of air on a moving body when the speed of that body becomes faster than the speed at which created shock waves can spread. In addition to these speeds, the air forms powerful shock waves which can cause noise nuisance and destructive effects 8-10 miles (13-16 km) below the aircraft. This is the so-called sonic boom. Due to the power required to pass through the sound barrier (flying at Mach 1), the supersonic transport requires a very much greater engine capacity than a subsonic airliner carrying the same pay-load. This single fact, leading to requirements for high technology and large fuel consumption, is the main economic drawback to supersonic travel.

Air friction passing over the structure at supersonic speeds causes further problems. Conventional light alloys used in aircraft construction become brittle after some time under stress at high temperatures. An airliner that cruises at Mach 2 requires special high-quality aluminium alloys, and Concorde contains in its structure many components made from materials such as stainless steel or titanium, particularly in areas of the engine nacelles.

Research continued in both Europe and the United States throughout the 1950s, and in the United Kingdom the first formal steps to build an SST were taken in November 1956 with the formation of the Supersonic Transport Aircraft Committee. This committee had representatives on it from most of the British aircraft and engine companies, together with government research workers. The Bristol Aeroplane Company, and its engine division, gave the STAC Committee the greatest support, and the company rapidly became the leading British experts on SST development. After some debate on the possible shape of the new airliner, in which consideration was given to swing wing designs pioneered by the late Sir Barnes Wallis, the committee concluded at an early stage that the likely design would be for a delta wing machine. It would cruise at Mach 2 and carry 100 passengers on a route length which approximated transatlantic conditions. Delta wings had been used extensively in military aircraft both in the United Kingdom and the United States, but it was a very different proposition to use the high-speed delta for civilian use, with all the safety requirements involved, when its main characteristic was its complete refusal to recover in stalled conditions. Extensive low-speed wind tunnel testing led to the develop-

Sir Barnes Wallis, the British aviation visionary who designed *inter alia* the R100 airship and the dam-breaking mine, proposed a supersonic airliner as early as the 1940s. He is seen here with a model of his *Swallow*, a swing-wing design, whose configuration changed as the aircraft moved from subsonic to supersonic conditions of flight. Today, swing wings are in use on military aircraft.

ment of a new pattern of delta wing, which swept back dramatically at the route, thus creating a vortex which would spread along a carefully controlled leading edge shape. This stabilized the air flow and was named the ogee form wing.

While this development work on the wing and the airframe was going on at Bristol, the engine company had produced proposals for a power plant, based on the Olympus engine, which had been developed for use in the Avro Vulcan bomber. In company with the aerodynamic designers at Filton, the Bristol engineers installed their Olympus behind a complicated variable orifice intake which could convert a supersonic air speed from Mach 2 conditions into an acceptable pressure and temperature to feed the engine.

In 1961, the ogee wing first took to the air in the Bristol 221 flying test bed. This little airplane had been remodelled from the Fairey FD2 which had been used for high-speed research in the 1950s and had held the world's air speed record during that time.

In the same year of 1961, a French consortium of Sud-Aviation and Dassault produced a model of their Super-Caravelle. This was a supersonic transport design that looked remarkably like the Bristol conception, but it was designed for medium-range rather than international routes. By this time the escalating costs of developing the airliner were becoming prohibitive, and there was much to be gained if a joint Anglo-French SST programme could be set up. The year marked the heyday of the late General de Gaulle; a series of very complicated and delicate negotiations between the two countries eventually led to the signing of an agreement between the British and French governments in late November 1962, to work

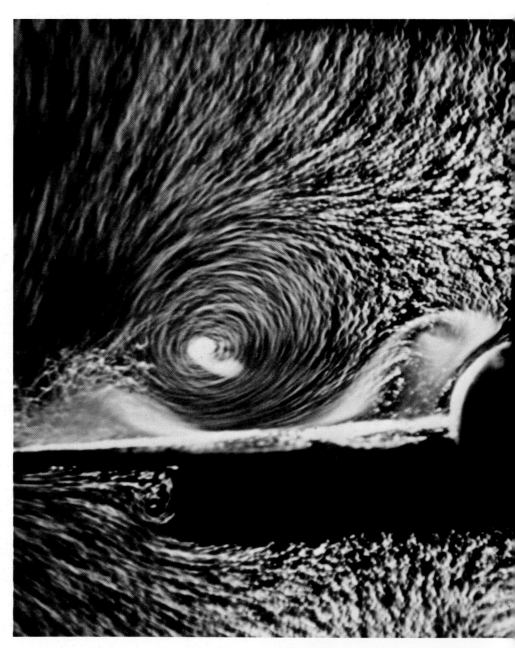

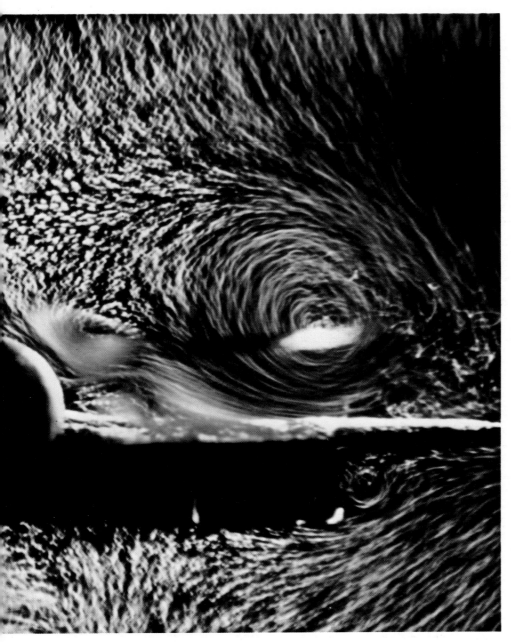

The Anglo-French SST project which
eventually became the BAC Aérospatiale
Concorde was the result of a sustained
development programme over two decades.
The vortices caused by supersonic flight show
up well in this wind tunnel photograph (above)
of a Concorde model undergoing tests. Left: The
Bristol 221 flying test bed was a rebuilt Fairey
FD2 with a scaled-down version of the
Concorde wing. It first flew in 1961.

together to produce a supersonic transport. The programme called for the
airliner to be in service on the world's
air routes by 1968.

Meanwhile, in the United States, aircraft manufacturers were gaining considerable experience of supersonic
flight from the vast military programmes
being carried out there. In particular,
Boeing and North American Rockwell
were involved, and American thought
developed along the lines of a delta
wing aircraft constructed from stainless
steel and using anything up to six
engines. This design conception came
from the North American Rockwell
Valkyrie bomber, but the project was
cancelled in November 1959. Nevertheless, Douglas, Lockheed, Convair and
Boeing all kept SST design teams
working.

Boeing, in particular, made studies in
depth and eventually came up with a
swing-wing design. However, after
wind tunnel research, the wing was redesigned to become a conventional
delta. In fact, support for the delta was
general among most American manufacturers. American efforts were
speeded up, following the agreement
between the British and the French, but
the high cost of development led to
American manufacturers refusing to put
their own capital into the SST as a
private venture. It was at this point, on
4 June 1963, that Pan Am placed options
for six Concordes. The very next day
President Kennedy announced the
development of an SST with the United
States government's financial backing.
The subsequent design was to be a
bigger and faster airplane than Concorde (as the British and French proposal was now called), and it was to
have a speed of Mach 3.

During the time that the argument
about the development of an SST raged

241

in America, the British and French project went ahead. However, early in the programme it became obvious that the joint manufacturers had badly miscalculated the time of construction and the cost of the project. Then, in 1964, the environmental argument began to be heard in Britain, France and the United States. The British government, in the person of the controversial Aviation Minister Tony Wedgwood Benn, carried out a series of boom tests over British cities and there was a resultant public outcry. This led to design changes which would allow Concorde to fly the bulk of its supersonic stages over the ocean, and the French concept of a medium-range airplane was dropped. This was only one of the problems. Throughout the 1960s, both BAC (Bristol had become part of British Aircraft Corporation in 1961) and Aérospatiale (the successor of Sud-Aviation) faced development problems which ranged from the complex intake design to the highly sophisticated cabin air system which was required in the new machine.

Meanwhile, in the Soviet Union, the Tupolev design organization headed by Russia's veteran aircraft designer, Andrei Nikolaevic Tupolev, had produced a programme for a third SST airliner. The Soviet Union was determined not to be left out of the race and so decided to develop a machine that proved to be very similar to Concorde. The design was first published in Moscow in late 1964 and named the Tu-144, although the world press inevitably nicknamed it 'Concordski'. The similarities between the two aircraft were obvious, and the only main difference lay in the arrangements of the engines, which were Kuznetsov NK-144 turbofans, rather than the pure jets of Concorde's Olympus 593s. These engines were much larger in size than the Olympus and were far less efficient. In all probability, they led to the indifferent performance of the Tu-144 when it eventually went into service.

In the United States, in the meantime, the field had been narrowed down to two manufacturers – Boeing and Lockheed. It was Boeing that eventually received a government contract in December 1966 with a design that, if it had ever been built, would have been the most technically complicated airliner ever to rise in the skies. It was a gigantic 300-ft (91-m) long delta with a massive tail plane, under which four General Electric Engines were hung. There was a double-jointed droop nose and in all the aircraft had no fewer than 59 moving control services. Boeing gave it the type number 2707 and began work on the prototype. If the Concorde builders had faced their problems, those experienced by Boeing were almost insuperable, and by 1968, with the Boeing aircraft months behind programme, Concorde 001 started runway trials. However, minor problems delayed the first flight and so on 31 December 1968, the Tu-144 became the first SST to fly. The first prototype Concorde, built in France, took off from Toulouse on 2 March 1969 and was followed by the British version at Filton on 9 April. It was now an all-out race betwen Russia and the Anglo-French team to get their super-jet into airline service. Development and flight trials went ahead smoothly, but by now problems of a different kind faced the British and French plane makers.

Opposition to the SST project was rapidly building up on both sides of the Atlantic. When the SST was conceived, aircraft noise had scarcely been considered, but by the early 1970s an alert public was demanding protection from the loss of the amenities that it enjoyed. This noise problem was the subject of numerous meetings and loud protest from environmental groups, and certain British economists were also questioning the profitability of the airliner. More importantly, the Boeing 747 had established its place in the world's airways, and it was clear that the industry was taking a very different course from that foreseen when the Concorde project was launched. Concorde costs had already risen to three times the original estimates and the British and French governments were becoming reconciled to the fact that there was little chance of recovering their investment.

In the United States, the anti-SST campaign reached its peak in 1971. The political lobby in Capitol Hill consisted mainly of senators who objected to large quantities of public money being used to finance a private venture. The end came in May of that year when, faced with an anti-SST vote in Congress, President Nixon cancelled the Boeing 2707. At that time the total cost of $980 million was almost exactly as much as the British government had spent on its share of the Concorde project, which by then had a number of aircraft flying. It was also more than Boeing had spent on the complete development of the 747.

With Boeing out of the race, development of Concorde and the Tu-144 went ahead. The Russian aircraft soon ran into trouble with its engine installation and the production version had its engines fitted in two pairs under the inner wing, rather like the Concorde.

Then the Russians suffered another blow when the second production aircraft was lost in an accident at the 1973 Paris Air Show. There were obvious problems with the low-speed handling characteristics of the machine and con-

Russia was the first nation to put an SST into the air when the Tupolev Tu-144 prototype flew on 31 December 1968 (top). The aircraft was bedevilled with aerodynamic and technical problems and, although it eventually entered passenger service, it was withdrawn in June 1978. Above: An early Boeing proposal for an SST in Alitalia colours. The Boeing design developed into the most complicated aircraft of modern times before its cancellation by President Nixon in May 1971.

siderable re-design took place. In addition to the splitting of the engines already mentioned, modifications were made to the main undercarriage, under-fuselage lines were re-designed and retractable stub wings or foreplanes were added on the side of the fuselage just aft of the cockpit.

The Tu-144 entered scheduled service on 26 December 1975, between Moscow and Alma-Ata. Only mail and freight was carried at first, but a passenger service began on 1 November 1977. Western journalists who travelled on the inaugural flights reported that the cabin noise was almost intolerable, although there was seating for up to 140 passengers and the range for this load was reported at 4000 miles (6437 km). The engines appeared to be at the root of the Tu-144 troubles, and the Soviet Union approached Aérospatiale for assistance. It is a matter of record that the Tu-144 was withdrawn from Aeroflot service on 1 June 1978, with only 102 scheduled flights carried out.

Concorde, therefore, is the only successful supersonic airliner flying today, even though its high development costs and operating economics have reduced the total number built to 16 aircraft. Economic considerations led Pan Am to cancel its order as long ago as 1973, although the builders had signed 10-year agreements with many of the world's major airlines almost a decade earlier.

However, the British and French national airlines, British Airways and Air France respectively, introduced the type into airline service in January 1976 with flights to Rio de Janeiro and Bahrain. Operations into Washington started in May of the same year, but local bodies in New York kept the airliner out of that city until late 1977. Since then Concordes have flown

successfully on transatlantic routes, although the high development costs have prevented any significant profitable operations. Nevertheless, agreements with Braniff and Singapore airlines have led to the extension of Concorde routes to Dallas-Fort Worth Airport and also to Singapore.

With the completion of the sixteenth Concorde, the brave Anglo-French venture which started in 1962 had ended. No further aircraft are likely to be built and the first generation of SSTs, while being a technical triumph, have proved to be commercially unsuccessful. What is the future of the supersonic passenger airliner as the world of aviation approaches the twenty-first century? The British and French governments have so far been unwilling to finance further development, but in America the main airframe manufacturers still devote considerable amounts of invest-

ment to work studying the possibilities of a second generation of supersonic transport. In this they have been joined from time to time by NASA, fresh from its triumphs in the exploration of inner planetary space.

The leading American supporter of SST aircraft now is probably McDonnell Douglas. The company has published a number of proposals for an advanced SST, which have concentrated on the NASA arrow wing layout. This is very similar to a delta, but has a more sophisticated wing design. The McDonnell Douglas project is for an airplane approximately the same size as the Boeing 747, making it nearly three times the size of Concorde. This would give a capacity for up to 270 passengers and the cruising speed would be at Mach 2.2. Other proposals from the American industry have allowed for a faster speed, but Mach 2 appears to be

sufficient in the calculations of most airlines, and it is unlikely that a Mach 3 airliner will appear in the foreseeable future. The engineering and production facilities needed to produce such a monster would inevitably mean that even the American industry, with all its other commitments, would not be able to tackle the problem economically. Therefore, the European industry is almost certain to be involved with America in any future programmes.

The problems are still immense, however. Any SST will still have to avoid flight over cities and developed countries, and this leads to inevitable limitations on operations and hence its marketability. The problem of noise remains a major drawback, but it is the quantities of fuel required by these aircraft that must make them of questionable economic liability as the cost of fossilized fuels continues to rise. Devel-

An artist's impression of the McDonnell Douglas SST (left), based on the NASA arrow wing design. If it is ever built the machine will be three times the size of Concorde and carry 720 passengers. The dream of supersonic flight (right) has persisted since the end of the Second World War. This fanciful illustration dates from 1952 and the idea is at least half-way to being realized.

opment costs would also be immense, making the resulting airplanes the most expensive that any airline would have to buy.

Therefore, while the future for supersonic aircraft in the 1980s-1990s looks quite bleak, the promise for subsonic types holds nothing but scope for advance and development. Throughout the next twenty years, the airlines of the world will be preoccupied with the launching and development of the new aircraft types that went into production in the United States and Europe during the late 1970s. First it must be said that the 'big three' of the wide-bodied airliners have proved themselves to be so advanced and profitable that they are likely to remain in production in developed versions well into the next century. It is likely therefore that the Lockheed TriStar, the Douglas DC-10 and the Boeing 747 will remain in airline service somewhat longer than other types. Following the tremendous expansion of business in the United States and on the North Atlantic during 1978 and 1979, some operators are flying their 747s for more than 14 hours a day. This will lead to the early production aircraft approaching the end of their useful life by the late 1980s or early 1990s. It can be well argued that the best replacement for the 747 when the time comes, is quite simply another 747. It could also be said, therefore, that while refinements in technology will lead to the improvement of existing designs – the TriStar 500 wing is a good example of this – the basic designs of the big wide-bodied jets are unlikely to change in the next two or three decades.

Engine design is another matter. Rising fuel costs have already been mentioned in relation to the development of SST aircraft, and there are many signs that industrial growth is already beginning to overtake the petroleum supply available world-wide. If shortage of fuel eventually becomes a reality of economic life, governments will obviously be forced to concentrate their research on fuel-saving technology and on the design of engines which give greater fuel economy than those in present use.

Another factor which influences potential design development in the 1980s and 1990s is the current state of airport supply. The building of a new airport is extremely expensive and political problems are inevitable, due to the environmental drawbacks that airports mean. There is, therefore, every incentive for aircraft designers to meet the twin pressures of traffic growth and airport congestion by stretching existing designs. An example of this technique is the improved version of the DC-10 which offers seats for 400 passengers on the United States' domestic services, and Airbus Industrie are studying a stretched version of the A300B. (Airbus Industrie is an international consortium of Aérospatiale, British Aerospace, CASA, Deutsche Airbus, Fokker VFW and General Electric.) Therefore, it is possible to forecast that by 2000, airlines wishing to replace their existing wide-bodied jets may well be ordering refined versions of the existing aircraft. These machines will possibly be fitted with power plants developed from the present generation of big turbo-fans, with more efficient noise control and the use of new composite materials.

During these decades, when it can be argued that a pause in the development of large airliners is not only desirable but necessary, research and development into new materials for aircraft structures could proceed. The application of carbon fibres to the construction of military aircraft is well advanced and the industry may well be on the verge of a very significant break-through in changing the main component in aircraft structures from metallic to non-metallic materials. However, the problems for civil aircraft construction that arise with the introduction of new materials means that several decades of research will be needed before the safety standards required can be met. Whole new techniques of testing, structural specimen construction and inspection will have to be invented and evaluated before new materials can become commonplace in aircraft production. This development programme means that although composite materials may have very desirable structural capability, the cost of development may mean that a conventional metal structure will still be produced because it is far cheaper.

It was in the field of the narrow-bodied medium-range airliner that exciting developments took place during the mid-1970s in the so-called 'War of the Paper Airplanes' which reached its climax in 1978. By the early 1970s, national aviation authorities were rapidly adopting new rules for the control of aircraft noise. These developments were outlined in the so-called Can 5 rules which were named after the International Civil Aviation Organization (ICAO) Fifth Committee on aircraft noise. The new rules meant that certain older designs like the Boeing 707 would no longer meet the noise specifications, and even well-tried designs like the Boeing 727 would require modification. These rules also coincided with the development of the big fan engines which, with their low fuel consumption, had reached the peak of refinement by 1975. Added to this, the continuing advance in avionics leading to more efficient control systems brought about a situation where development of new medium-range aircraft to operate the most profitable and crowded air routes became possible.

Boeing, as ever, were first into the field with a study for a replacement for its very successful 727 three-engined medium-range jet liner. Boeing were already the dominating concern in the American market. They produce over sixty percent of all aircraft flying in the United States and they were determined to maintain their position.

Following an unsuccessful proposal to United Airways, the largest American carrier, for a stretched version of the 727, Boeing produced, in 1975, a proposal for a new aircraft, under the title 7X7. It was a machine that looked very much like the Airbus and it seated about 200 passengers in lines of 8 abreast. At the same time, Airbus Indus-

trie announced a study for a very similar aircraft called the B10, while McDonnell Douglas were proposing a twin-engined version of the DC-10 to compete in the same field.

Both the American companies planned to subcontract components of their machines to European industry and considerable negotiations took place with possible collaborators. As well as the 7X7, Boeing also began to study a replacement for their existing smaller, narrow-body aircraft, and this became known as the 7N7. By 1977 the Boeing proposals for both types were so advanced that several airlines were expressing an interest in either machine.

This led to certain delays, and in April 1977 a significant break-through occurred for the European industries. In that month, the large American company Eastern Airlines signed an agreement to operate four Airbus A300Bs on a six-month trial, and a year later they placed orders for twenty of these big European jets. By the end of 1979, there were 180 Airbuses on order.

Boeing persisted in their sales campaign, and eventually their designs were firmed up in the Boeing 767, which was a twin-engined, wide-bodied, medium-range machine, and the 757, which was a narrow-bodied twin produced for British Airways and Eastern Airlines. Both these operators ordered the type and the eventual type turned out to be nearly as large as the 767, with two Rolls-Royce RB211-535 cropped fan engines. At the end of 1979, there were 43 Boeing 757s on order and 136 767s. The first prototypes are due to fly in 1982.

To compete with the American industry, Airbus Industrie produced a smaller version of the A300B, which became the A310, and this type was immediately

Above: The so-called 'War of the Paper Airplanes' reached its climax in 1978 with orders being placed for two new models offered by Boeing. The 757 (top) is a narrow-bodied jet with Rolls-Royce RB211-535 cropped fan engines and was ordered for Eastern and British Airways. The 767 is a wide body and 136 orders had been taken by January 1980. **Right:** The British Aerospace 146 Feederliner is a low-cost, low-noise small airliner designed for second line operators. It is the first all-British airliner design to go into production for over a decade. The first orders came from Argentina.

ordered in July 1978 by Lufthansa and other prominent European airlines.

So it was that the commercial battles of 1978 set the pattern for medium-sized airliners of the 1980s, and it is obvious that throughout the decade a tough commercial war will be waged between the American companies and Airbus Industrie. In the same section of the market, McDonnell Douglas are selling the stretched version of their well-known DC-9, which they call the DC-9 Super 80. During all these new proposals, it is not insignificant to note that orders for the Boeing 727, the well-tried triple jet dating back to the early 1960s, had reached 1720. There was no sign whatsoever that Boeing would yet run out of orders for this splendid machine. The Boeing 737 also looks well set to continue in production well into the 1980s.

A significant new type in the short-haul market is the British Aerospace Type 146. It is unusual in having four engines, supplied by Avco Lycoming with their type ALF502. It also has a high wing, reminiscent of Russian designs. The type offers a combination of low cost and low noise, and was developed from a Hawker Siddeley design. The project was launched in 1978 by the newly nationalized British Aerospace Corporation, and the first prototype is due to fly in 1981.

So stands the market for commercial airliners as the twentieth century enters its ninth decade. No review of the future of airliners would be complete without reference to the development of VTOL (Vertical Take-Off and Landing) and STOL (Short Take-Off and Landing) flight.

The helicopter is a commonplace machine today, with many specialist applications both in the military and civil role. Its industrial potential has

been proved in work carried out in oil exploration, in survey work and in short specialized passenger transport. Owing to the stringent safety requirements, its complexity and limitations make it largely an unsatisfactory airliner for the transportation of large numbers of people. Its actual development has never really fulfilled the expectations of its designers, although operators like New York Airways have pioneered commercial services. The Sikorsky S-61 has been the mainstay of civil helicopter flying and British Airways have used it on their routes to the Scilly Isles. The experience they have gained led them to order in 1978 a 44-seat version of the Boeing twin router CH-47.

The world's airlines have never shown themselves to be very interested in vertical or short take-off designs. In recent years, STOL projects have received large sums of government money in both America and Russia. However, largely with military application in mind, Boeing have developed a technique known as upper surface blowing, and this is used in their YC-14. Similar designs have come from McDonnell Douglas in the YC-15, although it is a four-engined aircraft, while Russia has produced the Antonov An-2272. The main problem with all these STOL designs, whether they use upper surface blowing or vectored thrust, as in the British Pegasus, is that they are all extremely noisy. In addition, there is considerable doubt about the economics of these very expensive aircraft. Despite a number of complex STOL designs that appeared in the early 1970s, there is really no further evidence on which to base a forecast of increased STOL development.

The carriage of freight by air is a growth industry, although it is remark-

Above: The helicopter has proved its usefulness in specialized situations but design complexity and stringent safety requirements have prevented its development as a mass carrier. Here a Sikorsky S-61 of British Airways is servicing a North Sea oil rig. Right: The McDonnell Douglas YC-15 first flew in 1975 as part of the United States Air Force medium STOL programme and is aimed at moving high density loads over short inter-city routes.

The airfreight market grew throughout the 1970s. Left: The gaping cargo hold of a Lufthansa Boeing 747 freighter. Top right: If it goes ahead, this McDonnell Douglas design study for the Span loader will introduce containerization to the airlines. Eight 8-ft (2-m) containers would be carried in the wings and the payload would be 600,000 lbs (272,154 kg). Bottom right: The Lockheed L100, the civil version of the Hercules, is the most successful freighter to date. The latest version, the L100–50, allows overnight deliveries of perishable goods anywhere in the United States.

© Aereon Corp.

able that very few airliners had ever been developed as specialized freighters from the drawing board. The Bristol Company produced its Type 170 Freighter as long ago as 1947 and sold over 200 before production ceased about 1960. The most successful commercial freighter since then has been the Lockheed L100, a civil version of the Hercules military transport. Otherwise, in the West, freighter aircraft are mainly passenger liners which have been down-graded to the freighting role. It is only in the Soviet Union that extensive use has been made of freighter aircraft in large numbers. The latest specialized jet freighter to go into service with the state airline, Aeroflot, is the 170-ton Ilyushin IL-76. It began service in 1975 and has been supplied steadily ever since. The IL-76 has been designed with the transport of heavy concentrated loads in mind, and is a versatile aircraft which can operate from short runways.

It is in the field of freight transportation that the most exotic ideas of the future development of aviation crop up from time to time. Recently, there has been a revival of interest in the airship as a freight-carrying vehicle. The supporters of practical lighter-than-air transport are arguing for a full-scale development programme with government funding, and point out the advantages that airships have over aircraft in the fields of environmental pollution and rising fuel costs. The development of modern materials has probably made possible the construction of very large, lightweight, strong airship hulls and helium can now be supplied in reasonably cheap and large quantities.

Recent reports indicate that the Soviet Union, West Germany, The Netherlands and France have all initiated preliminary studies for freighter airships in recent years. Amongst prominent designs that have come to the public attention, the most interesting are those put forward by the Aereon Corporation of Princeton, New Jersey. This company has advanced several of its delta wing concepts. The shape of a large, fat, flying triangle, the delta wing makes use of aerodynamic properties to obtain lift as well as that gained from helium gas carried internally. There would be a built-in cargo area with its own cargo-handling equipment, and initial design studies propose that six fully-loaded six-wheeled trucks could be carried into the air.

In the United Kingdom, the shipping industry has recently shown itself interested in airship design, and development studies have been carried out on behalf of European Ferries. However, much more research and development will be needed before practical designs

Half airplane, half airship (left), this scaled-down prototype from the Aereon Corporation takes to the air. It is proposed that the full-sized version will be able to carry six loaded trucks. The inter-city commutor ship of the twenty-first century? A proposal for a passenger and freight carrying airship from a consortium headed by a British shipping concern.

become a reality, and it is unlikely that airship proposals will get much priority from the restricted funds of Western governments. It is even more unlikely that this century will see again the huge dirigibles which graced the skies in the 1920s and 1930s.

More ideas about the re-introduction of the airship which are practical and possible are those proposals for the development of alternative fuels for aircraft. There appear to be two likely possibilities. The first is the application of nuclear power to airframe propulsion. The idea of atomic power for airplanes goes back to the 1940s, when the United States Air Force carried out studies for a nuclear-powered bomber. The programme developed far enough to allow a small nuclear reactor to be flown in a modified Convair B-36 bomber, but the idea was then discarded. It is obvious that nuclear power

has a potential in aviation if the problem of lightweight protected reactors can be solved, and advanced technology cannot be all that far from reaching this particular threshold.

A more practical alternative, although full of difficulties, is the possible use of liquid hydrogen in aircraft engines. This was the fuel that was used in the development of the large rockets which powered the Apollo programme in the late 1960s. As liquid hydrogen is produced by applying electrical energy to water, it is available in vast quantities and at relatively economic costs. The problem with the fuel is that it remains in a liquid state only at low temperatures and therefore it will be a major problem to insulate the fuel tanks of any future aircraft. The size of the tanks would probably equal that of the passenger cabin, but this is not so great a limitation as to prove impractical. How-

ever, it is likely that the reserves of fossil fuels will have to dwindle considerably before governments will begin to develop these alternative fuel sources with any sense of urgency.

The challenge of fuel supplies, the ever-increasing demand for more and more aircraft seats, the increase in the leisure time and the demand for high-speed routes are all factors which will lead to increased developments in aviation during the twenty-first century. The time will surely come when vast nuclear-powered airliners, perhaps 1000ft (305 m) in length and soaring to heights well above the stratosphere, will become a common sight at the world's airports. Many will say that this is an impossible dream but then the same thing was said to the Wright Brothers as they set out with their bamboo and canvas contraption to the sand dunes of Kitty Hawk less than a century ago.

Index